1,001 SMART TRAVEL TIPS

3rd Edition

Fodor's Travel Publications   New York, Toronto, London, Sydney, Auckland

www.fodors.com

FODOR'S 1,001 SMART TRAVEL TIPS

Editors: Laura M. Kidder (lead project editor); Stephanie Butler; Kelly Kealy

Editorial Production: Carrie Parker

Editorial Contributors: Alexis Kelly; Lisa McLaughlin; Doug Stallings

Design: Fabrizio LaRocca, *creative director*; Guido Caroti, *art director*; Melanie Marin, *senior picture editor*

Cover Photos: Left: John Foxx/ImageState/age fotostock. Left center: Rob Bouwman/Shutterstock. Right center: Igor XIII/Shutterstock. Right: Image Source Ltd/age fotostock.

Production Manager: Steve Slawsky

COPYRIGHT

3rd Edition

ISBN 978-1-4000-0506-2
ISSN 1541-289X

SPECIAL SALES

This book is available for special discounts for bulk purchases for sales promotions or premiums. Special editions, including personalized covers, excerpts of existing books, and corporate imprints, can be created in large quantities for special needs. For more information, write to Special Markets/Premium Sales, 1745 Broadway, MD 6-2, New York, NY 10019, or e-mail specialmarkets@randomhouse.com.

AN IMPORTANT TIP & AN INVITATION

Although all prices, opening times, and other details in this book are based on information supplied to us at press time, changes occur all the time in the travel world, and Fodor's cannot accept responsibility for facts that become outdated or for inadvertent errors or omissions. **So always confirm information when it matters,** especially if you're making a detour to visit a specific place. Your experiences—positive and negative—matter to us. If we have missed or misstated something, **please write to us.** We follow up on all suggestions. Contact the 1,001 Smart Travel Tips editor at editors@fodors.com or c/o Fodor's at 1745 Broadway, New York, NY 10019.

PRINTED IN THE UNITED STATES OF AMERICA

10 9 8 7 6 5 4 3 2 1

GETTING THE TRIP YOU WANT

Fodor's 1,001 Smart Travel Tips has the best advice gathered from our editors, writers, and readers. It covers every aspect of every kind of trip: deciding where and when to go; packing wisely for wherever you're headed; choosing the right way to get there; finding a great place to stay; figuring out what to see and do; and staying safe, healthy, and well fed the entire time. You'll also get the scoop on the best travel Web sites, on how to prepare for trips to dozens of countries, and on where to turn to when you encounter obstacles.

Above all else we hope the guidance in this book helps you to plan the trip of your dreams and allows your adventures to take shape as you want them to.

Who Says?

The tips in this book represent everything from tried-and-true strategies to quirky pearls of wisdom. They were contributed by many travel experts, including, but not limited to:

Stephanie Butler, Linda Cabasin, Erica Duecy, Robert Fisher, Carolyn Galgano, Maria Hart, Salwa Jabado, Kelly Kealy, Alexis Kelly, Margaret Kelly, Rachel Klein, Laura Kidder, Matthew Lombardi, Lisa McLaughlin, Molly Moker, Jess Moss, Doug Stallings, Cate Starmer, Caroline Trefler, Eric Wechter

CONTENTS

Be a Fodor's Correspondent

A great travel tip can make a nice vacation even sweeter and can also salvage a trip that might have begun to feel doomed. But the best travel tips will end up being the ones you learn through your own experiences, by exploring with an open mind and trying new things.

Your experiences and opinions matter. They matter to us. They matter to your fellow Fodor's traveelers, too. And we'd like to hear about them.

When you share your experiences and opinions, you become an active member of the Fodor's community. That means we'll not only use your feedback to make our books better, but we'll publish your names and comments whenever possible.

So please: tell us what to include. And tell us when we're right and when we're wrong. Give us your opinion instantly at our feedback center at www.fodors.com/feedback. You may also e-mail editors@fodors.com with the subject line "Tips Editor." Or send us your comments by mail to Tips Editor, Fodor's, 1745 Broadway, New York, NY 10019.

Happy Traveling!

Tim Jarrell, Publisher

Planning

WORD OF MOUTH

"July is the highest of high season in [many] places. And, finding flights may be very difficult, let alone finding accommodations."

—Janisj

"We have rented cars through Hotwire numerous times and have always been pleased, never had a problem and have saved many dollars"

—SandyBrit

Updated
by Alexis
Kelly
We hate to say it, but getting the trip you want takes work. Determining where to go and when, scouting the best deal, and doing a bit of guidebook and Internet research takes time and effort. But, as any successful traveler (or Boy Scout) will tell you, what you put into planning and preparing pays off in Vacationland, when you can relax knowing that you've taken care of all the potential pitfalls. For tips on what to do now so that your trip is effortless later, read on.

PICKING A PLACE

Determine what matters most in a destination. Domestic travel or international? By land, air, or water? City or country? Beach or mountains? Weekend or extended sojourn? Single destination or constantly on the move? Do you like adventurous activities, cultural opportunities, spa treatments? All three?

Go with your gut about where to go. Which of the following pops out? Rome and Florence. Caribbean beaches. Canadian ski resorts. Disney in Orlando. Camping in Colorado. A Napa Valley inn. Bird-watching in Central America. Cruising the Mediterranean. A safari in Kenya. Shopping in Hong Kong. This list represents broad types of travel, and your answer might reveal just what kind of travel mood you're in.

Mix and match destination activities creatively. With a little ingenuity, one destination can meet mixed needs. Cities have it all, or almost all: nonstop action for the go-getters, culture to spare, sophisticated spas. Outdoorsy types may not be in their optimal element, but they can usually find some kind of sporting activity (consider New York's urban adult playground, Chelsea Piers), and if not, there's always the hotel gym. Beach vacations can be weak on the cultural front: if that's a must, pick an exotic locale or one steeped in history.

Draw on a variety of trip-planning resources. The Web, guidebooks, media (magazines, newspapers, TV), friends and acquaintances, and travel agents are all helpful. Plop yourself down in the travel section of your local bookstore and pick up books that catch your eye. Check one source against another: That dreamy photo you clipped from a glossy magazine or a friend's rhapsodic recommendation might not give the whole story, and some Web sites, like

WHAT'S YOUR TRAVEL PROFILE?

The Go-Getter. You like to fill every moment, from dawn to midnight, with productive and/or pleasurable activities. Big cities, resorts with sports facilities, and theme parks will meet your need for constant stimulation.

The Culture Vulture. You're only happy when expanding your aesthetic horizons. Opt for big cities, foreign destinations, and places with unique festivals.

The Relaxation Seeker. You're intent on mellowing out at all costs. You might cope with plenty of stress in real life, but your ideal vacation means a chance to slow down—at a beach, in the peaceful countryside, at a spa, or on a cruise ship.

The Adventurer. You only experience life at its fullest when you're striving to meet new challenges (ace that tennis serve, tackle that mountain or Class III rapids). The answer is a beach, a ski or golf resort, the wilderness to be found within national parks, or an organized adventure tour.

brochures, can be guilty of glossing over potential downsides, such as dingy rooms or a major highway cutting right past a presumably peaceful retreat. The more sources you check, the more rounded the picture.

Be smart when researching multidestination trips. Sure, you can head to airport and airline Web sites to find out where the carriers fly into and out of and when. But you can save steps by heading to sites like Vayama.com and MontroseTravel.com, which have multidestination research and planning functions, or Flylc.com, a site with information on which low-cost carriers fly to which destinations in Europe. And if it's a really complicated trip—say, hopping from one Caribbean island to the next—you can't beat a travel agent who knows the region. AirTreks.com is a travel agent specializing in writing multistop international tickets.

Check out Web sites with user-generated travel info. On Fodors.com, head to the forums for on-the-ground pointers from like-minded travelers and to Ratings for user reviews of sights, hotels, and restaurants. Other Web sites include TravelChums.com (about 75% of their users are from the United States) or TravBuddy.com; Gusto.com (organizes advice thematically); TripAdvisor.com (has a collaborative writing/updating function); IgoUGo.com (for those who keep travel journals); VirtualTourist.com (lots of photos

WORD OF MOUTH: HOBBIES

"We definitely plan our vacations around our hobbies. If we can't bring our bikes or kayaks with us, we feel like we're missing out on something. Thank goodness so many cities are bike-friendly! One of our best trips to Chicago was when we took our bikes and cycled the lakeshore to the northern edge of the city." —Mermaid

"We've planned trips around certain bands' concert dates and hockey games—the event decided the location, and then we looked for other fun things to do while there. Saw Rush in Montreal and Las Vegas, [once planned] a trip to Detroit to see the Redwings play. . . ." —NewBe

"Hiking, walking, and visiting national parks/reserves is how we spend most of our vacation time because we *love* the outdoors. Every trip we plan revolves around outdoor activities (and wineries!), which is why we spend so much time in Australia and New Zealand." —Melnq8

as well as reviews of destinations and properties); and RealTravel.com (blogs and photos).

Look for "best of" lists for hotels, destinations, etc. Most newspapers, major travel magazines, and city-focused magazines publish (and post on their Web sites) "best of" articles or editions. On Fodors.com we post our Fodor's Choice Awards. These are a great resource for destinations as well as hotels, restaurants, sights, shops, clubs, and activities.

WORD OF MOUTH. "If I am going to visit 195 countries, I cannot afford to spend too much time in anyone of them unless I plan to live to 120! Three to four days on an island is usually enough for me." —DMB Traveler

TIMING YOUR TRIP

Determine the best travel seasons. In Central America, for example, the dry, peak season runs from mid-December through April. From mid-December until early February in particular, you have good weather and lush vegetation. Of course hotels will be full, making researching prices and booking ahead essential. Visiting off-season, on the other hand, may let you avoid crowds and high prices with only a few trade-offs. In rainy season, for instance, beaches might be wet in the afternoon but sunny and dry in the morning. That said, transportation could be a problem due to delayed flights and washed-out roads. And some climates might be unbearably cold or hot—turning your vacation into an episode of *Survivor*.

Travel in the shoulder season to save money. If your destination's peak season is from December through April and you want to travel in late April, you might save hundreds of dollars if you change your travel dates by a week or two. Note, though, that properties may charge the peak-season rate for an entire stay even if you straddle the change between peak and off-peak seasons; be sure to ask when the rates go down. Also, check out Offseason.CheapTickets.com, a quarterly report by CheapTickets.com based on an analysis of pricing information from its Web site.

Watch out for shifting shoulder seasons. The definitions of peak and off seasons were clearer before air-conditioning, and before tourism boards got the idea of expanding their markets. Online hotel room-rate charts will give you a good idea of peak booking periods.

Factor in travel patterns when scheduling your trip. Tourists crowd Europe's major art cities at Easter, when locals head to beaches and the countryside. From March through May, busloads of schoolchildren the world over take places of historical interest by storm. And you don't want to be, say, on an Italian beach in August if you can help it. You won't have a scrap of sand on which to lay your towel, and there won't be any deals on resorts. (Italian beach vacations are best taken in June and September.) On the other hand, from mid-July through August Paris is abandoned (albeit hot and stuffy), as the locals flee the city on beach trips of their own.

Brush up on international holidays. Many businesses close for holidays that aren't observed in the United States, so you might want to avoid travel at these times. On the other hand, elaborate, colorful celebrations make the Day of the Dead in Oaxaca, Mexico, or the week before Easter in Antigua, Guatemala, the main reasons to travel. A guidebook is a good source for information on local feasts and fêtes.

Watch the weather. Hurricane season in the Caribbean is from about June 1 through November 30, with greatest risk for a storm from August through October. December through early March is monsoon season in much of Southeast Asia. Accuweather.com is an independent weather-forecasting service with good coverage of hurricanes. Weather.com is the Web site for the Weather Channel. The World Weather Information Service (⊕ *worldweather.wmo. int*), the forecasting arm of the U.N.'s World Meteorological Organization (WMO), has weather updates for more than 1,200 cities. The WMO also has a site that tracks severe weather events (⊕ *severe.worldweather.wmo.int/*).

Avoid the busiest travel days. At Thanksgiving, for instance, get your traveling done on Tuesday or wait for Thanksgiving Day itself. Christmas Eve is actually a great time to travel—most people are already holed up with their loved ones.

Pick the best flight times and airports. Flying early in the morning might help you to avoid bottlenecks, but it depends on the day of the week and the route—these days, the proliferation of small commuter shuttles is what often clogs up runways, so if you're catching a 7 AM weekday flight in a busy business corridor (New York–Boston, say), your plane may get caught in the congestion. Also, not all airports are created equal. That's where the travelers' Web site of the National Air Traffic Controllers Association (⊕ *www.avoiddelays.com*) comes in handy. It will help you find the best time to fly from a particular airport, and the best airports for any connections. It's also a good place for flight-delay updates.

Travel when you get a good deal. Last-minute e-saver tickets and other deals can be the reward for adopting the drop-and-run lifestyle. (Heck, that's what "personal days" are for, right?) So even if you can't do all, say, of London in three days, you can still have an experience (and a deal) to remember and brag about indefinitely.

GETTING THE BEST DEALS

Dig deep when researching travel deals. Did you know that Internet prices aren't always the lowest? Brick-and-mortar travel agents may *still* be able to get you better deals, simply because it's their business to know their way around the reservations thicket. And online prices can be dramatically different from site to site—room costs alone can vary by as much as 200%. What's more, not all chains or carriers are represented on all sites. This is especially true of the smaller or discount airlines like jetBlue and Southwest. You may

TRIP BUDGET BASICS

■ **Plan your budget before you book.** Be comprehensive when calculating how much the trip will cost. Include pre-trip fees and purchases (passport renewals, visas, clothing, luggage); long-distance and local transportation; hotels (including all taxes); meals; beverages; entertainment; activities; gratuities; cell phone/long-distance calls; photography expenses. Also factor destination shopping (whether for local specialties or essential sundries) into your estimate. And after you've done this, add another 2%–5%—depending on how thrifty you are—to get a figure closer to what you'll probably spend.

■ **Research on-the-ground costs.** Meals, goods, and sometimes accommodations cost less overall in Latin American than in much of Europe or even the States. Likewise, certain European countries and U.S. regions are cheaper than others. A good travel guide will tell you the price of a local taxi ride, a beer or a cappuccino, a concert ticket, a museum entrance fee, a three-day bus pass, and so on. You can also contact a local tourist office, visit a local magazine or newspaper Web site, ask like-minded travelers on a travel forum, or e-mail businesses to get specifics. The U.S. State Department (⊕ *aoprals. state.gov*) surveys the cost of living in many countries to determine appropriate allowances for staff posted abroad. Although cumbersome, these quarterly indexes do give an idea of how expensive a given country is.

■ **Factor in exchange rates.** How much you get for your dollar affects the overall cost of a trip *and* the overall value for money of a destination. Check rates on Google (⊕ *www.google.com*) by typing in an amount and an explanation of how you want it converted (e.g., "14 Swiss francs in dollars"). Oanda.com (⊕ *www.oanda.com*) also allows you to print out a handy table with the current day's conversion rates. XE.com (⊕ *www.xe.com*) is another good currency conversion site.

■ **Don't forget at-home expenses.** Keep an eye on the bottom line at home. Do you have animals to board? Are there any major nontravel expenses looming (e.g., taxes, home improvement, auto repairs, medical bills, tuition)? Are you carrying high credit-card debt? Taking such concerns into account, you might want to curtail any overlavish plans.

just find the cheapest fare or best promotional room rate on an airline or hotel-chain Web site. Also, you can sometimes get a better price if you call a hotel's local toll-free number (if available) rather than a central reservations number.

Use travel aggregator sites to compare prices. Web sites like Kayak.com, Mobissimo.com, Quixo.com, Sidestep. com, and Travelgrove.com cull the best prices for airfares, hotels, and rental cars from many places. Most aggregators compare the major online travel-agent/booking-engine sites such as Expedia, Travelocity, and Orbitz. They also look at car-rental, cruise, and airline Web sites, though rarely the sites of smaller budget airlines. Some aggregators also compare such things as trip insurance or vacation packages.

Check out online travel companies' foreign Web sites. Changing that ".com" suffix to ".fr" (France), ".es" (Spain), ".mx" (Mexico), or ".ca" (Canada) might lead to better deals. Many airlines and car-rental agencies have foreign sites; so do online travel agents like Expedia and Travelocity. (To find out whether a company has international sites, you usually need only scroll down to the bottom of the Home page.) The catch? To purchase from these sites, you may need a credit-card billing address in the country on whose site you're searching. But friends or family living abroad can always buy for you; so can destination-based travel agents (just be sure that savings outweigh agent fees).

Don't shy from negotiating. It really can pay to haggle for a price below the published rates (known in the biz as "rack rates"). Research the norm, and then play on your strengths. Are you traveling off-season, when the property might otherwise have to absorb the costs of some empty rooms? Could the hotel match lower rates offered by nearby competitors? Or perhaps it could throw in a bonus, such as an extra night's stay or a sports-activity package? A little polite wheedling could result in choice dividends.

Check out your member benefits. Are you a member of the American Dental Association or the American Bar Association? Even if you do nothing more than carry your membership card and pay yearly dues, you can take advantage of low rates that many organizations and unions negotiate with hotels and car-rental companies.

Investigate credit-card privileges. Even if your credit card doesn't give you frequent-flier miles for purchases, you may still be eligible for discounts on travel products or services. Visit the company's Web site to check on hotel deals or promotions.

Have the best travel deals find you. On Expedia.com, Travelocity.com, and other sites you can sign up to receive e-mails the moment a fare meeting your price requirement is available to cities you specify. SmarterTravel.com will notify you weekly of the discounted flights departing from the gateways closest to you. TravelZoo.com and FareCompare.com send e-mails alerting you to great deals on packages and airfares, respectively. And many airlines e-mail a list of weekly specials (typically on Tuesday or Wednesday for the next or following weekend).

WORD OF MOUTH. "I get daily e-mails from Airfarewatchdog.com that alert me to sales and lower fares. . . ." —bettyk

Book trips on auction sites. If you bid wisely, there are deals to be had on auction sites like the name-your-own-price pioneer Priceline.com, as well as Skyauction.com and LuxuryLink.com. That said, these sites are best if you have a lot of flexibility and don't particularly care which airline you fly. If a specific itinerary or earning frequent-flier miles in a particular program is important to you, go elsewhere.

Read all the travel-auction-site rules. When entering a bid on sites like Priceline.com, make sure you know exactly what you're committing to and type things in carefully to avoid mistakes. Often changes aren't allowed—even for an extra fee—after a submitted bid is accepted.

Bid wisely in travel auctions. To get a ballpark figure before you start bidding on an auction site, research the regular prices, calculate the related taxes, and set yourself a bidding limit of 10%–15% below the total. Sites like Biddingfortravel.com are good for this. Also, auction sites don't let you submit repeat bids using the exact same criteria. For example, you can't start at $100 for an LA to NYC ticket and then keep "working your way up" to a price the booking service will accept. If you have to fly on particular dates to or from a town with multiple airports and want to make sure you pay the lowest possible fare, test the waters by listing just one airport for each town on your first bid. List the ones you prefer first, in case the bid is accepted. If it's not, add airports as you raise your bid.

WORD OF MOUTH: HOME SWAPS

"Homeexchange.com has the most listings worldwide (37,000) and includes insurance coverage, but it's the most expensive. It's also U.S. based so may not be the best choice if you are based in the U.S. and want to trade with someone in Europe. Ditto with Digsville.com . . . . Knowyourtrade.com is a good site for deciding which club to go and Homeexchanger.blogspot.com is a good blog on the subject." —Hastobe_Katt

"Since travel has become so expensive, and I live in a ski resort town, I thought I'd give it a whirl! I've had all good experiences. I joined Homeexchange.com, which seems to be very international. My exchanges have been with people from all over." —Dayle

"People exchange anything from small one bedroom apartments to large mansions. People also exchange pet care, plant care, etc. There are singles, couples, and families exchanging. It has been wonderful for us. We've traded in places that we never thought we would get to visit. Someone a while back expressed it well, when she said that by doing home exchange, she has managed to take a trip of a lifetime many times over. I concur." —annetti

SAVING MONEY ON HOTELS

Watch out for the term "from" when pricing hotels. That baseline figure, although an effective come-on, might apply to an undesirable hotel. The minimally acceptable, mid-level options could be quite a hike up.

Join hotel frequent-guest programs. You may get preferential treatment in room choice and/or upgrades in your favorite chains.

Ask about hotel packages and special rates. High-end hotel chains catering to business travelers are often busy only on weekdays; to fill rooms they often drop rates dramatically on weekends. And most hotels have special package deals and/or corporate rates.

Look for hotel price guarantees. For overseas trips, look for guaranteed hotel rates. With your rate locked in you won't pay more, even if the price goes up in the local currency.

Watch out for hidden hotel fees. It's almost unforgiveable the numbers of fees and surcharges hotels are adding to the room rate. It's truly unforgiveable that the fees are for services and amenities that you'd expect to be hotel-room basics. There are resort fees (for beach towels, chairs, use of the gym, etc., and lately adopted by hotels in cities), fees for in-room safes or refrigerators (so-called furniture fees), energy fees, housekeeping fees (yes, you read that correctly)—the list goes on. Check your bill carefully, and don't be afraid to request the removal of such charges. If a desk clerk refuses to oblige, ask to speak with the manager. If he or she won't help, contest the extra charges with your credit-card company.

Investigate home rentals and exchanges. Rental properties—including villas, houses, and apartments/condos—listed on sites such as Homeaway.com, VisitAlltheWorld.com, Forgetaway.com, Villas International (⊕ *www.villasintl. com*), and a host of other companies are often rented by the week. When you do the math, nightly rates may be better than at a hotel, particularly if you're with a group. Check out SlowTrav.com to read about home-rental experiences that other travelers have had. Home swaps through companies like HomeExchange.com aren't for everyone, but can save big bucks.

Don't rule out hostels. In some 4,000 locations in more than 80 countries around the world, Hostelling International (HI), the umbrella group for a number of national youth-hostel associations, offers single-sex, dorm-style beds and, at many hostels, rooms for couples and family accommodations. Membership in any HI national hostel association, open to travelers of all ages, allows you to stay in HI-affiliated hostels at member rates. A one-year membership through HIUSA.org is free to children under 18 and about $28 for adults. Rates in dorm-style rooms run about $15–$25 per bed per night; private rooms are more, but are still generally well under $125 a night. Members have priority if the hostel is full; they're also eligible for discounts around the world, even in restaurants, at attractions, and on rail and bus travel in some countries.

SAVING MONEY ON AIRFARE

Keep tabs on airfares. Check out FareCompare.com, which has historical and current airfares, and Farecast.com, which predicts fare changes based on historical data, to determine when to buy tickets. Unlike other sites, AirfareWatchDog. com includes rates for budget airlines like Southwest in its research.

WORD OF MOUTH. "For the lowest [ticket] price, check a couple of days before and after your desired date on each leg" —rizzuto

Check prices on budget airline Web sites. You'll need to go directly to their sites, as many low-cost carriers aren't included on the big travel sites. To save time, check out Whichbudget.com, which helps you find budget airlines the world over based on departure or arrival points.

Be sure that budget-airline savings don't get eaten alive. You might have gotten great prices on all those flights between countries for your grand tour of Europe, but is it really a deal? Checking bags, having overweight bags, wanting to guarantee a seat with your travel companions, or paying with a credit card can all lead to supplemental charges. As many low-cost carriers fly into secondary airports, your ground-transportation costs may be higher than with non-budget carriers. If you're a shopper, you may have to compare the costs of shipping goods home against baggage weight-overage fees—either way, you'll pay extra. And don't get us started on in-flight meals!

Use frequent-flier miles. The handy site Webflyer.com tracks current promotions and offers tips about maximizing your miles. On Flyertalk.com's forums travelers trade tips about hotel-loyalty programs as well as frequent-flier plans. Also check with the airlines themselves.

Keep abreast of airfares even after buying tickets. Some airlines give you credit for the value of the price reduction if the airfare goes down later (ask about this when booking). The innovative Web site Yapta.com monitors drops in airfares for just this purpose. You'll often have to pay a fee of $75 or $100 to rebook your flight, but if the fare drops substantially, the charge may be worth it.

Watch air-travel taxes and fees. Many airline Web sites—and most ads—show prices without taxes and surcharges. Some surcharges are obvious: for luggage, for flying on standby, and for changing your flight (and if your new flight is more expensive, you'll pay the difference, too). Others are less obvious. For instance, surcharges are added when you buy your ticket anywhere but on an airline Web site (that includes by phone—even if you call the airline directly), when you request the all-but-extinct paper tickets, and when you travel during peak periods. Don't buy till you know the full price: check out SmartTravel.com, which has comprehensive information on airline fees.

AIR MILES DO'S AND DON'TS

1

■ **Do get a credit card with an airline rewards program.** You might be surprised by just how many credit cards can be used to earn points good for airline tickets—it's not just cards that are affiliated with specific airlines or travel programs. Many other cards out there award points that can be used to buy products in special "rewards" catalogs, and these products often include airline tickets.

■ **Don't cash in frequent-flier miles for a cheap flight.** If you're getting a rate below $300, or even $500, for a round-trip flight, you're better off saving your miles for a pricey last-minute or high-season flight.

■ **Don't ignore travel restrictions with miles.** Only a certain number of seats on certain flights are set aside for travelers cashing in frequent-flier miles. Find out which blackout dates apply, and book your reservation as early as possible.

■ **Do use miles to upgrade.** As one Fodor's.com reader put it, "I can afford an $800 ticket to Paris. I cannot afford a $6,000 first-class ticket to Paris. I used 80,000 miles to upgrade my husband and myself a couple of years ago. Upgrades are the best use of frequent-flyer miles when you do the math."

■ **Don't let miles go to waste.** Although rules vary, some frequent-flier programs allow you to transfer miles to a spouse, partner, or member of the immediate family. And you can also cash in miles to buy a ticket in virtually anybody else's name. This can be handy if you have miles about to expire but no plans to travel soon yourself.

■ **Do be sure that miles are credited.** Check as soon as possible after your flight, either online or by phone, to see whether your account has been updated. If you wait until your next statement or even several days after you fly before noticing that you haven't received frequent-flier credit for a flight, it might be too late to get credit from the airline.

Look into air passes well before your trip. Discount air passes that let you travel economically in a country or region must often be purchased before you leave home. In some cases you can only get them through a travel agent.

Pick your air-travel days and times wisely. Look for departures on Tuesday, Wednesday, and Saturday, typically the cheapest days to travel. Flights on these days are often less crowded as well, so you may have room to spread out. Also check on prices for departures at different times of day.

Fly on a holiday. Just as the most expensive fares tend to be on the days or weekends at either side of a holiday, some of the least expensive are on the holiday itself, especially Christmas and Thanksgiving.

Look into flying to and from secondary airports. Discount airlines often use smaller, less chaotic secondary airports. Parking and car-rental rates may also be cheaper than at major airports. Just be absolutely sure that your ground-transportation costs and times don't cause your budget or your stress level to rise too much. For information on secondary U.S. airports, check out AlternateAirports.com.

SAVING MONEY ON RENTAL CARS

Research car-rental rates on the Web. You'll rarely save money and almost never save time calling a car-rental company's toll-free reservation number for rates rather than searching on the Web. Expedia.com and Orbitz.com allow you to comparison shop, and they sometimes list Web-only deals. You can also score good rates using a bidding site, like Priceline.com, which seems to work especially well if you're renting in less popular locations. Note, though, that these deals often come with restrictions, and require that you pay up front.

Check out travel packages that include car rental. Adding a car rental onto your air/hotel vacation package may be cheaper than renting a car separately.

Don't overlook local rental-car agencies. Price local companies as well as the majors. Avoiding the chains and renting through local agencies can save you big bucks, particularly in touristy areas like Florida and California, where competition is stiff. The potential downsides include limited counter/office hours, infrequent shuttle service, limited car selection, and no guaranteed roadside assistance.

Investigate car-rental wholesalers, particularly in Europe. Wholesalers don't own fleets, but rather rent in bulk from firms that do, so they frequently offer better rates. Prices are best during off-peak periods. Note that you must usually pay for such rentals before leaving home. Top European car-rental wholesalers include Auto Europe (⊕*www. autoeurope.com*), Europe by Car (⊕*www.ebctravel.com*), and Kemwel (⊕*www.kemwel.com*).

Look into leasing cars for long trips. In Europe, if you need a car for 17 days or longer you can often lease a spiffy luxury car at a discounted rate. Some rental companies in the United States, like Avis, offer "mini-leases." See their Web site if you're planning a three- or four-week road trip, or check prices on a short-term lease with auto dealerships.

Check out "drive-away" rental-car deals on long trips. Rental-car companies often need to move the bulk of their fleet to specific locations to meet seasonal demand. To do so they may offer excellent one-way rates to renters who can transport cars for them. Look for drive-away deals from Florida and Las Vegas, say, to the northeast at the start of the summer, and from California to the east coast at the start and end of the summer. Rates may go as low as $15 a day for a car with unlimited mileage. These deals are rarely advertised; sign up for special-deal e-mails, or call and inquire about discounted drive-away or one-way rentals.

Investigate all your member benefits before renting a car. Find out whether a credit card you carry or organization or frequent-renter or -flyer program to which you belong has a discount program. And confirm that such discounts really are a deal. You can often do better with special weekend or weekly rates offered by a rental agency.

WORD OF MOUTH. "I wanted to rent a Prius for a week in New Mexico and finally found it through Hertz at a cost of $406. I was chatting with my insurance company (USAA) and mentioned the upcoming trip. They asked if I had rented through them. They changed my reservation to go through them and my cost became $196.32! Check with your insurance company—they may have a better offer." —mpt33905

Join a rental agency's preferred customer club. If you rent a car more often than once a year or so, decide which car-rental company suits you best and join its preferred customer club. For a one-time fee of about $50, you'll get discounts, upgrades, and earn free rental days. You'll also get faster service at the counter and access to a wider choice of vehicles at airport lots. National's Emerald Club offers perks like full-size cars for mid-size rates, special pick-up lots reserved for club members, club members–only service counters, and toll-free phone assistance, among other things.

WHAT'S YOUR FEAR FACTOR?

Not everyone is an intrepid traveler. When choosing a destination, know your limits—and not only in terms of personal safety and political security. Some places also require tolerance for delays and cancellations, bumpy roads, badly labeled streets, crowded buses, poor sanitation, and big ugly bugs. Other places require a degree of strength when facing heartbreaking poverty—often made even more startling because it's juxtaposed with extreme wealth. Still other places require concerted efforts just to stay healthy by taking medication or daily precautionary measures or both. The following sources will help you determine just what health, safety, and other issues you'll face in a given destination.

■ **Centers for Disease Control** (⊕ www.cdc.gov/travel). The CDC has information on health risks associated with almost every country on the planet, as well as what precautions to take. If you're planning a cruise, check out the CDC's Vessel Sanitation Program (VSP)—which has, among other things, a list of cruise ships and their health-inspection scores and frequently asked questions about shipboard illness prevention.

■ **World Health Organization** (⊕ www.who.int). The WHO, the health arm of the United Nations, has information by topic and by country. Its clear, well-written publication "International Travel and Health," which you can download from the Web site, covers everything you need to know about staying healthy abroad.

■ **Central Intelligence Agency** (⊕ www.cia.gov). The CIA's online "World Factbook" has maps and facts on the people, government, economy, and more for countries from Afghanistan to Zimbabwe. It's the fastest way to get a snapshot of a nation. It's also updated regularly and, obviously, well researched.

■ **World-Newspapers.com**. There's nothing like the local paper for putting your finger on the pulse. This site has links to English-language newspapers, magazines, and Web sites in countries the world over.

U.S. State Department (⊕ travel.state.gov). The State Department's advice on the safety of a given country is probably the most conservative you'll encounter. That said, the information is updated regularly, and nearly every nation is covered. Just try to parse the language carefully. For example, a warning to "avoid all travel" carries more weight than one urging you to "avoid nonessential travel," and both are much stronger than a plea to "exercise caution." A travel warning is more permanent (though not necessarily more serious) than a so-called public announcement, which carries an expiration date.

■ **Other State Departments.** As different countries have different worldviews, look at travel advisories from a range of governments to get more of a sense of what's going on out there. Try the Australian Department of Foreign Affairs & Trade (⊕ *www.smartraveller.gov. au*); the Foreign Affairs and International Trade Canada (⊕ *www.voyage.gc.ca*); and the U.K. Foreign & Commonwealth Office (⊕ *www. fco.gov.uk*).

■ **ComeBackAlive.com.** The Web site of author, filmmaker, and adventurer Robert Young Pelton is, as its name suggests, edgy, with information on the world's most dangerous places. Finding safety information on other, seemingly safer places requires a little fiddling around, though. There are forums where danger junkies share tips, and there links to other relevant sites.

Factor in extra car-rental costs abroad. In Europe gasoline costs two to three times what it does in the United States, collision insurance (your own U.S. car insurer most likely will not cover you abroad) can be very costly, and renting a car as a walk-in—without a reservation—can be expensive.

Look for car-rental rate guarantees. With your rate locked in, you won't pay more, even if the price goes up in the local currency.

Ask about rental-car fees and surcharges. Most agencies charge a hefty fee for returning a car to a different location from where you picked it up. Also, most agencies impose a surcharge on drivers under age 25 (some won't rent to drivers under 25; for others the cutoff age is 21).

Don't rent a car at the airport. Airports often add surcharges, which you can sometimes avoid by renting from an agency whose office is just off airport property.

Rent cars weekly. Even if you only want to rent for five or six days, ask for the weekly rate; it may very well be cheaper than the daily rate for that period of time.

Study your car-rental contract. If you return your car before the minimum number of days (often five) specified in a weeklong contract, the weekly rate could revert to a higher daily rate. Be sure you can keep your car for the duration of the contract, or negotiate a better daily rate before you leave the counter. Likewise, don't expect to get the same great rate if you keep the car for an extra day or two. If your plans change, contact the rental company, discuss a new rate, and ask them to e-mail or fax you a new agreement.

Check prices on different-size rental cars. Smaller cars are more popular with renters, so prices may be lower for the larger models. Check the fees. You may be pleasantly surprised.

Get smart about rental-car fuel charges. Don't pay the rental agency for a tank of gas instead of refueling the car yourself before you return it. In some cases the per-gallon rate is much higher than you'd pay at a gas station. Even if the per-gallon rate is lower, you'll be charged for an entire tank whether you use it all or not (it's hard to work it so you can coast in on empty upon return). Fill up the tank at a station away from the drop-off point to get better prices.

Booking

WORD OF MOUTH

"Travelocity, Orbitz, Expedia, and the non-bidding portion of Priceline—all of these are vendors/middlemen. They don't buy the tickets for you, they just sell you tickets from the airlines inventory. Cheaptickets.com buys blocks of tickets cheaply and then resells them."

—mztery

Updated
by Alexis
Kelly

Unless your cousin is a travel agent, you're probably among the millions of people who make most of their travel arrangements online. But have you ever wondered just what the differences are between an online travel agent (a Web site through which you make reservations instead of going directly to the airline, hotel, or car-rental company), a discounter (a firm that does a high volume of business with a hotel chain or airline and accordingly gets good prices), a wholesaler (one that makes cheap reservations in bulk and then re-sells them to people like you), and an aggregator (one that compares all the offerings so you don't have to)?

Is it truly better to book directly on a hotel, airline, or car-rental Web site? What are the benefits and potential pitfalls of booking online? And when *does* a real-live travel agent come in handy? For answers to these and other burning questions, read on.

BOOKING BASICS

Understand online travel agents. Booking engines like Expedia.com, Travelocity.com, and Orbitz.com are actually high-volume, online travel agents. So are packagers like American Airlines Vacations and Virgin Vacations. You'll pay a fee for their services, which aren't always as comprehensive as those of brick-and-mortar agents. For example, Expedia and Travelocity aren't tapped into every hotel chain and don't search for prices on budget airlines or small foreign carriers. That said, some agents do have access to hard-to-find fares with savings that more than make up for any surcharges. Finally, to resolve any problems with a reservation made through such companies, contact them first.

Understand online travel wholesalers and discounters. A travel wholesaler such as Hotels.com or HotelClub.com can be a source of good rates, as can discounters such as Hotwire.com, particularly if you can bid for your hotel room or airfare. Indeed, such sites sometimes have deals that are unavailable elsewhere. They do, however, tend to work only with hotel chains (which makes them less useful for getting hotel reservations outside of major cities) or big airlines (so that often leaves out upstarts like jetBlue and some foreign carriers).

Set up a customized online travel page. Expedia.com and Travelocity.com, for example, allow you to select your preferred travel destinations, departure city, price, and more by signing up. Then every time you log on you'll get a pared-down selection of travel options that pertain specifically to your preferences. You can also store personal informa-tion, like your credit-card number and regular traveling companion's information—which make booking a quick procedure—and have the system keep track of your miles.

Allow yourself time when bidding in online travel auctions. The bidding period for travel auctions generally lasts several days, and you need to keep checking back to make sure you haven't been outbid. Also, you may need to pay the seller by check or credit card, which adds time to the transaction.

Know the terms and conditions of any trip. Find out about deposit and payment due dates (with attendant forfeits), refund policies and cancellation penalties, order process-ing and change fees, gratuity policies (an automatic 15% add-on can be a very big deal), complaint and refund pro-cedures, and trip-protection insurance options.

Print and carry hotel, airline, and rental car confirmations, itineraries, and receipts. You may need documentation (and, for electronic check-in, the credit card you used to purchase the flight) to get your boarding pass, which is required to get past security. Having printouts also makes it easier to troubleshoot things later. To play it extra safe, reconfirm airline reservations online a few days after booking, make sure you have the itinerary you requested, and double-check details such as seating requests.

Know when to work with a travel agent. A knowledgeable brick-and-mortar travel agent can be a godsend if you're booking a cruise, a package trip that's not available to you directly, an air pass, or a complicated itinerary including several overseas flights.

Look for travel agents with specialties. Travel agents that specialize in a destination may have exclusive access to cer-tain deals and insider information on things such as charter flights. Agents who specialize in types of travelers (families, senior citizens, gays and lesbians, naturists) or types of trips (cruises, luxury travel, safaris) can also be invaluable. One of the best resources out there is the American Society of Travel Agents' (ASTA's) TravelSense.org Web site. It has a search feature that allows you to find an ASTA–affiliated agent by area of expertise, including destination.

Get all promised trip services in writing. You need written confirmation of the arrangements you've agreed to in case anything should go wrong with the travel company or any of the service providers. If it does, a good travel agent will act as your advocate to resolve any complaints—either upon your return or, better yet, while there's still time to ameliorate the situation.

Look into travel packages. Packages combine airfare, accommodations, and perhaps a rental car or other extras (theater tickets, guided excursions, boat trips, reserved entry to popular museums, transit passes), but they let you do your own thing. They will definitely save you time, and may save you money. But you should price each part of the package separately to be sure. And be aware that prices advertised on Web sites and in newspapers rarely include service charges or taxes, which can up your costs by hundreds of dollars.

Don't rule out guided tours. These are perfect for busy people and/or for themed trips or trips to places where making arrangements is difficult (particularly when you don't speak the language). You travel along with a group—large or small—stay in prebooked hotels, eat with your fellow travelers, and follow a schedule. Your guide takes you to places that you might never discover on your own, perhaps enabling you to see more than you would otherwise.

Know what's included in your tour. Meals are sometimes included, sometimes not. A "land-only" tour includes all your travel (by bus, in most cases) in the destination, but not necessarily your flights to and from or even within it. In most cases prices in brochures don't include fees and taxes. And remember that you'll be expected to tip your guide (in cash) at the end of the tour.

Choose a reputable tour operator. Whether you buy a package trip or a tour, opt for an outfit that belongs to the United States Tour Operators Association (⊕*www.ustoa.com*), whose members must set aside funds to cover defaults. Your company should also participate in the Tour Operator Program of the American Society of Travel Agents (ASTA), which will act as mediator in any disputes. You can also check on a given company's reputation among travelers by posting an inquiry on one of the Fodors.com forums.

Protect your travel investments. Pay for everything with a credit card; if you have a problem, your credit-card company may help you resolve it. And buy trip insurance that covers default.

BOOKING ACCOMMODATIONS

Create a Web-site user profile with your favorite hotel chains. Many independent properties also offer a service that allows your preferences—for no-smoking rooms or a king-size bed—to be automatically included in each reservation. You can store your credit-card information, too, which will save time, and you'll usually be able to confirm or cancel reservations online even if you didn't book online.

Make your hotel-room desires clear. If you have preferences about the room you'll be staying in, make them clear to the reservations agent. Consider room size, smoking or no-smoking, king or two queens (or double or two twins), high floor or low floor, patio or balcony. Need quiet? Insist on a room away from the elevator or other high-traffic areas like bars, pools, restaurants, and service areas with ice and vending machines.

Know what to expect from the hotel. You don't want to discover on arrival that your double-room rate is in fact per person or that what is usually Modified American Plan rate (including breakfast and dinner) reverts to European Plan (no meals) off-season. Define what's meant by "all-inclusive." The wine that comes with dinner could cost you, as could that afternoon aperitif. Those much-vaunted water sports could incur an extra charge. Finally, inquire about such things as planned renovations on-site or nearby, guaranteed-reservation and cancellation policies, costs for children staying in your room, and parking options and fees.

Ask hotels about incidental costs. Seemingly petty details such as surcharges on local phone calls, local occupancy taxes, early check-in–checkout fees, resort amenity fees (for towels, use of the gym or pool, etc.), energy surcharges, and parking can really add up. Some hotels tack on hidden gratuities, too.

Get a clear picture of the view from the hotel. If you read the words "city view" or "ocean view," ask whether the view is obstructed or unobstructed. Also, in beach locations, be sure that your room is "beachfront" and not simply "waterfront." In Florida and many Caribbean destinations, for example, many visitors arrive at their "waterfront" hotels only to find themselves on the Intercoastal Waterway, a canal, or a bay, 10 or more minutes' drive from the actual beach.

CHOOSING AIRPLANE SEATS

Not all seats are created equal. Aisle seats are generally the most healthful, since you can more easily get up and stretch. On the other hand, windows are coziest for would-be nappers. Airline Web sites often have aircraft schematics, or you can try Seatguru.com, which not only has information on layouts but also on in-flight amenities (what few are left!). Below are few more pointers.

■ If you're traveling alone or as a couple on a plane with a two/three seat configuration, opt for a seat on the "two" side—this will at least ensure that you won't get stuck in the dreaded "middle" seat of a "three" section.

■ Avoid seats on the aisle directly across from the lavatories. Frequent fliers say those are even worse than back-row seats that don't recline.

■ When flying early in the day, book a seat away from the sunrise side of the plane so you're not bothered by the intense early morning rays.

■ For the best views of clouds and terrain, avoid window seats that are over the wing.

■ Try for a seat in an exit row. The plus side is more legroom. The minuses include having to stash your carry-on in an overhead bin for the duration of the flight and possibly having to pay a fee for the privilege of sitting in these popular seats. Also, you can't sit in exit rows when you have kids in tow. Just note that some airlines charge extra for such seats.

Look for a floor plan. Some Web sites contain floor plans of the hotel or of individual rooms. These will tell you definitively whether the photos have distorted the reality or conveyed it accurately. They will also show the relative locations of different features, and help you avoid a room by the elevator or at the remote end of a long corridor.

BOOKING FLIGHTS

Know your flight type. "Nonstop" goes from city A to city B without stopping. A "direct flight" stops, then flies on but does not require a change of planes. "Connecting" means that you will change planes. And a "through flight" requires you to change both your plane and your airline.

Pick the flight with the best on-time record. Major U.S. airlines are required to publish in the computer reservations

2

system a one-digit code for each flight that indicates how often it arrives on time (within 15 minutes of schedule. A code "6" means that the flight arrived punctually between 60% and 69% of the time, a code "3" 30% to 39% of the time. This information is available on airline Web sites. Travel and reservations agents also have it.

Arrange connecting flights with care. Don't buy a ticket if there's less than an hour between connecting flights. Although schedules are padded, if anything goes wrong you might miss your connection. If you're traveling to an important function, depart a day early.

Book flights for early in the day. Early flights are most likely to be on time. If they are delayed or you miss a connection, you stand a much better chance of getting on another flight and not being stranded overnight.

In winter, make flight connections through warm-weather cities. If you're flying from Phoenix to Boston with a choice between a connection in Dallas and a connection in Chicago, choose Dallas. Even if this option takes slightly longer, you're much less likely to encounter the weather-related delays that plague northern cities.

Get in-flight meal specifics when booking. Airline meals are increasingly a thing of the past, and when food is offered, it often costs extra. That said, meal choices can be wide (e.g., children's menus, diabetic, kosher, vegetarian).

WORD OF MOUTH. "United is a poor airline for long distance to Asia compared to Asian competitors (worse meals, fewer flight attendants per passenger, worse service in the air, and hopeless to deal with if you need to telephone them), unless you are willing to spend the extra money for their Economy-plus seats." —rizzuto

Choose a good seat on the plane. Often, you can pick a seat when you buy your ticket on an airline Web site. But it's not guaranteed; the airline could change the plane after you book, so double-check. You can also select a seat if you check in electronically.

BOOKING RENTAL CARS

Be sure you have the right driver's license. Most rental-car agencies accept your valid state driver's license with another form of photo ID; some agencies (and destinations) also require an International Driver's Permit (IDP), which states

RENTAL CAR INSURANCE

Everyone who rents a car wonders whether the insurance that the rental companies offer is worth the expense. No one—including us—has a simple answer. It all depends on how much regular insurance you have, how comfortable you are with risk, and whether or not money is an issue.

■ **Check your car-insurance policy first.** If you own a car and carry comprehensive car insurance for both collision and liability, your personal auto insurance will probably cover a rental to some degree, though not all policies protect you abroad; read your policy's fine print.

■ **Have CDW or LDW at the very least.** If you don't have auto insurance, buy the collision damage waiver (CDW)—also called the loss-damage waiver (LDW)—from the rental company. This eliminates your liability for theft of or damage to the car.

■ **Inquire about the rental agency's insurance requirements.** Some agencies *require* you to purchase CDW coverage through them; many will even include it in quoted rates. All will strongly encourage you to buy CDW—possibly implying that it's required—so

be sure to ask about it. U.S. rental companies sell CDWs and LDWs for about $15 to $25 a day; supplemental liability is usually more than $10 a day.

■ **Weigh other car-insurance options.** It may be cheaper to buy CDW coverage on its own or add a supplemental CDW to a comprehensive travel-insurance policy than to purchase it from a rental company. Through Travel Guard (⊕ *www.travelguard. com*), for instance, you pay $9 per day for $35,000 of coverage (with a $250 deductible)—about half the price you'd pay at some car-rental companies. That said, you don't pay for a supplement if you're required to buy from the rental company.

■ **Don't buy more coverage than you need.** The rental agency may offer you all sorts of policies with coverage beyond collision and liability, but they're rarely worth the cost. In the U.S., personal accident insurance, which is basic hospitalization coverage, is a rip-off if you already have health insurance.

■ **Check out credit-card coverage.** Some credit cards offer CDW coverage, but it's usually supplemen-

2

tal to your own insurance and rarely covers SUVs, minivans, luxury models, and the like. If your coverage is secondary, you may still be liable for loss-of-use costs from the rental agency (again, read the fine print). And note that no credit-card insurance is valid unless you use that card for all transactions, from reserving to paying the final bill. Finally, all companies exclude car rental in some countries, so be sure to find out about the destination to which you are traveling.

Know the destination's insurance quirks. For example, in some European countries collision policies that car-rental companies sell typically do not cover stolen vehicles. (All agencies operating in Italy require that you buy CDW and a theft-protection policy, but those costs will already be included in the rates you are quoted.) And MasterCard is one of the few companies that offer Americans CDW in Ireland. (At the rental counter you'll need to present a letter from MasterCard stating that it does, indeed, provide this coverage, or you'll be forced to buy it.)

in a number of languages the type of license you have and its expiration date. Even if an IDP isn't required, it's easier for foreign authorities to understand, making it especially worthwhile if you're traveling in rural areas and aren't fluent in the language. You don't need to take a test to get an IDP; you just pay a fee of about $15. Permits are available through the AAA and other agencies.

WORD OF MOUTH. "It's good to have an International Drivers Permit whenever you are traveling internationally. In case of an emergency, it's another form of important information for authorities. It's very easy to get one; if you have an AAA office nearby, the staff there can get you one in minutes. Make sure you have your passport with you when getting your permit." —Oregongirl777

Choose the right rental car for your trip. Avoid tiny economy cars if you're driving in mountainous, high-altitude areas. Make sure the car can accommodate not only you and your passengers but also everybody's luggage. Will you need air-conditioning where you're traveling? A ski rack? In some countries you're more likely to find cars with manual rather than automatic transmissions. Also, be aware that a mid-sized European car is probably more like a compact model in the United States.

Know where you can—and can't—drive a rental car. In Hawaii, rental-car companies routinely forbid drivers from taking their car onto certain dangerous but popular roads. Crossing the border into Canada or Mexico from the United States is also a no-no. Because of the high car-theft rate, many European agencies don't want their cars taken into Eastern Europe. You'll need a special sticker in order to drive on the autobahns of Switzerland and Austria. Make sure your agency knows where you plan to use the car.

Preparing for the Trip

WORD OF MOUTH

"I prefer to arrive with $50 or so in the local currency and wait until the following day, when I am alert and awake, to withdraw my main stash of cash."

—enzian

Updated
by Alexis
Kelly

OK. You've picked a vacation destination, booked your hotel, and made all your transportation arrangements. You're all set to go. Not so fast! Have you devised an itinerary or made reservations for that fancy, of-the-moment restaurant? Have you looked into travel insurance or pre-trip vaccinations? Have you gathered all your necessary documents, including a current passport?

Thoughtful preparation—sooner rather than later—can be as important to a successful trip as research, planning, and booking. For tips on what to do now so that your trip is effortless later, read on.

Devise a rough itinerary or wish list of sights. You don't want to waste time on the ground trying to figure out where to go. Include things of interest to you and all your traveling companions. Plan things day by day, and keep the itinerary (and your minds) flexible—with lots of room for breaks. All this makes it easier to avoid the three feelings that lead to bickering: resentment, disappointment, and fatigue.

Plan your time realistically. Look over a guidebook or Web site about the area you're visiting, and really assess your options. Some places, like laid-back beach locales or secluded countryside B&Bs, lend themselves to outright rest and relaxation. Others have so many activity options that you can easily feel overwhelmed. If you don't fret about simply taking it easy or about seeing it all, you may get the hang of simply relaxing much more quickly.

Research the best times to visit tourist hot spots. It's understandable that you've just *got* to see Stonehenge, but crowds can put a damper on your experience. Check your guidebook, the Web, or call in advance to ask about the best seasons, days, or even hours to avoid crowds. Also find out about less-visited areas nearby.

Assemble a travel documents kit. This is a pouch or envelope of the stuff that, if you lost everything else, would still leave you basically OK. Include transportation confirmations or tickets; hotel and rental-car confirmations; copies of your passport's first page and any visa pages; copies of prescriptions for medications and eyeglasses; list of credit-card numbers and assistance hotlines; contact info for travel insurance or medical-assistance providers; contacts for family, neighbors, doctors, work associates. Travel Stix (⊕*www.mytravelstix.com*) compact flash drives have sets of essential travel forms and documents. There's a set for college kids, babysitters, older travelers, children, business travelers, adventure travelers, pets, and international travelers. Just download the forms, fill them out, and then upload them. Sets run between $20 and $25.

Plan to hand-carry your travel documents. Put your documents kit in your carry-on as backup, adding maps and guidebooks as necessary. When it's time to go, carry on your person your passport, airline tickets, hotel confirmations, or other necessary receipts.

TIPS FOR THE SUPER-ORGANIZED

Book activities well before takeoff. National, regional, and city tourist-board sites often have links to theaters, non-profit associations, or commercial companies with calendars and online booking capabilities. So do sites like Citysearch.com. Some of the world's top museums let you buy tickets to special exhibitions with a few clicks or a phone call. And did you know that Ticketmaster.com serves not only the United States but also several foreign countries? For discount tickets, try the Theater Development Fund (⊕*www.tdf.org*). AllAboutJazz.com has a calendar page listing festivals and concerts. Domestic, as well as international events, are listed. But the mother of all sites has to be Viator.com—it lists and lets you book shows, tours, day trips, and other activities all over the world.

Ship your luggage ahead. Shipping luggage via an air-freight service like LuggageConcierge.com, LuggageFree.com, SportsExpress.com, or VirtualBellhop.com is a great way to cut down on backaches, hassles, and stress. Plan to send your bags ahead by several days to U.S. destinations and by up to two weeks to some international destinations. It will cost at least $100 to send a small piece of luggage, a golf bag, or a pair of skis to a domestic destination, much more to places overseas. All the freight services insure bags (for most the limit is $1,000). Some cover a certain amount automatically. Each item shipped with Virtual Bellhop, for instance, is automatically insured up to $500 for loss or damage, and you can buy additional coverage ($1 for each additional $100 worth). Note, though, that insurance coverage is charged per leg of the trip—in other words, multiply the charge by two for a round-trip.

Pick the cleanest beach. The Blue Flag Programme (⊕*www. blueflag.org*) acknowledges beaches that meet high standards in terms of environmental management, water quality, and safety and services. It was started in France by the Foundation for Environmental Education (FEE) during the "European Year of the Environment" (1987 to you and me), and has since spread to the rest of Europe and beyond. Today the list includes both beaches and marinas—2,949 beaches and 662 marinas, in fact—in 41 countries, with more countries adopting the program each year.

Plan your theme park strategy. Founded and edited by a former attractions host at Walt Disney World, ThemePark-Insider.com now taps readers for ratings and reviews of and tips for parks around the world. Listings have sections on hours, tickets, strategy, and current park buzz. Also, look into new technologies that give you park updates that will help you on the ground. For example, Disney and Verizon have teamed up to update you via cell phone on real-time attraction availability, character meet-and-greet locations, and the like.

Find Wi-Fi hot spots. You can find information (including user reviews) on Internet connectivity and other tech services offered by hotels, restaurants, bookstores, and other business on sites like WiFi Hotspot List (⊕*www.wi-fihotspotlist.com*) and WiFiFreespot.com—which list spots in the Caribbean, Canada, Europe, Asia, the Middle East, Africa, and Australia. JiWire (⊕*www.jiwire.com*) is a private company (a mobile audience media company, to be precise) that offers a very public service. Its Web site helps you find Wi-Fi-verified public hotspots—roughly 299,000 free and pay-for locations—in 144 countries. There's even a free app for the iPhone and iPod Touch that helps you find Wi-Fi hotspots anywhere in the world.

Book an airport parking space. A couple of clicks on Airport-ParkingReservations.com and a small deposit (the equivalent of the fee for one day of parking) are all it takes to book a space at one of more than 65 airports in the United States, Canada, the United Kingdom, and Ireland. Choose from self-park, valet, outdoor, and indoor lots. Free shuttle service and luggage assistance and discounted rates are among the perks of using this site. Booking spots through Avistar Parking (⊕*www.avistarparking.com*) may yield a 10% discount (via a downloadable coupon) on already low rates. And ParkSleepFly.com has money-saving packages from airport-area hotels that offer a week or more of discounted or free parking to overnight guests.

Check out airport wait times. The Transportation Security Administration helps to make up for the hassles of beefed-up security with a section on its Web site (⊕ *waittime.tsa.dhs. gov*). Its Wait Times Calculator estimates—based on historical data, not current situations—how long it takes to clear checkpoints (i.e., processing time) on departure in U.S. airports. United States Customs and Border Patrol (⊕ *apps. cbp.gov/awt*) provides similar information for arrivals. Many airports also have such information on their sites.

Check out your flight status. Flightstats.com reports on flight delays, airport weather conditions, and on-time performance—among other things. You can sign up for e-mails or mobile-phone alerts. Official Airline Guides for the Traveler (⊕ *www.oagtravel.com*) can fill you in on flight status for free, and flight duration, airline routes, and more as part of a free trial. Orbitz (⊕ *updates.orbitz.com*) was one of the first booking sites to include updates on things like airport delays. You can also sign up for mobile phone alerts and view itineraries, flight status, etc.

Check in online. More and more airlines are not only allowing you to check in online but also to pick a seat, book bags in advance, and print e-tickets. Hyatt, Hilton, and Far East Hotels are among the hotel chains that allow electronic room check-in. More companies will certainly follow their lead.

Firm up those dinner plans. Research restaurants on Fodors. com and online reservation services like OpenTable.com, which covers all 50 states and Washington, D.C., and has limited listings in Canada, Mexico, the United Kingdom, Dubai, and elsewhere. DinnerBroker.com has restaurants throughout the United States as well as a few in Canada. For good nonfranchise road-trip options, check out Roadfood. com. MenuPages.com has menus for more than 30,000 restaurants in New York, Boston, D.C., Philly, Los Angeles, San Francisco, South Florida, Chicago, London, and Paris.

Calculate how much your drive will cost. Input your route and the make and model of your car on the AAA's fuel-cost calculator (⊕ *www.fuelcostcalculator.com*) and voilà! Although figures assume there are no traffic jams (which you probably should factor in), gas prices are updated regularly. Use it to budget for a road trip or to decide whether to fly or drive.

Find a decent bathroom. BathroomDiaries.com is flush with unsanitized info on restrooms the world over—each one located, reviewed, and rated. SitOrSquat.com provides the same info and has a mobile app.

Map out public transportation. Hopstop.com has transit maps and can give bus and subway directions between sights in Boston, Providence, Hartford, New York, Philadelphia, Baltimore, Chicago, Atlanta, San Francisco, and Washington, D.C. There's also information for Long Island Railroad, Metro North, and New Jersey for those in New York's tristate area. Amadeus.net also has numerous helpful travel tools, including subway maps.

PASSPORTS AND VISAS

Get a passport. You and every member of your family should have one. It verifies both identity and nationality, and you need one now more than ever. U.S. citizens must have a passport when traveling by air between the United States and several destinations for which other forms of identification (e.g., a driver's license and a birth certificate) were once sufficient. These destinations include Mexico, Canada, Bermuda, and all countries in Central America and the Caribbean (except Puerto Rico and the U.S. Virgin Islands). You'll also need a passport when traveling between the United States and such destinations by land and sea.

Get a passport card if you live near the border of Canada or Mexico. If you'll be traveling by land or sea between the U.S. and Mexico, Canada, Bermuda, or the Caribbean you can get a passport card; the same rules and regulations that apply to passport books apply to passport cards. The card fits easily in your wallet and lasts as long as a passport book but is less expensive: $55 for adults and $40 for children under 16. It's also only $30 to renew. However, this card can *not* be used for air travel.

Take the right steps toward getting a passport. You must apply in person if you're getting a passport for the first time; if your previous passport was lost, stolen, or damaged; or if your previous passport has expired and was issued more than 15 years ago or when you were under 16. All children under 18 must appear in person to apply for or renew a passport. Both parents must accompany any child under 14 (or send a notarized statement with their permission) and provide proof of their relationship to the child. If you're simply renewing a passport, you can do so by mail.

Don't let a name change invalidate your passport. If you've changed your name, you must have your current, valid passport amended. To do so, mail your passport with your court order, adoption decree, or marriage certificate showing your name change, and a completed passport application form DSP-19 to the passport agency nearest you.

Know the destination's passport and visa requirements. Some countries require that your passport be valid for at least six months after the date you arrive. Some countries also require a visa in addition to a passport. And still other countries require that you have blank pages (for a visa stamp) at the very front and/or very back of your passport. Knowing the rules will allow you time to renew your passport early, get the necessary visa, or have extra pages added to your valid passport.

Know where to go to get a passport. There are 18 regional passport offices, as well as 9,400 or so passport acceptance facilities in post offices, public libraries, and other governmental offices. See the State Department's Web site (⊕ *travel.state.gov/passport*) for details.

Know your passport fees and forms. Forms (for passport books and cards) are available at passport acceptance facilities and online (⊕ *travel.state.gov/passport*), where you'll also find detailed application instructions. The cost to apply for a new passport book is $100 for adults, $85 for children under 16; renewals are $75. Passport cards (good for travel by land or sea only) cost $55 for adults, $40 for children under 16 and $30 to renew.

Breeze through customs. U.S. Customs and Border Protection offers Trusted Traveler Programs (⊕ *www.cbp.gov/xp/cgov/travel/*) that speed up the reentry of Americans from abroad. These programs are only available to citizens who already have passport books and aren't deemed a security threat after background checks and one-on-one interviews. Those who qualify for the Global Entry program, for instance, are issued a card that contains information on biometric signifiers. On reentry from abroad into one of the 20 participating U.S. airports, they simply swipe a card at a kiosk and have either a fingerprint or iris scanned rather than showing a passport. The cost is $100 and approval lasts for five years. The NEXUS card ($50) is

WORD OF MOUTH: GLOBAL ENTRY

"My wife just completed the [Global Entry application] process. It was pretty painless; all done online followed by an in-person interview (20 minutes) at the regional GOES office. Start-to-finish was about one week." —Josh

My travel buddy and I just signed up and were approved. It will be well worth the $20 per year [that it works out to] to get through immigration and customs quicker. We've been backed up multiple times in Miami and New York and almost missed our connecting flights. Plus, it's just pretty cool to have. We can't wait to go someplace, so we can use it coming back!" —sandy_b

"I used it for the first time at Dallas/Fort Worth International (DFW).... It took about two minutes from start to finish. And there was a special (quick) customs inspection desk for Global Entry travelers. I am amazed that it only costs $100 and lasts for five years. I think our government should increase the price." —lovely2c

"We are very pleased with Global Entry, especially... after a long, exhausting flight. We've used it at both Dulles and DFW airports. In all cases, it took us less than five minutes to complete the entry process. The lines at Dulles are usually long, so we save a great deal of time after an eight to nine hour trip from Europe. However, you do have to be in an area that has a border/passport control office to do the personal interview, picture-taking, and digital fingerprinting." —lilla

"The basic membership for Privium [the EU equivalent of Global Entry] is 115 euros per year. The United Kingdom is the only country where it's free, I believe. Global Entry members can join Privium and Privium members can join Global Entry, so if you often fly from, to, or through, say, Amsterdam, a joint membership might be nice." —travelgourmet

used for expedited crossings between the United States and Canada. The SENTRI pass ($122.25) is for use between the United States and Mexico.

Time it right when getting a passport. U.S. passports are valid for 10 years. Allow six weeks for processing, both for first-time passports and renewals. For an expediting fee of $60 you can reduce this time to about two weeks. Know that wait times can be much longer just before or during the busy summer travel season.

Don't panic if your trip is coming up and you don't have a valid passport. If your trip is less than two weeks away or you need your passport quickly so there's enough time to get a foreign visa, you can expedite matters by going to a passport office with the necessary documentation. Call the National Passport Information Center for an appointment (☎ *877/487–2778*). There are operators (best for emergencies) available weekdays 8 AM to 10 PM, EST, but there's automated service (best for nonemergency situations) 24 hours a day.

Look into private passport-acquisition expediters. Companies like Travisa.com, G3 Visas & Passports (⊕ *www.g3visas.com*), and A. Briggs (⊕ *www.abriggs.com*) can get things done in as little as 24 hours. Fees can be hefty: roughly $300 for 24-hour renewal, $200-plus for 48 hours; and $100 to $150 for 5–7 days. Add in courier-service fees and the U.S. Government's renewal and expediting fees, and you're talking a nice chunk of change. To find out more about these companies and to check prices, visit the Web site of the National Association of Passport and Visa Services (⊕ *www.napvs.org*).

Track your passport application. The state department's Web site (⊕ *travel.state.gov/passport*) has a nifty tracking feature that lets you check the status of your application. You can also inquire about it via e-mail; just know that in the busy spring and summer months the wait time for an e-mail response can be as much as two to four days.

Make copies of your passport. Before your trip, make two copies of your passport's data page (one for someone at home and another for you to carry separately from the original). Or scan the page and e-mail it to someone at home and/or yourself. Passportsupport.com is an Australian company that allows you to scan passports and other documents into their secure system for access via the Internet should you need them. The annual fee for the service is about US$13 (A$15).

WHAT, EXACTLY, IS A VISA?

A visa is essentially formal permission to enter a country. It allows countries to keep track of visitors and to generate revenue (from application fees). Some countries participate in the visa-waiver program, which allows U.S. citizens to travel to them without a visa—usually for stays of less than 90 days for leisure or business—and vice versa. Other countries routinely issue tourist visas on arrival, particularly to U.S. citizens, though sometimes you have to stand in a separate line and pay a small fee to get your stamp before going through immigration at the airport on arrival. Still other countries require that you arrange for a visa in advance of your trip. There's usually—but not always—a fee involved, and said fee may be nominal ($10 or less) or substantial ($100 or more).

If you must apply for a visa in advance, you can usually do it in person or by mail. When you apply by mail, you send your passport to a designated consulate, where your passport will be examined and the visa issued. Expediters—usually the same ones who handle expedited passport applications—can do all the work of obtaining your visa for you; however, there's always an additional cost ($50 per visa and up).

Most visas limit you to a single trip—basically during the actual dates of your planned vacation. Other visas allow you to visit as many times as you wish for a specific period of time. Remember that requirements change, sometimes at the drop of a hat, and the burden is on you to make sure that you have the appropriate visas. Otherwise, you'll be turned away at the airport or, worse, deported after you arrive in the country. No company or travel insurer gives refunds if your travel plans are disrupted because you didn't have the correct visa.

HEALTH AND WELL BEING

Take stock of your health. Get a checkup, discuss your travel plans, and look into your last batch of shots including your MMR (measles, mumps, and rubella immunization) and tetanus. Make a list of medical issues that might affect your plans—from serious conditions like asthma and high blood pressure to more minor complaints like tennis elbow or foot calluses. Create a "health" checklist with such things as medications, ice packs, and so on. Iron out ways to cope with your health needs on the road, like having your prescriptions called into a pharmacy in your destination, or bringing extra medication with you. If you have your prescription filled at a national pharmacy chain like CVS or Rite Aid, prescriptions can be filled at any location in the United States.

Investigate health issues in remote destinations. Some countries require immunizations of international travelers; for others, especially remote destinations in southerly climes, you might want to take some extra precautions. The Centers for Disease Control's Web site (⊕ *www.cdc.gov*) lists health issues and vaccination requirements by country. WebMD.com is a great place to get more information on particular diseases, conditions, and medications.

Consult a travel-medicine expert when needed. These doctors know all about things like which vaccinations are truly necessary for a given trip and which antimalarial drug is best for a given destination. They can also advise you on items to pack in a travel medical kit. The International Society of Travel Medicine (⊕ *www.istm.org*) has a list of practitioners and clinics around the world.

Don't put off pretrip getting shots and medicines. Some preventative inoculations, like those for hepatitis B, require three shots over a period of six months. You must get the first two within a month of each other before you travel; the third can usually be administered after your return home. You also have to start taking antimalarial drugs before departing for an affected area.

Carry plenty of your prescribed medicines. Bring more than you anticipate needing, just in case you get stranded. And pack them in their original containers in carry-on bags, not checked luggage, which could go astray. Have your doctor use the generic name and note potency/dosage information on any prescription refill slips you need.

Sign up with a medical-evacuation assistance company. A membership in one of these companies gets you doctor referrals, emergency evacuation or repatriation, 24-hour hotlines for medical consultation, and other assistance. International SOS (⊕ *www.internationalsos.com*) and AirMed International (⊕ *www.airmed.com*) provide evacuation services and medical referrals. MedjetAssist (⊕ *www. medjetassist.com*) offers medical evacuation.

Determine what your insurance company covers abroad. Inquire about your company's provisions for emergency care outside your coverage area. What kind of documentation should you bring? Who should you contact if you fall ill? It's likely that your existing policy won't cover you internationally. A short-term travel-insurance policy with medical and evacuation coverage is a wise investment if you plan to cross the border for an extended period of time.

Find out whether your foreign destination has free national health care. If so, the country may also provide foreigners with free outpatient or other medical services. Some European countries have this.

STAYING FIT

Write down your current fitness plan before heading out. You'll find it easier to follow your exercise regime if you put it in writing. Or list daily on-the-road fitness goals. As an example: (1) walk whenever possible; (2) eat smaller portions; (3) go for a run on the beach; (4) stretch for five minutes morning and night. But don't go on a guilt trip if you miss a few goals: the point of the list is to keep you healthy, not stress you out.

Screen your hotel's fitness facilities. It's not enough to know that there *is* a gym: How big is it? What are the hours? What kind of equipment is available? What classes are offered? Are they free? Does the pool have lap lanes, or is it a family free-for-all? Are there in-room fitness offerings like treadmills or yoga mats and DVDs. Do rooms have enough floor space for an in-room workout? Are there in-room whirlpool baths? What about on-site saunas or steam rooms? Call for information and/or take a virtual tour of the hotel on its Web site or on a booking site. Use the screening features on booking sites to be sure fitness facilities meet your needs.

Look into local workout options. Ask your hotel for recommendations, or check out sites like Healthclubs.com and Airportgyms.com. Swimmersguide.com, created and maintained by two lifelong lap swimmers, has listings of pools around the world that are accessible to the public, as well as some hotel pools. On RunthePlanet.com you can research the world's races and routes; the latter are provided by fellow runners. Yogafinder.com does just what its name implies—in about 85 countries. Athletic-MindedTraveler.com charges less than $5 a month for access to well-edited information on where to work out, run, buy equipment, or play your favorite sport in more than 60 U.S. and Canadian cities.

Research workout routines and portable gear. All the major fitness magazines (e.g., *Health, Fitness, Men's Health, Women's Health*) have workout routines in their issues and on their Web sites. The American Council on Fitness (⊕*www.acefitness.org*) has an exercise library with illustrated moves that target every part of the body. Jfit.com sells a portable travel workout kit with resistance bands, bars, and ankle straps. All of Lifeline USA's (⊕*www.lifelineusa.com*) exercise products are portable.

Opt for destination-specific activities. Can't find any of the activities you know and love? Try a new one—perhaps one for which the destination is known. Sign up for tango lessons in Buenos Aires, surfing sessions in San Diego, rock-climbing courses in Grand Teton, guided walkabouts in the Outback, or tai chi classes in Hong Kong. Tourist-board, national park, and city Web sites have information on many such activities. Maxlifestyle.net has information on everything from getting started to gearing up to planning a trip around 20 different activities—from hiking to snowboarding to meditation.

Book a fitness-oriented trip. If you want the focus of your trip to be on fitness, wellness, and health, look into tours offered by operators like Fit Tours (⊕*www.fitnesstouring.com*), which does custom trips as well as organized ones geared to people of different fitness levels—from active senior citizens to high-performance endurance athletes—to places like Costa Rica, Mexico, St. Lucia, Colorado, and Austria.

STAYING TRIM

Map out diet and exercise strategies before traveling. Don't want to be munching airline peanuts all day? Bring your own snacks. Your hotel lacks an exercise room? Call ahead to find out whether there are pleasant walking/running routes nearby. As long as you look around for smart ways to adapt, you can find a way to adhere to your fitness goals.

Try to eat normally during your trip. Travelers often joke that on the road "calories don't count"—if only! If your usual morning meal is a bagel and juice, a solid week of breakfast buffets could get you into trouble. Avoid sabotaging

TRIP INSURANCE 101

What kind of coverage do you honestly need? Do you even need trip insurance at all? Take a deep breath and read on.

Comprehensive trip insurance is valuable if you're booking an expensive or complicated trip (particularly to an isolated region) or if you're booking far in advance. Such policies typically cover trip-cancellation and interruption, letting you cancel or cut your trip short because of a personal emergency, illness, or, in some cases, acts of terrorism in your destination. Such policies also cover evacuation and medical care. Some also cover trip delays because of bad weather or mechanical problems, as well as lost or delayed baggage. Insurers include Access America (⊕ www.accessamerica.com), CSA Travel Protection (⊕ www.csatravelprotection.com), HTH Worldwide (⊕ www.hthworldwide.com), and Travel Guard (⊕ www.travelguard.com).

Another type of coverage to look for is financial default—that is, when your trip is disrupted because a tour operator, airline, or cruise line goes out of business. Generally you must buy this when you book your trip or shortly thereafter, and it's only available to you if your operator isn't on a list of excluded companies.

Medicare, Medigap, or some private insurers do not cover medical expenses outside the United States (including aboard a cruise ship, even if it leaves from a U.S. port). Medical-only policies typically reimburse you for medical care (excluding that related to preexisting conditions) and hospitalization, and provide for evacuation. You still have to pay the bills and await reimbursement from the insurer, though. International Medical Group (⊕ www.imglobal.com) and Wallach & Company (⊕ www.wallach.com) are among the companies that offer medical-only coverage.

Some online booking sites also have insurance. Expedia.com offers Package Protection Plus plans, which start at $40 per person, on air-hotel vacation packages it sells. If you cancel or change—for any reason—you're entitled to a refund on trip deposits, airline-change fees, and booking fees. The plan also includes travel- and baggage-delay reimbursements, travel-accident protection, and other things. Airfare refunds are contingent upon whether the fare was a published one or an Expedia-negotiated one. If you want coverage for airfare alone, you can buy a separate, more restrictive plan.

When investigating policies, press for details. With trip-cancellation insurance, for instance, be sure to ask whether you're covered should you back out because of terrorist attacks, civil unrest, or natural disasters in the destination, you're laid off from a full-time job at home, or you have an unforeseen conflict at work. With medical insurance, inquire about preexisting condition issues and coverage if you're injured participating in risky sports (mountain climbing or skiing, say). If the things that concern you aren't covered, you may need to look into add-ons like "any reason" cancellation coverage or adventure-sports coverage.

Expect comprehensive travel-insurance policies to cost about 4% to 7% or 8% of the total price of your trip (it's more like 8%–12% if you're over age 70). A medical-only policy may or may not be cheaper than a comprehensive policy. Always read the fine print to make sure that you're covered for the risks that are of most concern to you. The easiest way to compare policies is on InsureMyTrip.com and TotalTravelInsurance.com, which have information from 17 insurers; Squaremouth.com, which has lists prices and policies for 15 insurers; and QuoteMyTrip.com, which has prices and policies for more than 40 insurers.

To get the most of your coverage, buy insurance when you book your trip. And, before you *do* buy, go over not only your personal insurance coverage but also coverage that may be provided by a credit card used to purchase travel services. It's a waste of money to be covered for the same things twice.

3

your fitness goals by asking yourself the question: Is this what I'd do at home? Do your best to approximate normal eating routines while still allowing for opportunities to sample local cuisines.

Create an on-the-road meal plan. Use guidebooks and online resources to find the kinds of restaurants you prefer. Check online menus or ask your hotel to fax you its menus and, if possible, those of restaurants nearby. The Web site GoodFoodNearYou.com has menu nutrition information for 220,000 U.S. restaurants—making it much easier to create healthful meal plans. The site also has a free app so you can continue your research during the trip. If your hotel room has a mini-refrigerator or a larger minibar, ask your hotel about good groceries and delis in the neighborhood so you can stockpile some healthful nibbles.

Eat big at lunch. Try eating one big meal each day in the middle of the day, followed by a light dinner. You'll save money, too, as lunch is always cheaper than dinner.

Avoid international fast-food chains. McDonald's, Burger King, Wendy's—this junk food is everywhere, so why would you eat it on vacation? Use your precious time in London, Moscow, or Honolulu to seek out local flavors.

Sign up with WeightWatchers.com. One of the country's most acclaimed weight-loss programs has a fantastic Web site with all kinds of tools and support that will help you set goals and stay on track—during your vacation as well as before and after if you like. Although the three-month online membership package saves money, you can sign up for one month—just so you can log in on the road—for a reasonable price (occasionally a free month membership is also available). WeightWatchers now has a free app for iPhones.

Plan ahead for special dietary concerns. If you have food allergies and are traveling to a non-English-speaking destination, consider having a detailed explanation of your allergy translated so that you can carry it with you to show staff in restaurants. The Food Allergy and Anaphylaxis Network (⊕ *www.foodallergy.org*) has lots of helpful hints about traveling with food allergies. If you're a vegetarian, hop online to check restaurant menus or call ahead to be sure that your options aren't limited. Or pick an all-vegetarian dining spot through a Web site such as Vegdining.com.

Have fun staying fit and trim. Staying healthy should be fun—otherwise, why bother? If you're making yourself miserable by trying too hard to stick to the straight and narrow, lighten up a bit. Don't get too fixated on your routine. You don't need to dread every restaurant visit: sharing a dessert from time to time can be salubrious. Keep your mind open to the possibilities—that's why you're traveling, after all.

FROM DISTRESSED TO DE-STRESSED

Book spa treatments as soon as you book a trip. What better way to transition from everyday stress and routine into vacation-time relaxation and renewal? Guaranteeing you'll get in means making appointments well in advance. To feel refreshed after a lengthy international flight, schedule a massage for as early as possible the day you arrive. Follow it with a snack, a sauna, and a nap, and you'll be a whole new person. A salt glow or loofah body scrub is the perfect way to prep your skin for beach attire. A mid-trip pedicure will combat sightseeing fatigue. Spafinder.com links to all types of spas around the world.

Figure out which type of spa suits your style. Spas come in all shapes and sizes, but according to the International Spa Association (⊕ *www.experienceispa.com*) there are seven types: day spas; club spas (essentially, fitness centers or gyms with day spas); destination spas (stays are all about fitness, diet, and treatments); hotel/resort spas, cruise-ship spas; mineral-springs spas (with mineral springs, thermal baths, and hydro- or thalassotherapy treatments); and medical spas (with medical professionals overseeing prevention/wellness programs or cosmetic procedures and recovery). Deciding on your interests and goals will enhance your spa experience.

Don't think that spas are just for women. About 80% of spagoers are female, but men are a fast-growing market. Many spas have lounge areas, treatments, and programs designed specifically with men in mind.

Jump-start your fitness program at a destination spa. If you're looking to begin a weight-management program, embark on a fitness regimen, or make other lifestyle changes, a destination spa is best. You'll be totally immersed in an atmosphere of wellness along with other like-minded people, away from the temptations found at most resorts.

MONEY MATTERS

Start your trip with a little local currency. Before a foreign trip, convert about $100 to $200 into local currency—enough to cover a cab ride from the airport, a few incidentals, and a meal or two. Have enough small bills to cover tips. It won't hurt to have a few unexchanged bucks stashed away, either. Get the rest of your cash from an ATM upon arrival. Avoid converting at currency-exchange booths in airports and on streets or at hotels, where fees are often high and rates are often low.

Don't wait till the last minute to get foreign currency. Banks rarely have every foreign currency on hand, and it may take as long as a week to order. If you're planning to exchange funds before leaving home, don't wait till the last minute. International Currency Express (⊕ *www.foreignmoney.com*) will exchange dollars into any of 54 foreign currencies and ship it to you within five business days. You'll pay for the exchange and the shipping, though, so it pays to plan ahead with your own bank.

Make sure you'll have access to your money abroad. Are ATMs available? Is your ATM pin number four digits (six digits are uncommon in some places) and wired for your destination? Are credit cards widely accepted? These are things you'll want to know before you go. Also, for more flexibility bring a debit card as opposed to a card designated for ATM withdrawals only.

Know the monetary import and export rules. You can leave from or return to the United States with as much money (currency, coin, traveler's checks) as you wish. But if the value is more than $10,000 you must fill out a Currency Reporting Form, available from U.S. Customs. The penalties for failing to do this are severe. The regulations involving importing and exporting money to/from other countries may vary, so if this is an issue, do your homework.

Set a daily budget so you exchange only what you need. It would be a shame to have to exchange huge amounts of foreign currency back into dollars, hence paying exchange fees twice. Setting a daily budget will help you avoid this scenario.

Use credit cards for travel-related and large retail purchases. Many credit-card companies offer purchase-protection plans, dispute resolution, and other consumer services that might come in handy.

CREDIT CARDS

Find the best credit card for you. Credit cards aren't all the same. Most major card companies tack on a foreign transaction fee of 2%–5% on any charge made internationally. The issuing bank might also add similar fees. Call your credit-card company before you go away—fees change often and you don't want to be stuck charging the majority of your trip on a card with hefty ones.

Look into cards issued by smaller banks and credit unions. These institutions might charge lower rates. After checking rates, check that the exchange rates are consistent with your other cards.

Notify your credit-card company before you travel. If you don't do this, the company might put a hold on your card due to "unusual" activity—like a charge for a restaurant in Kraków. If you call ahead, the company may append a memo to your account. Hopefully, your call will prevent a needless interruption of your shopping spree along Paris's Avenue Montaigne.

WORD OF MOUTH. "You should *never* use a credit card to get cash from an ATM. Your credit card will begin charging you a high finance charge as soon as you make the withdrawal. It will be considered a loan, which is treated differently than a charge." —ellenem

Know your credit-card numbers. Record all your credit-card numbers—as well as the phone numbers to call if your cards are lost or stolen—in a safe place, so you're prepared should something go wrong. Both MasterCard and Visa have general numbers you can call (collect if you're abroad) if your card is lost, but you're better off calling the number of your issuing bank, since MasterCard and Visa usually just transfer you to your bank; your bank's number is usually printed on your card.

Be savvy about chips and PINs. Many European countries have adopted "smart" or "chip and PIN" systems. Credit cards have embedded chips—rather than magnetic strips—and purchases are confirmed with a PIN, not your signature. If you have a traditional card or a chip card that requires a signature, you might have difficulty making purchases from automated machines, like ticket machines. You will need a human being's intervention, like a teller at a ticket window, so that you may sign for the purchase.

BEST CARDS FOR TRAVEL

CREDIT CARDS

Although you may not know it, many credit cards tack a 3% currency-conversion fee for all foreign charges. This fee generally includes a 1% fee levied by Visa or Master-Card; your card company passes the charge on to you. That's not small change when you consider all the hotel stays, meals, souvenirs, and museum entrance fees you will charge on that sucker.

Best of the Bunch. Capital One has had zero conversion fees and has even absorbed the 1% fee that Visa and MasterCard charge to process purchases. American Express charges a flat 2.7% fee and doesn't allow merchants to tack on additional fees at the point of sale, namely the Dynamic Currency Conversion fee (DCC). By charging with an Amex card you are completely avoiding the DCC altogether, which is just one less thing to worry about.

DEBIT CARDS

Debit cards are the most convenient means of procuring local currency at a favorable rate. It's a godsend to be able to skip the airport exchange desk to make a beeline for an ATM, as long as you know what sort of fees to expect with every withdrawal. Some debit cards, like their credit-card counterparts, tack on a 3% currency-conversion fee plus a fee if you use the card at a machine that isn't affiliated with your home bank. You may also be charged for withdrawing money by the owner of the machine.

Best of the Bunch. HSBC, as there's peace of mind in knowing that there's likely a branch relatively close should something with your account go awry. The bank has more than 150,000 ATMs and close to 8,000 branches in 119 countries and territories. Fees for purchases and withdrawals (including from non-HSBC machines) have been low.

Bank of America is another good choice, according to SmarterTravel.com, as it's part of the Global ATM Alliance, a group of banks in seven major countries with reciprocal no-fee withdrawals. That means access to almost 18,000 ATMs operated by Barclays in the United Kingdom, BNP Paribas in France, China Construction Bank in China, Deutsche Bank in Germany, Santander Serfin in Mexico, Scotiabank in Canada, and Westpac in Australia and New Zealand.

REWARDS CARDS

If you spend more time in airport lounges than your own living room, chances are you'll be logging enough miles and trips to make carrying a rewards card seem

3

like a no-brainer. There's a dizzying array of options; you may be surprised to find that some hotel-based cards offer greater flexibility and value than many airline frequent-flyer cards. Keep in mind that participation in many rewards programs and clubs, including those mentioned here, don't require that you sign up for the connected credit card. The cards are a means to accumulate points at a faster rate.

Best of the Bunch. Starwood Preferred Guest American Express Card: it has consistently been voted the best travel card by users of the FlyerTalk.com forum. You accumulate "Starpoints" with every dollar you spend on the card; you can then cash in the points for free stays and upgrades at Starwood hotels or for tickets on over 30 airlines.

The Capital One Venture Rewards Credit Card was voted top dog by Creditcard.com. Miles don't expire, there are no foreign transaction fees, you accumulate 2 mi for every dollar you spend, and the yearly fee of $59 is waived for the first year.

Deal in local currency. Before you charge something, ask the merchant whether he or she plans to do a dynamic currency conversion (DCC). In such a transaction the credit-card processor (shop, restaurant, or hotel, not Visa or Master-Card) converts the currency and charges you in dollars. In most cases you'll pay the merchant a 3% fee for this service in addition to any credit-card company and issuing-bank foreign-transaction surcharges. DCC is optional—speak up to avoid these hidden charges. American Express card carriers needn't bother; DCC is not offered at all.

Keep track of transaction dates. If you're traveling in an area where the currency fluctuates wildly, you might want to note the transaction date of your purchase. Shifty merchants will sometimes wait a few weeks (or months) to submit the charge to your credit-card company in the hope of getting a better exchange rate. Your credit-card statement shows both the transaction date, which is the date you made the purchase, and the posting date, which is the date the merchant presented your card company with the charge. If something seems wrong, call your credit-card company and ask them to research the transaction.

DEBIT CARDS

Research ATM locations the world over. Make sure your debit card is a member of the major networks that operate where you're headed. Look on the back of your card for participating networks. Check your individual network's ATM locator to be sure that there are ATMs available where you are headed. Both Visa (⊕ *http://visa.via.infonow.net/locator/ global*) and MasterCard (⊕ *www.mastercard.com*) networks feature ATM locators on their Web sites. MasterCard also has the ATM Hunter App available for free on iTunes.

Find out about ATM charges. There are two possible charges— one from the ATM side and one from your bank back home. If you're using an ATM that is within a network alliance that your card is a member of, it's less likely that the foreign bank will levy a fee. One caveat—many convenience store–type ATMs (machines not connected to a formal bank) charge. Check with your bank to see what sort of fees they charge—some levy a flat charge of $1–$10 for every withdrawal.

Have a cash withdrawal strategy. To save time tracking down machines and reduce the fees associated with withdrawing, take out larger amounts than you would normally. Note, though, that there are withdrawal limits, and these vary by both bank and machine. Also, if you do withdraw a large amount, choose one that can be fulfilled with a variety of bills to avoid being given solely large bills. Chances are you'll want a drink or coffee soon after landing, and some vendors may refuse to make change for larger bills.

Be sure your PIN number will work abroad. PIN numbers with more than four digits aren't recognized at ATMs in many countries. If yours has five or more, remember to change it before you leave. Also, if your PIN number is a word, you should learn the numeric equivalents of the letters on the keypad, because the keypads on some foreign bank machines have numbers only.

TECHNOLOGY FOR THE ROAD

CELL PHONES

Find out if your phone works internationally. In the U.S. most cells are "locked" and won't work with other carriers' networks. Elsewhere, people pay more for their phones but can choose what networks to use them on. Your locked U.S. phone may work internationally, depending on whether it supports GSM (Global System for Mobile Communications), alternate bands, and who provides your wireless service. Verizon and Sprint aren't the best for international travel; AT&T and T-Mobile are better bets.

Look into renting a phone. If you travel abroad infrequently and/or expect to make a lot of calls, a rental may be the best way to save money. If you anticipate limited usage, your own phone may be the least expensive option. Weigh the rental fees and service against your home service provider's roaming rates to determine the best deal. If you travel abroad frequently, you may want to buy, however; figure that the cost of a phone that works internationally is equal to the cost of three or four rentals.

If you buy, get an unlocked GSM phone with quadband support. "Unlocked" means you can use the phone with any wireless service provider; "GSM" is the Global System for Mobile Communications; quadband means the phone supports the two bands—wireless operating frequencies—used in North America as well as the two used elsewhere in the world. You'll also need a SIM card to use in your phone.

SIM CARD ESSENTIALS

A SIM card is a small insert that slides into your phone and stores information such as your phone number, the carrier that supplies your service, and the rates you pay. SIMs are available for single countries or as multilocation "global" cards, and are associated with a particular calling plan.

If you own an unlocked Global System for Mobile Communications (GSM) phone, you can swap SIM cards in and out as needed, buying a SIM for Italy this year and one for France the year after. Your phone will have a different number each time you swap the SIMs. A global SIM card gives you one phone number wherever you may roam.

Single-country SIM cards (about $45) give you a local to-that-country cell-phone number. The calling plans associated with local SIM cards typically offer inexpensive rates for local calls and free incoming calls. Most offer long-distance calling to overseas phone numbers. But check each card's long-distance capabilities and fees; costs vary widely depending on the local carrier. Some cards offer roaming services, so you can use the phone in a different country, but this tends to be very expensive—a dollar a minute roaming charge plus the per-minute cost of the call isn't unusual.

A global roaming SIM card (about $60) has one rate for incoming calls and another for outgoing calls, no matter what country you're in when you place a call. Usually you'll pay $1 per minute for outgoing calls and $0.40 a minute for incoming (note: *you* pay the cost of incoming calls, not the caller.) Global cards are good for those who travel often to more than one destination, or travelers who will be visiting more than one country in one trip.

You can purchase SIMs from Rebelfone.com, Brightroam. com, and WorldSim.com, among other companies. Depending on the SIM card or rental plan, you'll either be billed after the fact or be required to buy a prepaid SIM for whatever amount you choose. With postpaid options, expect to provide a credit-card number to be kept on file, pass a credit check, and if you're renting, possibly pay a deposit of $150–$200 (the fee will be put on your credit card and released when you pay the bill).

Shop for an international calling plan. Cell-phone rental
fees vary widely by destination and calling plan. AllCell-
Rentals.com has a good plan for Italy. For trips to France,
CellularAbroad.com offers a one-month rental plan priced
at $109 ($49 weekly) plus $69 for a SIM card (which is
yours to keep). The company also has good deals in the
United Kingdom. TravelCell.com is also a good bet for the
United Kingdom, as well as for Italy and China (including Hong Kong). For Singapore and Taiwan, look into
InternationalCellular.com. If you're traveling to Japan or
Korea, you'll need a country-specific phone, as telecom-
munications systems in these countries are not compatible
with other countries' systems. In Japan, MyJapanPhone.
com has a good plan.

COMPUTERS

Shield your computer from the traumas of travel. Pack it in
a padded case, and, if you're flying, avoid placing it in the
overhead bin, where it will be bumped and jostled. And
when the flight attendants push the drinks cart near your
seat, close your laptop. A bit of turbulence or just plain
klutziness can result in a spill, and a doused laptop is almost
always a dead laptop.

Have the right computer gear. Bring along the system-restore
or operating-system software that came with your computer in case some tech trauma occurs while you're away;
a backup memory stick with essential files; a power adap-
tor if you're traveling out of the country (check with the
manufacturer for these, and remember to get adaptors for
all the electronic gear you're bringing); and perhaps a short
extension cord so you can work anywhere in your room
instead of right up next to the room's only power outlet.

Lengthen your computer battery's charge. To get the longest life possible from your PC laptop's battery, go to
Start>Control Panel>Power Options, and on the "Power
Schemes" pull-down menu choose "Max Battery." Windows will now conserve your battery power by shutting
off your screen and spinning down the hard drive when
you aren't actively using the computer. Mac users: go to
System Preferences>Energy Saver>Settings for Battery and
Optimization>Better Battery Life. Also, to save the life of
your battery, decrease the screen's brightness–look for the
key on your keyboard with the little sun icon on it and

CHOOSING A TRAVEL LAPTOP

Choosing the right laptop can make even a nerd nervous. The best place to start is by deciding what sort of laptop you want from the four basic formats: desktop replacement, thin and light, ultraportable, or ruggedized? Here are a few tips.

Desktop replacements. These brawny machines weigh 8-plus pounds and have full-size keyboards and large display screens. They usually provide the best bang for your technology buck, as they're powerful, sturdy, and reasonably priced. Lugging them around can be a pain, but if your portable will be your primary computer, you'll probably want a desktop replacement model.

Thin and lights. These machines have all the features of a desktop replacement but in a more svelte form. They weigh around 7 pounds and are noticeably slimmer than desktop replacement models. They're easier to travel with than their beefier brethren but may feel more fragile.

Thin and lights are typically (but not always) more expensive than a similarly powerful desktop replacement. Portability, it seems, comes at premium price.

Ultraportables. About the size of a hardcover book, these machines are typically less than 5 pounds. They're a dream to travel with, but their small keyboards and display screens can feel too cramped for everyday use. If, however, you're looking for a computer that will be used solely as a travel companion, an ultraportable is your dream machine.

Ruggedized laptops. Ruggedized laptops aren't bothered by liquid, dust, or dirt. You can drop, squash, and otherwise harass them and they will survive. Due to their special disaster-blasting features, they're more expensive than other portables and are best for travelers who use their computers in conditions likely to damage less-armored machines.

press it and the function key simultaneously. (No such key? Check your computer's manual.)

Thwart computer thieves. Put your laptop in your room safe or the hotel safe when not in your room (not under the bed or in the drawers underneath your undies—two of the first places a thief will look). If the hotel safe seems dicey, or you need to bring your laptop to a conference room or onto a convention floor, most laptops have a security slot

(Kensington lock). Get a locking device with an attached cable (available at any well-stocked computer supply store), wrap the cable around a heavy, stationery object, and insert the lock into the security slot.

Get connected. Check WiFiFreeSpot.com and Wi-FiHot-SpotList.com for exhaustive listings of public wireless networks around the world. Jiwire (⊕ *www.jiwire.com*) has a public Wi-Fi hotspot locator. Jiwire also has a free Wi-Fi finder app on iTunes.

Make sure you're good to go on e-mail. Once you're connected to a public wireless service you'll be able to receive mail through an e-mail program like Outlook, but you probably won't be able to send it. That's because most Internet service providers block e-mail sent through their network via any other ISP, including wireless ones (as a spam-fighting measure). To send e-mail, use your ISP's Web mail service or set up a Web mail account with a free service like Google's Gmail, Yahoo, or Hotmail.

Keep your computer healthy. Viruses and worms can run rampant on the wide-open public wireless services offered by hotels, coffee shops, bookstores, and libraries. Protect your computer from other electronic germs by making sure your operating system's firewall is active, blocking most incoming threats. Also make sure that you're running an up-to-date antivirus program.

Stop snoops. Public wireless service is open to any and all, which means that any data you have stored on your computer is accessible to all other users on the network. The best way to ward off snoops is to disable your wireless card's Ad-Hoc (peer-to-peer) mode. This helps to prevent anyone else from connecting to your computer. The software for your wireless modem will allow you to disable Ad-Hoc with a single click. And again, make sure you're running a firewall on your computer.

Packing

WORD OF MOUTH

"Use contact lens cases for cosmetics. Moisturizers, foundation, etc., work great in these. I use a Sharpie to label them. I can get over a week's worth of my items in just one side of a case."

—mms

"I use stackable screw-type pill containers to put my cosmetics in order of use: cleanser, serum, moisturizer, sunscreen, foundation [nothing too watery, though]. I do a test run before my trip to be sure I won't run out of an item. Because they're screwed together, I don't hunt in my cosmetics bags for things."

—Allivian

www.fodors.com/forums

Updated
by Lisa
McLaughlin

Although we want to get away from our daily cares when we travel, we also feel oddly compelled to bring along everything from our everyday world when we do. It's not enough that we're going on vacation, as outfit after outfit is layered in the suitcase like an enormous wedding cake; it's as if we want our things to have the experience, too.

Below are some ideas on how to lighten your load, navigate the tendency to overstuff bags, and meet the ever-tightening luggage requirements without feeling like you're missing anything more than the delivery of your hometown paper.

THE PACKING PLAN

4

Consider your itinerary. How will you be spending your days—in a series of meetings or lolling, sarong-wrapped, on the beach? Will you be staying put or moving nightly? Seeing the same people for the duration or meeting new ones daily? Knowing what you'll be doing is the first step toward planning what to wear.

Look into local dress requirements. In some resort areas an anything-goes dress code applies; others might expect fancy dress for dinner. If you're going abroad, local mores may vary. In the fashion capital of Milan women visiting the famous cathedral are expected to cover their heads and bare shoulders with a scarf. In the Middle East, women are expected to dress modestly (long skirts, no pants). Before you start assembling your wardrobe, do your homework.

Look into local fashion. Each place has its fashion quirks. In New York City you'll stand out in a windbreaker and waist pack, because locals tend to leave home confidently attired like they're film stars acting in a city street scene. In Paris women are far less likely to wear open-toed shoes, especially in any kind of business setting. In Italy the jeans, sneakers, and baseball hat combo doesn't go over too well. If not standing out is important to you, know before you go.

Anticipate the weather. If you're traveling fairly soon, check the *New York Times,* CNN International, the Weather Channel, or the Web to get forecasts. If your trip is a few weeks (or months) off, consult guidebooks and tourism boards so you'll know what conditions to expect.

Scope out your hotel. Inquire about laundry services, hair dryers, irons, ironing boards, cribs, high chairs, toiletries, and other amenities. Knowing that you can maintain your

WORD OF MOUTH: THE BANDANA

"I bought a bandana on a whim. Since then I've used it (this list is not in chronological order):

■ Over my mouth to screen out sand/dust in a wind storm.

■ Over my hair in an open Jeep.

■ Around my neck in the supermarket's freezer section (to stay warm).

■ Around my neck in the boat (wetted down, to stay cool).

■ Tied around a handful of seeds I poached from a botanical garden.

■ Tied around my forehead to keep sweat out of my eyes when working on the boat.

■ Tied around my dog's neck as an impromptu collar when I forget the real one.

■ As a [handkerchief] when I was allergic to something unknown and caught unawares without tissues.

■ As a way to hold ice on an impending bruise.

■ As a napkin to wrap around a roll I took from a breakfast buffet.

■ As a rag to wipe my hands when I slipped and accidentally touched dog poop.

■ As a rag to wipe off my camera/lens when it got rained on.

■ To lay out in the hotel room to put my rings/watch on bed so I would have a visual clue to remember them when I got up early the next day for a flight." —spcfa

wardrobe on-site and dispense with some of these accoutrements could make your suitcase a bit lighter.

Make a comprehensive packing list. Think about everything you'll need to take, from medical kits to incidentals and electrical items. Write everything down. Check your itinerary and note necessary gear or possible outfits next to each activity or meeting, including shoes and accessories. In this way you'll become aware of your clothing needs and begin to form a tentative travel wardrobe.

Make a separate clothing list. This list should include only the clothing you've chosen. Study it carefully, noting how many times you've listed a specific item and assessing the palette. If shorts are listed seven times for the week, for instance, you can probably make do with two or three pairs. Are those lime-green Manolo Blahnik pumps the only articles of lime-green attire? Better leave them home in favor of more versatile shoes.

Leave appliances at home. Although they should work fine anywhere in the United States, Canada, Mexico, Japan, Korea, Jamaica, Bermuda, and the Bahamas, elsewhere you'll need an adapter (other countries have four different pin configurations) and possibly a converter. Most hotels provide irons and blow dryers; manual razors and toothbrushes are really easier on the road. Unless having your own device is absolutely essential (e.g., a laptop, phone, or cameras), leave it home.

CLOTHING

Play the numbers game. A good rule of thumb for trips less than one week is one shirt per day, one layering jacket or sweater, one bottom per every two days (but never less than two pairs of pants), no more than two pairs of shoes (one you wear and one you pack), underwear for every day, and seasonal additions, like a bathing suit.

Plan to wash it out. If you're traveling for more than a week, follow the same numbers as above and plan on washing clothes instead of bringing more. If you're in a country with a good exchange rate, or aren't on a tight budget, take advantage of the hotel laundry service or dry cleaning. Otherwise, bring individual packets of Woolite and a travel stain-treatment stick (Tide to Go is the best one).

Stick with the "two pairs of shoes" rule. It might be hard to imagine that two pairs of shoes can cover all occasions, but they can. Bring a dressy pair that looks great with a skirt or pants, and a casual (but not beat-up) pair that you can walk across Rome in. Unless you plan to run, you won't need running shoes.

Layer, even if you think you won't need to. Forget what you've read about sunny California: San Francisco in summer is subject to finger-numbing fogs, and even Los Angeles has its chilly days. Also, malls, museums, cinemas, and airline cabins are often air-conditioned to a wintry degree. The best bet is a lightweight, waterproof jacket, stuffable into your carry-on. A shawl-size scarf—virtually weightless and warm—is a woman's best friend, and can act as a beach cover-up or a wrap.

Consider the multiple uses of a jacket. A navy or olive-green blazer looks great over jeans as well as with business slacks. A windbreaker makes for a waterproof shell. A long, fancy coat dresses up casual outfits.

GOOD-TO-GO GOODS

Several retailers sell stylish mix-and-match clothing in fabrics that travel well. Look for such lines at J. Jill, Spiegel, and Chicos. Travelsmith sells travel clothing and lots of other handy items. Coldwater Creek also has travel togs, and many items are reversible. The Container Store and L.L. Bean have lots of great totes and toiletry cases.

Flight001.com sells sets of refillable containers in 1-quart clear zip-top bags ($10–$22). The company 3floz.com stocks carry-on friendly sizes of luxe and green toiletries and cosmetics. Real road warriors should log onto Mysmartpac.com and order a TSA-compliant, eco-friendly kit of toiletries in resealable pouches. Each his or hers kit has a razor, a toothbrush, and several high-quality personal-care products that last for as many as six uses.

The Avid Traveler Essentials Gift Set ($53.95 ⊕ www.minimus.biz) comes with two clear vinyl zipper bags, hand sanitizer, Imodium, Neosporin, duct tape, four single-use thermometers, toilet paper and a seat cover, and lots of other stuff. Everything's in TSA-approved sizes. The Large Ready Organized First Aid Kit ($15.99 ⊕ www.drugstore.com) by Johnson & Johnson has 170 items, including Imodium, a cold pack, a variety of band aids, cleansing wipes, antibiotic ointment, Tylenol, and more. Or you can create your own kit.

Focus on a couple of colors. If you coordinate your wardrobe around two or three complimentary colors (e.g., black, gray, and red or brown, green, and beige), you'll have greater latitude in your outfit choices because everything goes with everything else, and you'll get more mileage out of fewer accessories.

Go shopping. Yup. You read this correctly. If there's one key element that will tie your wardrobe together (e.g., a dressy blouse that transforms that suit skirt into a dinner outfit, pants with legs that zip off to create shorts or capris) and enable you to pack fewer things, then go out and get it. If your children have outgrown key clothing items, budget the time to get them reoutfitted.

Mix and match, then edit. Try to have everything you pack serve at least a couple of different purposes. Figure out how many outfits you can make with each article of clothing. Black pants, for instance, are the perfect multifunctional item; they can be dressed up or down. Most women find that separates work better than dresses, although you may need a few dresses for certain occasions. Don't take an item you'll wear only once unless you absolutely can't live without it. Considering all the variables calmly, you can begin to edit your wardrobe.

WORD OF MOUTH. "I only take one big trip a year and pack any old clothes that are still wearable but I don't like anymore—those that would be off to a charity. At the end of the trip or en route I discard what I don't need anymore or I may have replaced on the way (such as shoes and purse). . . ." —Leelauirno

Opt for lightweight, wrinkleproof fabrics. As you evaluate your options and narrow your choices, go for items that are light in weight, wrinkle resistant, compact, and washable. If you notice the resilience of a particular item over the course of a workday, pack it! If you've considered a microfiber skirt, buy it now.

Choose a travel outfit. Drawing on the items you've selected, select an outfit to travel in. You might want to opt for the heaviest clothes on your list; wearing those means you'll have less to pack. If traveling casually, wear neat-looking, loose-fitting clothing that breathes, and do a bit of layering: cabin temperatures often vary. If you're heading south, leave your heavy winter coat in the car trunk or back at home.

Get your clothes travel-ready. Go over the clothes you've selected and see which ones need washing, dry-cleaning, and mending—and get it done. If traveling with children, have them try on their vacation clothes in advance—they may have outgrown some since the last trip.

TOILETRIES

Keep a toiletries travel kit. Frequent travelers would do well to double up on toiletries and keep one set at home, the other permanently packed inside their luggage. Even if virtually every hotel now provides the basics, you never know what key items may be missing (or not to your liking). As long as you have your own essentials, you're set.

Follow the 3-1-1 rule. The Transportation Security Administration allows you to carry on personal-care products in 3-ounce or smaller containers. All containers must be in a clear 1-quart resealable bag. Each person is allowed one

TRAVEL MEDICAL KIT

Obviously, you shouldn't pack your entire medicine chest, but you also don't want to skimp when it comes to necessary or potentially lifesaving supplies. What bare medical necessities to bring? Although the contents of your medical kit will vary depending on where you're headed, most travel-medicine experts agree that there are some items that ought to be in nearly every traveler's black bag.

☐ **Prepackaged antiseptic towelettes, bandages, and topical antibiotics.** The more you're out and about, the more likely you are to get a few scrapes. There's no sense letting a minor scratch develop into a major infection, especially if you're traveling to a remote area.

☐ **Flashlight.** Although not necessarily a medical supply, a flashlight is necessary for many situations, from unlighted city streets to midnight trips to the bathroom in jungle resorts that run on generators.

☐ **Pepto-Bismol and Imodium.** Rich food or bad food can give you stomach troubles. Plan for them by bringing these tablets along.

☐ **Moleskin.** Although not lifesaving, this adhesive padding can be the key to preventing the activity-limiting blisters that are likely to develop as you trek from site to site.

☐ **Sunscreen.** A sunburn is not only annoying but also cancer-causing. It can also hamper your skin's ability to perspire, which is essential for preventing your body from overheating in hot climates.

☐ **Motion-sickness remedies.** Dramamine tablets and Scopamine patches can relieve a lot of discomfort if the boat crossing is rougher than expected or the bus ride is wickedly bumpy.

☐ **Thermometer in a sturdy case.** The best way to assess whether you have an infection needing a doctor's care is to take your temperature to see if you have a fever.

☐ **Pain relievers.** Such pain relievers as Tylenol or Advil can come in handy for treating headaches, joint pain, and fever.

☐ **Hydrocortisone 1% ointment or cream.** The alien bacteria you may encounter when you go swimming in the sea or other natural bodies of water can trigger itching or a rash, which this cream can counter. It can also help relieve those unbearable symptoms of a poison ivy rash.

☐ **Allergy medicine.** If you are an allergy sufferer, take along some antihistamines. Your allergies may not be acting up at home prior to departure, but changes in altitude and a different clime at your destination may trigger even an occasional allergy. Of course, if you have food allergies, reactions to bee stings, or other specific conditions requiring medications or an EpiPen, make sure you have an ample supply before you hit the road.

☐ **Special ointments.** If you are a woman prone to yeast infections, over-the-counter creams for these infections, such as Monistat, should also be in your medical kit. And if you are a person who suffers from athlete's foot or jock itch, don't forget an antifungal cream.

☐ **Repellents.** A mosquito repellent containing DEET (N,N-diethylmetatoluamide) is especially critical if you are traveling to tropical areas where malaria, yellow fever, dengue, and other mosquito-borne diseases are likely to lurk. Skin-So-Soft and Naturapel are two DEET-free repellents for areas without malaria. Depending upon your lodging conditions, you may want to bring mosquito coils and a mosquito net for sleeping; you could even take it a step further and have the netting dipped in permethrin insecticide.

☐ **Antimalarial drugs.** These are also essential if you are traveling to an area where malaria is prevalent, such as Africa, central and northeastern South America, India, and southeastern Asia. You will need a prescription for an antimalarial.

☐ **Water purification tablets, packets of oral rehydration salts, and Cipro or Bactrim.** As many as half of all travelers experience the dreaded traveler's diarrhea. Water purification tablets (found in sporting-goods stores and pharmacies) or a SteriPEN, a pocket-sized device that purifies water with UV light, can help prevent it, and oral rehydration salts (found at pharmacies) and the antibiotics Cipro or Bactrim are used to treat it. You need a prescription for the antibiotics, which should be used only to treat—not prevent—traveler's diarrhea.

☐ **Condoms.** These can be lifesaving, no matter where you travel—and they may not be of the highest quality or even available everywhere.

such resealable bag. Have yours pulled out of your bag when you get to the security line, as you'll need to put it in the plastic bins separately from your carry-on.

Be smart about packing toiletries in checked luggage. Buy inexpensive, reusable, travel-size containers and fill them with your own products. Never fill containers to the top, though: changes in air-pressure during a flight could cause the contents to expand and leak. To play it extra safe, put toiletry bottles in a resealable plastic bag within your kit. And put the kit itself in a plastic bag. If, after all this, you still end up with sunscreen on your Bruno Maglis, the travel gods simply have it in for you.

Double up. Look for ways to make your daily routine more travel-friendly. Why pack hand, body, and face creams when one all-purpose moisturizer will do? Why pack clothes cleaner when your shampoo will do? Or forget shampoo, and go with a Dr. Bronner's soap that's everything in one.

OTHER GEAR

Bring resealable plastic bags in different sizes. Plastic bags are indispensable, and can be used for anything from packing shoes and wet swimsuits to trash in the car.

WORD OF MOUTH. "One of my favorite travel hints that I learned on Fodors.com is the Ziplock washing machine. Take a large resealable plastic bag, and put in the clothes and squirt of soap (or shampoo), Shake it, dump water, shake it, dump water, add water and shake again. Easy." —LSky

Pack bubble wrap and tape. If you're traveling to a place where ceramics, glass, or other breakable goods are must-haves on any self-respecting shopper's list, bubble wrap and tape make it easy to get things home in one piece.

Pack an all-in-one tool. A Swiss Army knife or the equivalent provides a scissors, toothpick, nail file, bottle opener, screwdriver, and small knife in mere inches of space. But remember: Pack it in your checked bag, not your carry-on, or it'll be confiscated at the security gate.

Include a basic sewing kit. Pick one up at a drugstore or grocery store (some hotels provide little kits). Or make your own, with a credit-card-size piece of cardboard: pierce it with a couple of needles and pins, wind on various colored threads, then attach a safety pin with a couple of buttons.

Throw in a collapsible duffel or large tote. Will you buy out the store? Be prepared. Store an empty bag inside your medium-size checked bag rather than bringing a huge suitcase to accommodate future purchases—you can use it as a day pack in the meantime.

LUGGAGE

Check weight and size limitations. In the United States you may be charged extra for checked bags weighing more than 50 pounds (but let's face it, you may be charged for *any* checked bag, these days). Abroad, some airlines don't allow you to check bags over 60 to 70 pounds, or they charge outrageous fees for every excess pound—or bag. Carry-on size limitations can be stringent, too.

Decide now: Check it or carry it? Most airlines now charge fees for checked baggage on domestic flights, starting at $25 for the first checked bag and $35 for the second. International flights generally allow for two checked bags at no charge. Check with your carrier for the most up-to-date fees before you pack, and decide whether it is worth the cost to check a large bag, or whether a carry-on bag packed with only the essentials could be enough for your trip.

Don't just use any old suitcase. Consider your particular trip. Do two small bags make more sense than one big one? They may if you're flying on tiny airplanes. Find out whether you'll have to claim your luggage and recheck it or whether you'll be required to make a 500-yard dash to make a connecting flight and need wheels.

Rethink valuables. On U.S. flights, airlines are liable for less than $3,000 per person for bags. On international flights the liability limit is less than $700 per bag. But items like computers, cameras, and jewelry aren't covered, and as gadgetry can go on and off the list of carry-on no-no's, you can't count on keeping things safe by keeping them close. Although comprehensive travel policies may cover luggage, the liability limit is often a pittance. Your homeowner's policy may cover you sufficiently when you travel—or not.

Be wary about locks. If TSA employees must inspect your checked bags, they will literally break locks or even slash and retape the material if your bags are locked shut. Two

LUGGAGE QUALITY CHECKS

Not all luggage is created equal. Even bags of a similar type vary tremendously from manufacturer to manufacturer. Here are some things to check:

Frame. Fiberglass inner frames ensure both strength and light weight. Inner structures may also be made of aluminum, wood, durable molded plastic compounds, or any combination of the above. A weighty frame will make a case heavy even before it's packed. Frame materials are often listed on the luggage tag; your luggage salesperson should also be able to tell you what they are.

Construction. On cases with zippers, look for taped seams, in which a strip of cloth reinforces the zipper and bag connection; this prevents fraying. Exterior joints should be covered with leather, nylon piping, or welts to reinforce the seams and absorb wear and tear. Seams should be lockstitched—a method in which each stitch is reinforced, or locked, to stay in place and stand alone. This way, if one stitch happens to break, it won't take the next one with it and unravel your seam.

Fabric. Leather luggage can be very durable and looks marvelous, but it is often too heavy to be carried even when it's empty. Top-grain or full-grain leather, the outermost layer of the hide, is stronger and more durable than leather made from splits, the layers of hide that are split off from underneath the top grain. Luggage made from splits costs less but is more likely to show wear.

Heavier synthetics protect the bag's contents better and stand up to sharp objects that might cause tears or rips in transit. Ballistic nylon is very strong but a bit expensive. Bags made of Cordura or Cordura Plus cost less and are still pretty sturdy. Although tweed and brocade bags may appear sturdy, they're slashable, and the thicker fabric adds weight.

There are some other unusual fabrics that are perfect for the traveler concerned about the environment. These include Fortrel EcoSpun, a durable material made from recycled plastic bottles, and fabric woven from hemp.

Waterproofing. Whether you're trapped in an Indian monsoon or a heavy downpour, waterproof luggage comes in handy. The best all-around fabric is a Cordura or ballistic nylon with a waterproof seal—most bags aren't waterproofed on the outside, but treated on the inside with a moisture-resisting sealant. If you require special protection from water for camping, rafting, or some other adventure, buy at a store that specializes in rugged gear.

Closings. The simpler, the better. Zippers should be tough and run smoothly. They should also be double-stitched (stitched on both sides of the zipper) and self-repairing or large, very sturdy, and smooth-running. Zippers made of polyester coils that have been woven or sewn to tapes can take a lot of pressure and can be fixed if they pop open.

Handles. On pullmans opt for side *and* top handles, and check to see how they're attached. Those attached with screws can be replaced; when riveted handles come off, they can't be easily fixed. Also note whether the handle is padded on the underside and whether it's covered with leather or only sturdy plastic. Check telescoping handles: some can be locked in place, whereas others remain free to slide in and out at random. The handle system should be well protected, whether it's housed inside the bag or outside. Be sure the handle is sturdy, especially if you plan to hang a briefcase or tote bag over it.

Straps and webbing. Shoulder straps should be made of wide webbing, and ideally they should be padded where they rest on your shoulders. Note how the webbing is attached to the bag. Is it reinforced with box and cross stitching? Choose a duffel with a shoulder strap in addition to two center handles—this increases your carrying options for times when you'll need your hands free. It's equally important that backpack straps be padded, because they will be resting on your shoulders for long periods of time. Look for a padded waist or hip strap as well, to steady and center the bag on your body. All straps should be adjustable.

Wheels. Four wheels make a suitcase more stable and easier to roll than two wheels (think car versus motorcycle). The wheels should be spaced as wide apart as possible and should be recessed into the frame—an exposed wheel can be neatly severed from your bag by a pothole, an uneven cobblestone, or a seemingly innocuous curb. Large, sturdy, in-line-skate wheels provide the ultimate in rollability. Insist on smooth-rolling wheels that are firmly bolted in place.

companies, Travel Sentry and Safe Skies, make so-called TSA-approved locks, but many passengers have complained that TSA employees have simply cut those off as well. A better option may be to secure bags with plastic zip ties, available in hardware stores.

Mind those bag tags. Old tags may look good on your ski jacket, but at check-in if an old tag remains, you're just asking to have your luggage sent to the wrong airport. That said, be sure that the new tag affixed to your bag by the check-in attendant has the correct three-letter destination code.

Label your bags clearly, inside and out. Make sure your address, phone number (including cell), and e-mail address are filled out clearly on luggage tags. (Skip your home address: If thieves get a look at it, they might head off on a little business trip of their own.) Place tags or cards with your contact info inside your luggage, too, in case the external tags are lost. Also pack a copy of your itinerary—or at least information on your hotel—so that the airline can track you down if need be.

Individualize your luggage. Inevitably, someone's going to have your exact bag. To prevent them from innocently taking off with it, add a distinguishing mark—a bright ribbon, an identifiable sticker or kitschy luggage tag, a pause-inspiring strip of duct tape. This distinction will help not only on the baggage carousel, but anywhere luggage accumulates, such as in a crowded hotel lobby.

CARRY-ONS

Keep important items in carry-ons. The carry-on is the place to keep your travel documents kit (itineraries, tickets, confirmation printouts, passport); prescription medicines (in their original packaging); an extra pair of contacts or eyeglasses; and slippers, socks, or flip-flops to wear on the plane.

Anticipate having to check carry-ons. Carry-on bags can be no larger than 45 linear inches (the total length, width, and height). Not much will help your case if yours are simply too big or if you and your luggage has been selected for checking because your flight is full and the overhead compartments are stuffed. You'll probably feel more comfortable cooperating if you've put a sturdy luggage tag on your bag and segregated all onboard must-haves—including jewelry, medications, and paperwork—in one section of the bag so that they can be easily removed.

GETTING IT INTO THE BAG

Refine and record your packing list. Some travelers recommend halving the packing list at the last minute, but if you've prepared well, you'll probably only need to do some light editing. Place a copy of your revised list in your personal documents kit—as a checklist for when you're repacking to head home, for reference on the next trip, and also as a record in case your luggage is lost or stolen. Or e-mail the list to yourself. To play it double-safe, add a photograph of your luggage to your personal documents kit.

Customize a "night before" routine. Packing can be stressful, so set aside enough time and set the desired mood (whether classical and calming, or pumped-up Rolling Stones). If you're a perfectionist, set up an ironing board next to your suitcase: Ironed clothes lie flatter and arrive neater.

Pack outside your bag. Before you actually pack your suitcase, pile everything you plan to bring on your bed. This is your opportunity to eye your clothes and cull a few more items. If you pack directly into your suitcase, you'll be tempted to throw in a few extra items (trust us, you will). Once you've made the final edit, pack only what's in front of you. If you've followed our advice, your suitcase should now be a lean, mean, traveling machine.

Weed out anything you'd hate to lose. Packing your favorite electronic gadgets and jewelry is risky. A plastic watch is the way to go if you wear one at all—in many places, you can keep perfectly on top of the time by checking clock towers and clocks in other public places. If you do take good jewelry, make a point of never removing it, even when sleeping; once it's off, it's too easy to forget.

Pare every ounce of extra weight. The small stuff adds up. Packing pros know, for instance, to remove facial tissues from their bulky boxes and slip them into resealable plastic bags. Ditto for baby wipes—useful for waterless hand washing and, some contend, stain removal.

Divvy the load. If you're traveling with a spouse or companion, figure out where you don't need to double up. She's got the shampoo? You'll get the toothpaste.

PACKING CHECKLIST

ADULTS

■ 1 pair of khakis or other dressy-casual trousers

■ 1 pair of jeans

■ 1 pair of long pants that convert to shorts or capris

■ 1 pair of shorts or capris

■ 1 sundress or set of casual-dressy separates

■ 1 coordinating blazer (men) or elegant wrap (women)

■ 2 collared shirts (e.g., oxfords, polos)

■ 3 T-shirts or turtlenecks

■ 1 pullover sweater or cardigan

■ 1 pareo or sarong

■ Workout outfit (including sports bra if applicable)

■ 1 pair of sneakers good for walking and your sport of choice (e.g., running, tennis)

■ 1 pair of dressy boots or shoes

■ 1 pair of sandals or flip-flops

■ Necessary accessories: scarves, belt, handbag, hosiery or socks, sunglasses

■ Sleepwear, underwear

■ Bathing suit, goggles, cap

■ Sun hat

■ Rain poncho or all-purpose windbreaker, jacket with a zip-out lining, or winter coat (wear on the plane)

■ Umbrella

■ Collapsible tote bag or day pack and duffel (for big shoppers)

■ If winter, hats, scarves, gloves

LITTLE ONES

■ 2 outfits and pajamas per day

■ Outerwear, socks, under-shirts

■ Swimsuit, swim diapers, diaper cover

■ Diapers, rash cream, changing pad

■ Baby wipes, baby powder

■ Toilet-seat adapter or potty seat

■ Car seat

■ Baby carrier

■ Collapsible stroller

■ Baby formula

■ Can opener, if needed

■ Bottles or holders, liners, nipples, rings, caps

■ Bottle brush

■ Breast pump

■ Baby cereal

■ Bibs

■ Terrycloth hand towels

■ Collapsible hook-on high chair

■ Blankets

■ Sleepwear

■ Pacifiers

■ Nightlight

■ Portable crib

■ Safety gizmos

OLDER KIDS, TWEENS, AND TEENS
- 1 outfit per day
- 2 extra tops
- An extra pair of pants
- 1 dress outfit
- Sweatshirt, sweater
- Windbreaker, outerwear
- Shoes, extra laces
- Socks, undies
- 2 swimsuits, swim goggles
- Snacks
- Familiar foods
- Drinks
- Toys, books, games, iPod or MP3 player, DVDs and players
- A tote for all the toys, books, games, iPod or MP3 players, DVDs and players

WHAT TO WEAR ON THE PLANE
- Your bulkiest clothes and outerwear
- A sweater or other cover-up
- Loose clothing in soft, natural fibers
- Low-heeled leather or canvas slip-on shoes

WHAT TO CARRY ON THE PLANE
- Travel documents
- Money, valuables
- Electronics, breakables
- 311-compliant toiletries kit
- Prescription medications
- Eyeglasses, sunglasses
- Change of clothes

- Reading material, paper, pens
- Neck pillow
- Sleep mask, earplugs
- Soft slippers or warm socks

4

Cross-pack. A pair of people flying together could also pack some of each person's essentials in the other's suitcase. That way, if one bag doesn't make it to the destination, both will still be covered.

Try different folding techniques. Each school has its passionate advocates. You might do best to match the method to your luggage. Rolling items works well with duffels and soft-sided bags, and will meet the needs of a casual traveler. "Interlocking" (wrapping slacks, say, around a bulky sweater) and the "dressmaker's dummy" approach (layering your garments progressively over one another) are other good ways to minimize wrinkles.

Use the proper packing material for the job. As friction is what causes wrinkles, plastic, which reduces, friction, is your friend. Put individual items inside dry-cleaner bags and they'll arrive in a perfectly preserved state. Resealable plastic bags are good for stowing miscellaneous items. Inexpensive nylon-mesh laundry bags are great for delicates. Not only will this keep them safe and clean, if your bag is inspected, no one need touch your undies because an inspector will be able to see into the bag.

Organize for efficiency. Lay your bag flat and put folded clothes in piles down the center. If you're packing your toiletries kit, put it at what will be the bottom of your bag when it's standing (this should now be the heaviest item in your bag; in this position it won't crush other items). Rolled clothes fit into the spaces around the stacked clothes. Shoes should never be empty: They're ideal for stuffing with underwear, socks, or a travel umbrella. Nor should they travel in pairs: one by one (and wrapped, of course), they're easily wedged into unused crannies. Socks fill in remaining holes.

Family Travel

WORD OF MOUTH

"Don't underestimate the difficulties of flying with a little one especially when there's many time zone changes. Plus it is different when you have to carry all of the "stuff" that goes along with taking a child."

—Lynnaustin

Updated
by Alexis
Kelly

"I need a vacation to get over my vacation." It's a common refrain from parents who've just come home from the family schlep—um, trip. To be sure, vacationing is never going to be the way it was pre-children, when all you needed was a book, a margarita, and a bikini (or not). These days, add a couple of cherubs whose meltdown schedule doesn't know the difference between East Coast and West Coast time, and, well, sometimes it feels like you probably never should have left home.

But believe it or not, it is possible to put the "vacation" back into family travel. Some of it's a simple matter of changing expectations. You probably won't finish a good read; you might not even get past "Call me Ishmael." But if you pick the right place, reserve the right room, and plan the right diversions, you might even end up more rested than when you started. Honest.

WHERE TO GO

Set a goal. What kind of vacation do you want? Rest and relaxation? Unencumbered family time? Nonstop action? An all-inclusive resort or a cruise with childcare will no doubt give you more R&R—in fact, parents and children may see little of each other. A house at the beach is more likely to net family time, with the potential risk of too much togetherness. A theme park will keep you plenty busy if your brood likes to keep moving.

Ask "What is there to do?" That idyllic Berkshires retreat looks perfect, but the lovely view of the rolling hills won't entertain the kids. And card games and jacks may wear on mom and dad. Before renting, ask your agent about local activities—swimming, bike trails, alpine slides. Visiting a hotel in the city? Call the concierge ahead of time and ask about "must-do" activities that might require reservations.

Think "location, location, location." It may seem pennywise to book off-the-beaten-trail accommodations. But such remote areas can be lonely, especially if you've got kids who like other kids for company. The arrangement may also be impractical if it translates into long drives for food and entertainment.

Involve children in planning. Unusual destinations can become more interesting for children if you pique their curiosity. Show them maps and brochures of the area; rent movies or read books about it. Movie buffs-in-training will

VISITING THEME PARKS

■ **Cater to the kids.** Half the fun of a theme park is watching the kids experience it for the first time. The misery comes when we grownups try to inject thrills the kids aren't ready for (as in "You'll love Space Mountain. It's not scary at all") or devote hours to lines for attractions only one parent will be able to ride. Consider the stage the kids are in and enjoy accordingly. The big rides will still be there for you to enjoy together when they're older.

■ **Don't try to do everything.** Setting the alarm clock and rushing around on a schedule is way too much like a job. Choose a couple of things you consider "must-dos," and then let the adventure take you where it leads.

Think of it as leaving things for next time.

■ **Take time off.** Anyone who's endured an over-stimulated kid knows there's truth in the saying "You can get too much of a good thing." Some quiet time spent swimming or even lounging in the pool will recharge everyone for more "fun."

■ **Know when to forego the vacation touchdown and accept a punt.** It's easy to lose perspective, as in "No, we are not going swimming! We paid a fortune for these passes and we're going to stay here until we're done!" Remember, it's a vacation. When all is said and done, what you paid for is a good time. Be prepared to change courses to keep it that way.

probably get a kick out of knowing about any films that have been shot there, and budding athletes are sure to like details about local sports heroes and pro teams.

WORD OF MOUTH. "I think the biggest difference when traveling with children is their pace. The travel itself isn't the big adjustment; it's the slowing down once we get there. I've learned to plan one activity in the morning and one in the afternoon and come back to the hotel for a nap in between. Any more than that, and my kids are tired and cranky. You just can't plan to do too much." —sanibella

Be realistic. Theme and water parks are natural family destinations. But be mindful of such things as height restrictions before committing. A park's bent for high-speed thrills or height minimums may leave little for small children to do—or worse, frustrate wannabe riders who don't make the cutoff.

Use a family-friendly travel agent. Such experts can point you to the latest and greatest in family resorts. Apart from the planning, a knowledgeable agent can avert disaster, reminding you about things you might not think of, like car-seat rentals and child-care program reservations. They can also run interference should something go wrong.

Get the inside scoop on family travel. Check out posts on Fodors.com, where many of the Fodor's community discuss general and destination-specific family travel issues. On FamilyTravelForum.com, articles are written by families who travel for families who travel. There are destination-specific and thematic (cruise, adventure, road trips) features, an active forum, and a free custom-trip planning tool.

KIDS AND HOTELS

Be sure the hotel is child-friendly. Many, but not all, high-end haunts welcome kids. Clues are in the descriptions. "Premier family resort" is a keeper. "Romantic boutique hotel," maybe not. Some places tread the middle ground, as in "Children over 12 always welcome." Such a disclaimer may be a hint to look elsewhere, or risk facing withering stares upon arrival. When in doubt, ask.

WORD OF MOUTH. "Wondering what to do about the gross remote control in the hotel room? Take along an extra zip lock baggie and zip it in. Zip it and click it!" —mom23rugrats

Mention the ages of your children when booking hotels. Sometimes hotels have special rooms (such as rooms with bunk beds) just for families. Such things aren't necessarily offered up front, so be sure to ask when making reservations.

Inquire about in-hotel child equipment. Most, but not all, hotels have amenities such as cribs. Some need to be reserved in advance. Ask whether there will be an additional charge, and make sure it is a crib that meets current child-safety standards.

Bring your own safety gizmos. Hotel rooms have outlets just like home—only without the safety covers that keep kids from electrocuting themselves. Such peace-of-mind items are easily packed, and worth the few pennies.

BOOKING FAMILY HOTEL STAYS

■ **Talk to the person in charge.** Some hotels won't guarantee a particular room arrangement (such as connecting) at booking; if so, call the front desk to plead your case. If you still can't get assurances, book elsewhere.

■ **Define suite.** All suites are not created equal. Sometimes a junior suite is merely an L-shaped room with a sitting area, meaning you won't have that all-important door separating you from the kids. Ask the question: Is this a suite with two separate rooms?

■ **Ask about family suites.** Not all hotel suites are presidentially priced. Some, like the new breed of family suites offered at a growing number of places, are more moderate. Reservation agents won't often check inventory unless you ask.

■ **Don't share a room.** The family that sleeps together... hates each other in the morning. Cramming the whole bunch into 400 square feet of hotel hardly seems like a vacation. A better bet: Check out an all-suites hotel, or ask a standard-room hotel whether they offer multiroom discounts.

■ **Get connecting rooms.** In hotel speak, "connecting rooms" means there's a door leading directly from your room to the kids' room. "Adjoining" only means you'll be next to each other. Be specific when making reservations.

5

SIZING UP HOTEL CHILD CARE

Ask what kind of child care the hotel offers. Garden-variety kids' clubs with coloring and videos are good for occasional nights out. Look for something more elaborate if your vacation hinges on keeping the kids busy. Find out whether all-day programs include field trips, or whether the kids will be primarily inside. Some resorts only contract with in-room sitter services, an arrangement not everyone finds comfortable.

Find out what ages are allowed. The most elaborate programs have clubs for infants all the way up to teens. Not all do. Many require preschoolers to be potty trained. Some clubs don't start at age 3; others end at age 12. Make sure your child fits the bill, or risk being disappointed upon arrival.

Investigate capacity. Some programs have enrollment limits, meaning you'll have to be quick to sign your kids up. Ask if you can sign up in advance; if not, head straight to the kids' club desk when you check in.

Be clear about kids-program hours. Some kids' clubs are seasonal. Others only operate evenings. Still others take weekends off. Make sure the operating hours fit your needs.

Research caregiver qualifications and ratios. What's the number of children per adult? Are providers first-aid trained? If they'll be at the beach, do adults have water-safety training?

WORD OF MOUTH. **"Stop at a market area and grab some bread, veggies, and cheese as soon as you get there. I take a couple of extra large resealable plastic bags to contain everything."** —mom23rugrats

---

PACKING FOR KIDS

Give everyone his or her own bag. Individual suitcases (preferably different colors—red for one, blue for another) help you locate items in a hurry. This will make life easy at the airport, as even little kids are not only capable of toting around a mini-Pullman—they often enjoy it.

Assemble one toiletry kit for all the kids. Today's rules regarding carry-on liquids mean more shampoos in checked baggage—and more potential for messy spills. Checking one bag with all spillable items (as well as beauty items such as hair dryers and makeup) saves you from a potential trip to the Laundromat upon arrival. It also eases unpacking, allowing you to deposit the entire case right in the bathroom.

Make packing lists for each child. List each item as it's packed, and stow the complete itemization in the suitcase. The arrangement will help you repack at the end of the trip and give you the peace of mind of knowing everything that came is going back home.

Pack a family carry-on. One bag of essentials saves heartache if a bag is temporarily lost. Include one outfit for everyone, as well as prescriptions and other must-haves. A communal bag also simplifies car travel, giving quick access to overnight necessities for midway stops instead of unpacking the whole car.

Consider creative carry-ons. Soft coolers make great carry-on luggage. Roomy and crushable, they're perfect for nonbreakable items (such as those extra outfits) and help you cut your food bill by becoming picnic baskets for takeout meals.

Think plastic. Plastic bags protect delicate items from spills inside your suitcase. They'll also be invaluable at trip's end for dirty laundry and any wet clothes coming home.

CAR TRAVEL WITH KIDS

Schedule road trips wisely. Toddlers do well when their sleep schedule is factored in. Leaving at naptime guarantees at least a few hours of snoozing. It's tempting to depart at bedtime, but you may end up with wide-eyed kids upon arrival at your destination, and you risk becoming drowsy yourself during the late-night ride.

Bring diversions along for the ride. Few things are worse than bored offspring on a long trip. In addition to electronic gizmos (MP3 players, portable game consoles), good diversions include books, audiotapes, clipboards, action figures, toy animals and vehicles, sticker books, coloring–activity books, dolls, colored pencils (avoid markers and pens that can become messy when uncapped). The License Plate Game (see how many states you can find) and Start a Story (create a tale with each person adding one sentence at a time) are fun distractions. For really long rides, a portable DVD player could be your ace in the hole when the kids are on the edge.

Install car seats correctly. The National Highway Traffic Safety Administration (⊕*www.nhtsa.dot.gov*), a division of the U.S. Department of Transportation, estimates that three out of four car seats are improperly installed. Contact the NHTSA or your state's department of traffic safety for locations of child safety-seat inspection stations.

Anchor luggage in the car. Heavy bags and equipment become lethal projectiles in an accident. Strap in DVD players. Put luggage in the trunk. If you're driving a wagon, invest in a barrier between the cargo and passenger areas.

Bring pillows for car naps. The comfy accessory creates prime nap conditions, and can be used as a barrier between two quarreling kids.

Limit on-the-road junk food. Treats are great, but too many can lead to carsickness. Too much caffeine can wire up

5

RENTING A CAR WITH THE KIDS

■ **Bring a car seat.** Most rental companies charge extra for safety equipment like car seats—upward of $10 per day—an arrangement that adds up, especially if you're bringing more than one child. It costs you nothing to bring your own. Seats can be checked as luggage, or, if they meet airline requirements, they can be brought on board the plane for a snug, safe flight.

■ **Get a big car.** It's tempting to skip the pricey minivan and rent the less expansive family sedan. But "full-size" in rental speak isn't as big as it sounds. Strollers and such take up lots of trunk space. Although your family of five may fit, your luggage probably won't.

■ **Join the preferred-renters' club.** Almost every rental company has one. Such memberships allow you to breeze past those notoriously long counter lines and right to your car. Time-savers like this are invaluable for families who are likely tired and hungry after a long flight.

the kids and make you crazy. Lean toward healthy snacks (fruit, veggies, peanut-butter crackers) and moderation.

Let the kids navigate. Equip each kid with a road map to your destination. It's a great way to school them in geography; older kids might even get a kick out of estimating distances. Add stickers from each stop (preferably those that represent the area) and you've got the makings of a great keepsake of the trip.

Plan to make pit stops. Gone are the days when you were kid-free and could drive straight through from Syracuse to Daytona. Enjoy it; stop and smell the roses. Throw a ball. Toss a Frisbee. Better yet: Make getting there half the fun. Stop at quirky museums or landmarks. Plan an overnight at a hotel with a pool. No matter your timetable, avoid the "I gotta go now" emergency by offering frequent bathroom breaks, especially for potty-training toddlers.

Research changing-table locations. A first-time mom who quickly tired of having dirty diapers and nowhere to put them founded ChangingTableLocator.com. Users report on locations (there are about 300 locations throughout the country) for four categories: family-friendly (tables in both men and women's rooms), nursing room, limited access (table in the women's room only), or no table.

FLYING WITH KIDS

Buy your child a seat. A long trip with a child on your lap is uncomfortable. And if you hit turbulence it can be unsafe. International travel generally requires a ticket (albeit a discounted one) even if the child is occupying a lap, so you might as well buy a seat.

Ask about children's fares. Sometimes infants and toddlers fly free if they sit on a parent's lap and older children fly for half price in their own seats—though this is less and less common.

Bring the car seat. Kids used to sitting in car seats are more likely to sit happily if they're in them on the plane. Inquire about policies involving car seats, though; having one may limit seating options. Also ask about seat-belt extenders for car seats. (Note that you can't count on a flight attendant to produce an extender; you may have to ask for one when you board.)

5

Tell the airline if you're flying with a newborn. Some airlines may require a doctor's note to fly with a newborn. Some limit travel while pregnant, requiring doctors' notes during late term, and restrict travel completely for seven days before and after a due date. Check with the individual airline for rules.

Watch your seat selection. Children cannot be seated in emergency-exit rows. Avoid them when booking, or you may have the unpleasant surprise of finding your family split up in flight.

WORD OF MOUTH. "Our kids were asleep about 30 minutes into the flight and slept the entire way. We reserved four seats in the middle together and put parents on the outside and the girls on the inside. They each put their heads on our laps and lay down as much as possible with the seat arms up. They ended up kicking each other occasionally during the night, but did OK." —surfmom

Bring food. Once upon a time, airlines used to serve actual in-flight meals. These days you're most likely to get a bag of peanuts and a coke. Ask the reservationists if there are special meals for children. After they stop laughing, start planning for snacks.

Pack smart. Bring sippy cups to avoid spills. If you're travel-ing with a baby, bring a change of clothes (for both of you) and more diapers and wipes than you think you'll need.

Ease the pressure. Be prepared with something to chew or suck on (bottles or pacifiers for little ones) for pressure changes during takeoff and landing.

Bring in-flight diversions. Crayons, markers, coloring books, paper, pencils, scotch tape, and children's safety scissors are invaluable, as are playing cards, books, music players, and books on tape. Travel games are a bonus, but beware of loud gizmos that rattle the passengers in front of you. Wrap a few inexpensive trinkets to hand out at desperate moments. Gifts don't have to be elaborate—the act of opening is often entertainment enough.

Enlist help. One child increases 100-fold the amount of stuff you're hauling. Forget machismo and economy and use the skycaps.

Time pit stops well. Hit the bathroom before the FASTEN SEAT-BELT sign is lit for the last time. The time between initial descent and arrival at the gate can be an eternity if your potty-training toddler has to wait for the bathroom.

Skip the red-eye. Flying all night to Paris may seem like a good idea, until your toddler is awake all night, throws up in the cab on the way to the hotel, and remains miserable for the next seven days. You may lose some time traveling by day, but the rest of your vacation will be better for it.

WORD OF MOUTH. "If you [must travel overnight], a nonstop flight is the way to go. I've also found that splitting up the trip into shorter flights is better for younger kids who tend to get antsy after being in the air for three or four hours. . . . It's ideal if kids can burn off some energy for an hour or two in an airport between flights." —hlphillips

Leave plenty of time. Nothing starts a vacation off on the wrong foot like having to sprint to the gate. Reduce pre-flight stress by arriving early enough to calmly navigate security and deal with the inevitable bathroom and food stops on the way to the plane.

Keep a tight reign. It's one thing to take your child for a walk down the aisle, and quite another to let him run loose. Air travelers generally frown on children staring at them while they're trying to sleep. Beware of seatback kicking and endless games of peek-a-boo.

Avoid colored liquids. Don't let kids consume anything red or purple unless it's in a sippy cup. This includes tomato juice, red wine, and colas. Your seatmates will thank you.

Get creative when changing diapers. Surprisingly, not all planes have restroom changing tables. If this is the case, your best option is to sit on the toilet and change baby on a changing pad in your lap. Or put a changing pad on the floor and give it a go.

CHILDREN FLYING ALONE

Make sure your child can handle a solo flight. Most airlines don't allow children under age 5 to fly unaccompanied. But even older children may not be well suited for traveling alone. If your child is very anxious or very defiant (i.e., doesn't follow instructions without arguing), he or she will have a difficult time navigating a busy airport, especially if he or she encounters delays.

Choose your carrier wisely. Some airlines are better equipped to aid children flying solo. For example, British Airways has dedicated child lounges at its London airports.

Talk to the airline before booking. Different airlines have different rules. Some allow young children only on direct flights. Others won't allow them to fly after a certain hour (to avoid the potential for an overnight delay) or on connecting flights. Some carriers define "unaccompanied minors" as kids under 15; others insist that kids 13 and older fly as adults. These days, airlines do a lot of code-sharing, so make sure that a flight isn't being handled by a partner airline, which may have different rules. In most cases it's best to book by phone; some airlines will not allow you to book unaccompanied minors online.

Expect to pay more for supervision. Many airlines charge a "supervision" fee to assign a person or persons to look out for your child. This fee should ensure that someone will escort your child to the gate, escort them at their destination to the adult designated to pick them up, and keep an eye on them if their ride at either end is late. Ask about an airline's specific policy when booking.

Safeguard your child. Don't put his or her name on anything that's outwardly visible. Remind your child not to speak

DOCUMENTATION FOR KIDS

Certain types of travel with children require documentation. For more information, don't hesitate to bring up some of the following issues when talking to your airline.

■ **Obtain passports for your kids.** Some people neglect passports when their kids are infants; all U.S. citizens are required to have them for international travel from birth on.

■ **Know the rules about getting passports for kids.** Both parents–guardians must be present when trying to obtain a child's passport. If it's not possible for both parents–guardians to be present, the absent party must provide a notarized Statement of Consent. If one parent has sole legal custody, specific paperwork must be present.

■ **Watch passport expiration dates.** Under age 16, passports are good for only 5 years, unlike the 10-year span of an adult's passport.

■ **Observe single parent rules.** Parents flying solo with a child will need written consent from the other parent when flying internationally. Not all agents ask for it domestically (some phone reps will tell you not to bother), but it's best to be prepared.

■ **Know what unaccompanied minors will need.** Children flying alone require Unaccompanied Minor forms, and some airlines, particularly on international routes, also require notarized proof (sometimes from both parents) that the child has permission to travel alone. Contact the airline to make sure you know exactly what forms will be needed.

to or show his or her boarding pass to anyone but airport personnel. When you arrive at the airport, point out members of airport personnel and security, so your child will know how to recognize them. Check the child's ticket and boarding pass to confirm that names are spelled correctly. Children have "gone missing" over this.

Prepare your child. Explain the process ahead of time. Tell her about the airline-issued badges that often must be worn at all times and who will hold her tickets and documentation (generally flight attendants do so during the flight). Define terms and instructions she's likely to see and hear, such as "lavatory" and "seatbelt sign." Check out in-flight entertainment options online, and explain how the headphone jacks plug into the armrest. As most airlines won't administer medication of any kind, give your child instructions about doses.

Pack essentials in your child's carry-on. Beyond the obvious—books or video games to keep them occupied, a few snacks, a change of clothes, a sweatshirt or jacket in case they get cold on the plane, money for emergencies, printouts with contact info at home and at their destination and important medical information, and, if possible, a cell phone (or calling card; make sure they know how to use it).

Don't leave the airport before the plane takes off. Depending on the airline's policy (and the ever-changing security policies), you may be required to escort your child to the gate. For this, you'll need documentation to pass through security. (Ask for it at the check-in counter.) Even if you're not allowed past check-in, don't leave until you confirm that the plane has taken off and that your child has gotten on the flight. Make sure that whoever is seeing your child off on the return flight does the same.

Confirm pickup. To pick up your child, the person at the other end must present proper identification, as well as a signed and perhaps notarized document, often called an Acceptance of Responsibility form. Check with the airline for the specific documentation you will need.

EATING WITH KIDS

Be a little daring. Sticking to familiar chain eateries seems to negate a big part of visiting a foreign place. Ask around for appropriate eateries, preferably establishments that are emblematic of your destination. It will be much more fun than dining at the same places you could visit at home.

Be realistic. The time to introduce a new food to your child is not at the end of a long day, when he's missed both his naps and he's starving. An unadventurous palate at home is likely to be equally unadventurous on the road. Choose eateries that allow you to introduce local flavors while offering more familiar foods as well.

Avoid arriving overly hungry. Famished children are notoriously miserable, and Murphy's Law dictates that the hungriest people in the restaurant will be served last. Avert disaster with bread, crackers, or the Cheerios or graham crackers you have stashed in your bag.

Order for the kids first. There's no shame in staggering everyone's meals—the timing will benefit everyone. Before your server even finishes saying, "Hello my name is . . .," place your order for the little ones. Request grown-up drinks and fare when the server returns.

Let them eat cake. Feed kids their main dish via room service and later let them eat dessert while you enjoy dinner. It may raise eyebrows among fellow diners, but as long as the kids are well behaved, who cares?

Be creative. Don't feel shackled by the children's menu, and don't despair if there isn't one: Many restaurants will be happy to adjust grown-up meals. Linguine without the clam sauce and chicken Parmesan without the Parmesan (but maybe with ketchup) are good bets. On the other hand, ask ahead about the kitchen's flexibility, and find out whether kiddie meals have grownup prices.

Pack a stash of little packages of ketchup. If your child usually slathers it on everything, come prepared. For the record: The French don't have a word for "ketchup."

Take a hint. You may have the most well-behaved cherubs on the planet, but that will be irrelevant if the restaurant doesn't want them. "We don't prohibit children, but we don't recommend bringing them" is a hint. Take it and move on.

Know when to give up on table manners. The fancy macaroni and cheese made with real cheddar and Parmesan pales next to the freeze-dried cheese-food product your children love at home. The restaurant's pasta is too saucy, or your child is simply cranky. Whatever the cause of the fussiness— especially if it escalates into a meltdown—be considerate of the hapless diners around you. Pay your bill and leave. Enjoy your gourmet doggie bags back in your hotel room after the kids have gone to bed.

Try takeout if all else fails. Grab some picnic fixings at a local food shop and head for a playground. Without the stress of a full-service meal, your kids might just become adventurous enough to sample a new flavor or two—and actually enjoy them.

TRAVELING WITH TEENS

Give teens some freedom. All-inclusives and cruises give older kids their first taste of independence. The finite space of a boat or resort means a rare opportunity to play and dine at will. Buses at places like Walt Disney World afford the chance to motor around independently.

Give yourself peace of mind. Organized activities entertain teens while allowing parents to keep track of them. Many resorts now offer teen clubs, exclusive spots open only to certain ages. Such clubs are often equipped with soft drinks, game rooms, karaoke, and dance floors.

Set a budget. Motorized sports are the mama of all extras. Teenagers will zero in on them the moment they arrive. Jet Skis and parasailing can cost upwards of $60 an hour. Little things like soft drinks and virgin cocktails—$1 to $5 each—not to mention arcade games, can add up in a hurry, especially since they're often bought with resort charge cards that don't seem like actual money. Use prepaid cards when possible. Either way, set a budget and stick to it.

Bring a friend. Nothing entertains a kid like another kid. Before offering an invitation, talk to the parents of the potential guest. Agree on who's paying for what, and how much supervision will be offered. Written permission—signed by the guest's parents and notarized—is needed to fly. Such documentation, plus insurance info, is also needed to get health care in an emergency.

FAMILY REUNIONS

Plan well ahead. Large groups require as much as a year's advance notice. That includes air, hotels, restaurants, villas, shows, and anything else you can think of. It will also help you be mindful of individual budget preferences.

Reserve an apartment, a condo, or a house. This works best for families who thrive on the chaos of communal living. The only potential hang-up: Who gets the master suite. If it's a birthday event, the big room naturally goes to the guest of honor. Garden-variety reunions have a harder choice. One solution: Donate it to some of the kids. The suite will be plenty big for a slumber party, and you'll love the fact that their war-torn bathroom is blissfully out of sight. On that note, designate chore duties. Nothing ruins a vacation faster than doing all the work.

SAMPLE PERMISSION LETTER

Here's the text you might use for a typical letter of permission.
You should type this up yourself, putting in all the specific details
of your trip in place of the blanks.

CONSENT FOR MINOR CHILDREN TO TRAVEL

Date: ....

I (we):..

authorize my/our minor child(ren),......................................

....

to travel to...

.... on ....

aboard Airline/Flight Number: ....

and/or Cruise Ship...

with.. .

Their expected date of return is ....

In addition, I (we) authorize: ....

....

to consent to any necessary routine or emergency medical
treatment during the aforementioned trip.

Signed: .... (Parent)

Signed: .... (Parent)

Address: ....

....

Telephone:...

Sworn to and signed before me, a Notary Public,

this .... day of .... , 20.......

....

Notary Public Signature and Seal

Reserve a block of hotel rooms. This is the optimal choice for families that tend to get in each other's hair. Add a courtesy suite, and you have all the benefits of togetherness, plus a place to retreat to when you need it.

Ask about group discounts. Your large brood may qualify for rates normally offered to schools and corporations. Talk to the group-sales office, and ask about discounts on flights as well as hotels (for multiroom blocks), theme parks, and shows.

Consider the spread of age and abilities. Kiddie parks are going to bore teenagers. Museum-heavy itineraries are poison for tots. Mega coasters? Let's just say grandma will probably be on the sidelines. The best destinations have something for everyone, including those with disabilities. Some places like San Diego—with theme parks, museums, and beaches—have built-in entertainment for all.

Consider individual preferences. Planning a group trip can't be a 100% democracy, but there are some situations that definitely call for a vote. Before booking a grown-up night, for example, make sure all parents are on board with child-care. Avoid booking your favorite steak house if you know there are vegetarians.

Provide goodies. Welcome baskets are a festive way to begin the adventure. Making them at home and shipping ahead costs less than having them custom-made at the hotel. For a beachside adventure, fill sand pails with disposable cameras, dollar-store photo albums, water bottles, Frisbees, and other goodies.

Look into childcare. Keeping the kids busy frees the adults to catch up.

Schedule apart time. Not every moment has to be a group hug. Build in optional daytime activities for individuals, with set meeting times, such as 7 PM for dinner, for the group.

Make a big finish. A special, last-night dinner doesn't have to be a budget-busting affair. Group-sales offices at many restaurants and concierges at hotels can help arrange gala feasts for any budget. Many—even lower-end eateries— offer private rooms and special menus for such events. If money is really tight, look into doing a luncheon instead of a dinner, as the midday meal is usually cheap.

Pet Travel

WORD OF MOUTH

"Go to www.petswelcome.com for a listing by state of hotels, motels, B&B's etc. who take dogs. We use it all the time."

— Plan2GoSoon

"I don't object to dogs on flights at all. In many cases, they're better-behaved than some of the humans I've encountered on planes!"

— bookchick

Updated by Alexis Kelly

It's no secret that dogs can be perfect companions on the great American road trip, but today, with tiny muzzles peeking out of nearly every oversized designer bag, pets have become much more visible in less obvious arenas like airports and luxury hotel lobbies. After all, if Leona Helmsley can bequeath millions to her Maltese, surely you can at least give your furry friend a proper summer vacation.

Before you hit the road with Rover, though, keep in mind that your pet will require much of your time, just as he does at home. In fact, your pet will probably be a major focus of your trip, which is fine if you're camping and hiking, but harder to deal with if you yearn to spend leisurely hours shopping, dining, or visiting museums.

And just as with people, some pets travel better than others. If your dog's disposition bears a striking resemblance to the high-maintenance aunt that ruined last year's family reunion, perhaps you don't want to spend six hours on a plane with him. The best candidates for travel are pets that are even-tempered, well behaved, sociable, and in good health. If yours is anxious or aggressive, it's probably best to board him or hire a pet sitter.

6

PET-TRAVEL BASICS

Leave young pets at home. Kittens and puppies are more easily frightened by new environments and more susceptible to illnesses.

Hire a pet sitter. After considering your options, if you do decide that the best choice for you and your pet is to let the little guy stay at home where he'll be more comfortable, look into the services of the National Association of Professional Pet Sitters, or NAPPS (⊕ *www.petsitters.org*), which offers a cadre of trained, professional pet sitters who will take care of your pet in your home. This kennel alternative allows you to interview the potential sitter and make sure personalities match.

WORD OF MOUTH. "I've used a professional pet-sitting service and never had a problem. I feel much better knowing my kitty is at home in a familiar environment. The sitter pets and sits with my cat for about an hour each day, scoops her poop, and even brings in my mail and waters my plants. If you decide to go with a sitter, have them come to the house to meet you and the cats.

This way you can interview them and see how the cats and sitter react to each other." —laurieco

Consider having your pet tattooed or microchipped. Both processes are humane and effective for tracking lost pets.

Know your pet's "normals." You should know all your animal's normal vital signs, including temperature, heart rate, respiration rate, and the frequency of eating, drinking, and eliminating. Consult your vet to help compile this list. Any variation in your pet's normals may be an indication that something isn't right.

Just say no to drugs. Never give your pet any drugs, especially tranquilizers, without your veterinarian's approval; most do not recommend tranquilizers because they can have adverse side effects at high altitudes. All options (including holistic remedies) should be discussed with your vet, and new drugs or treatments should be administered to your pet in small doses before travel to ensure that he or she does not have adverse reactions.

Ask your vet for referrals for vets in your destination. You should get at least one referral for all areas to which you plan to travel. Alternatively, contact the American Animal Hospital Association (⊕ *www.healthypet.com*) or the American Veterinary Medical Association (⊕ *www.avma. org*) for referrals.

Ask your vet about the necessary shots. Rabies vaccinations should be up-to-date and verified on your pet's tag, as some states require proof of vaccination before allowing pets entry. Other shots might be wise depending on where you're heading: Lyme disease is prevalent in the northeastern United States, and your animal should be vaccinated if you plan to spend time outdoors in that area.

Introduce crate feeding early. Many animals suffer from a lack of appetite when they are traveling or under stress in general. If you plan ahead, you can train your pet to eat in the car and/or his crate. Feed him in his crate in and out of the car for at least a few weeks prior to your trip. By doing so, you will train your pet to think of his crate as his portable dining room.

Be vigilant about dehydration, heatstroke, and hypothermia. Common car-trip problems for pets relate to temperature: hypothermia in cold weather and dehydration or even heatstroke when it's warm. Hypothermia is manifested by prolonged shivering; prevent it by keeping your pet warm in the car, perhaps with an extra covering. You can avoid dehydration (indicated by a dry mouth and sunken eyes) and heatstroke (you'll see significant panting and frothing) by keeping your car cool, giving your pet plenty of cool water to drink, and watching to see that he drinks it. If you think your pet's in trouble, talk to a vet immediately.

Be aware of your surroundings. Many public areas and lodgings use poisons to get rid of insects and rodents. These are poisonous to pets, too. When you register, ask if any poisons are used. If you're traveling to an unfamiliar region of the United States, it's advisable to contact a local animal hospital to inquire about destination-specific health issues for dogs and other outdoor pets—especially problems with ticks and Lyme disease, thorny or poisonous plants, snakes or predatory animals, or high incidences of heartworm and fleas.

Don't assume all parks are pet-friendly. What could be more fun for a dog than trotting along scenic mountain trails or in dense forests full of new smells? Unfortunately for your hirsute companion, many national and state parks restrict dogs from hiking trails—and many public areas for that matter. Before planning a hiking trip, make sure your pet is welcome. It would be a real bummer to drive halfway across the country only to leave the poor guy in a hotel room or kennel.

Bone up on water safety. Many dogs love water and will relish an afternoon at a beach or on a boat. Remember that watercraft should be given the same scrutiny as any other new environment. Make sure that there is a way to secure your pet to prevent him from falling into the water or injuring himself if the ride gets rough. Provide him with a space of his own that feels protected (and is protected from the sun) and has a cushion or towel for him to lie down on. And even if your dog is a strong swimmer, it's a good idea to fit him with a life jacket or other flotation device—many calm-looking rivers can have strong currents that may confuse or overwhelm a dog.

Be aware of public transportation snags. In cities most public transportation options are off-limits to dogs. If your adventures may include buses, trains, subways, or ferries, research ahead of time whether you'll be able to bring your pet aboard.

CAMP GONE TO THE DOGS

Do George and Gracie run the other way from you when you call? You may want to take them to Camp Gone to the Dogs (⊕ *www.campgonetothedogs.com*). Every year, more than 400 dog lovers and more than 500 dogs do just that, coming from as far away as Australia and Japan to Marlboro College in Marlboro, Vermont, in June, and to the Mountaineer Inn in Stowe, Vermont, every September, for a week.

Dogs get obedience and agility training from top instructors. They dash through tunnels and over (or around) obstacle courses, learn to track by following a scent, play with Frisbees, try their paws at freestyle dancing, tricks and games, and much more—all in a noncompetitive atmosphere. At the Marlboro session there are some 50 events each day, where you'll learn about herding, hunting, Tellington Touch, competition obedience, and other topics; there's even a dog costume contest.

Reserve well ahead—the camps have been featured on national TV shows and in national magazines, and are extremely popular. Some people even come without their dogs, and many return year in and year out. The single all-inclusive price runs around $1,325–$1,500.

PACKING FOR YOUR PET

Bring verification that your pet is approved. Have handy the information that your airline, car-rental agent, or hotel e-mailed or faxed to you, so you have proof that someone has endorsed your pet's transportation or stay.

Bring copies of health and vaccination records and extra ID tags. You and your pet are out of your normal surroundings, so it's good to take extra precautions in the event anything goes awry.

Have your pet wear two tags when traveling. One tag should list your permanent address and telephone number and the other a way to contact you on the road. A trick for that second "tag" is to staple a card or matchbook from your lodging to your pet's collar.

Pack a current photo of your pet. Taking every imaginable precaution doesn't guarantee your pet won't get lost on your trip. As a safety measure, be sure to have some current photos and a detailed description of your pet's markings in case you need to put up signs.

Bring a good leash and consider a bell. Pets may be fine on a junky, chewed-up leash for their local walks, but for new places and modes of transportation a sturdier one is worth the investment. For added safety, outfit your travel companion with something jangly.

Pack comfort objects. If your pet has a personal attachment, say, to a particular plastic bone or a certain stuffed toy, be sure to bring it along.

Don't forget a flashlight. It'll come in handy for those night-time walks.

Pack a pet first-aid kit. Some items to consider: elastic bandages and tape, tweezers for removing burrs and ticks, antiseptics and antibacterial creams, eyewash, cortisone, hydrogen peroxide, antihistamines, and hand wipes.

Include some grooming supplies. Consult your vet for other suggestions and instructions.

6

Go disposable and portable en route. Paper plates are easy to toss, and a collapsible water bowl is light to carry. You can bring plastic bowls for your destination.

Pack the familiar kibble. If you routinely use a local brand that may be difficult to find while traveling, pack enough for the whole trip. A sudden change in your animal's food could cause an upset stomach.

Bring a container or two of water from home. If your pet has a sensitive stomach and may be affected by drinking new water, bring enough along, or stick to bottled water.

AIR TRAVEL WITH PETS

Book a flight on a pets-only airline. Yup. Such a thing exists. PetAirways (⊕ *www.petairways.com*) serves New York, D.C., Atlanta, Los Angeles, Phoenix, Denver, Omaha, Fort Lauderdale, and Chicago. You, your pet, and its carrier check into the pet lounge on departure, company representatives board and secure your pet in its carrier. All pets are monitored regularly during the flight, and then are picked up at the pet lounge at the destination airport about a half-hour after arrival. Flights eastbound leave on Tuesday and Wednesday; westbound flights leave on Thursday and Friday. Fares start at $149 one-way.

Look for written guidelines for pet travel. Airlines that have taken the time to put pet policies in writing are more committed to safely transporting animals. If airline employees can't articulate pet policies for you, err on the side of safety and choose a different company.

Check the Department of Transportation Web site for complaints. The DOT's Aviation Consumer Protection Division (⊕ *airconsumer.ost.dot.gov*) keeps data on airlines that have been fined for mishandling animals entrusted to their care; you may want to check out your airline's record.

Book pet travel well in advance. No matter where on the plane your four-legged friend will be located, book well in advance, as a limited number of pets can be transported on any given flight. Sometimes no more than two pets are allowed in a cabin per flight, so it's especially important to book early for carry-on pets. Restrictions vary for cargo quotas.

Opt for nonstop flights. Dealing with multiple connections, particularly ones that require a change of plane, will be as stressful on your pet as it is on you. Stick with nonstop flights, and try to get on the first flight of the day—it will cause fewer disruptions in your pet's routine.

Travel with pets on a weekday. Weekday flights, especially midweek, are usually less hectic than weekend flights; both you and your pet are more likely to receive attentive service.

Get your pet's paperwork together. To travel by plane, your pet will need a health certificate that has been issued no more than 30 days prior to the flight if he will be in the cabin and no more than 10 days if he will be traveling in cargo.

Remember that Hawaii has its own rules about pet entry. The state of Hawaii, which is rabies-free, has more stringent health requirements for pets flying in from the mainland. Even if your dog meets all requirements, he may still be quarantined for one to five days. It can take several months to get the proper paperwork together. The Web site for Hawaii's Department of Agriculture (⊕ *www.hawaii.gov/ hdoa/ai/aqs*) has quarantine information.

Don't overfeed your pet on departure day. Avoid feeding your pet a large meal within six hours of departure time. It's usually best to feed dogs a small meal before you leave the house and then a larger meal upon arrival at your destination at the end of the day. Cats usually won't eat once they see you packing, so when you get to your destination be sure to set up a quiet spot for your cat to enjoy a meal.

Remove the muzzle. Keeping your pet muzzled may inhibit its ability to breathe and/or pant. If your dog cannot behave without a muzzle, perhaps he or she shouldn't fly. Choke, pinch, or training collars should be removed also, especially on pets traveling in cargo.

Protect your pet's ears. Hours of engine noise can be unnerving to us, so imagine how upsetting it is to a cat or dog. Consult your vet about earplugs, especially if your animal is very skittish around loud noises.

CARRY-ON PETS

Flying the pet-friendly skies. Petflight.com has information on which airlines will allow pets as carry-ons, which except pets as baggage, information about flying to Hawaii, airline incident reports, and more. There's even a list of airport spots where you can take your pet to walk and wee.

Weigh Fluffy. As a rule, pets permitted to travel in the cabin can weigh no more than 20 pounds.

Avoid the aisle seat. Opt for a window or center seat, as they generally have more room to stow carry-ons. Of course, business and first-class seats have even more room.

Keep the leash and paperwork handy. When you arrive at the security gate, you will be required to remove your pet from its carrier and send the carrier through the X-ray machine. Be sure to have a harness and leash attached to your pet. To avoid delays, also be sure to have your pet's health certificate and boarding pass ready when you approach the security gate.

Invest in a Sherpa bag. Most airlines have approved soft-sided carriers, such as the Sherpa bag, for cabin travel. You can buy a model with a removable "travel tray," which is lined, washable, and absorbent. Better yet, you can get one with wheels for when your shoulder's had enough of lugging around a 15-pound tabby.

6

GLOBE-TROTTING PETS

The average purse poodle has probably traveled more than the average travel writer. But while taking Bijou to see the Eiffel Tower and the canals of Venice may make her a better dog, getting her out of the airport may make you a more frazzled person—thanks to strict health laws.

Some countries have lengthy quarantine requirements. Many require an International Health Certificate that must be signed by a vet accredited by the Animal and Plant Health Inspection Service (APHIS ⊕ *www.aphis.usda. gov*). Countries in the European Union require pets to have microchips or tattoos; your vet must fill out an EU-approved health certificate and do a full work-up on your pet no more than 10 days before travel. The United Kingdom has made the transition a bit easier by introducing the Pet Travel Scheme, or PETS (⊕ *www.defra.gov.uk*), under which cats and dogs (and ferrets) from several EU and non-EU countries can bypass the protracted quarantine routine if they have been fitted with microchips and successfully vaccinated against rabies.

Contact the consulate or embassy of the country you plan to enter for a full list of requirements. Local APHIS offices can also help you muddle through the process, as well as recommend accredited veterinarians. Whatever you do, don't wait—it may six months or more to collect all the paperwork needed to admit your pet to a foreign country. Contact the consulate again four weeks prior to departure to reconfirm the country's requirements.

For people embarking on long trips around Europe, Cunard's *Queen Mary 2* (⊕ *www. cunard.com/QM2*) is a viable way to cross the Atlantic with pets in tow. The ship has kennels on its upper deck and the animals are given exercise several times a day. Owners can stop by to visit their pets and play with them during designated hours.

PETS IN CARGO

Consider the risks of flying your pet in cargo carefully. Flying as cargo is one of the most hazardous ways to transport pets; before you stow Fido down below, know what she'll be up against. Besides considering your pet's tolerance for anxiety-inducing situations and temperature variations, also consider that if she's pregnant or ill she shouldn't fly because the stress can cause serious complications. It's not the best idea to send little ones via cargo, either; pets must be at least 8 weeks old to fly within the United States, and most airlines don't recommend flying cargo at less than 12 weeks.

Know the rules for pet's traveling below. To travel on your flight as excess baggage, the total weight of your pet and its carrier must not exceed 100 pounds. If the weight of the animal and carrier combined is greater than that, most airlines will only allow the pet to be shipped as cargo. When flying as cargo, pets are not guaranteed to be on the same flight as you are. Pricing also changes: It will be based on the weight and/or the measurements of the kennel.

Be aware of breed restrictions on pet travel. Some airlines prohibit short-nosed animals (Boston terriers, pugs, bulldogs, and Himalayan and Persian cats) in cargo during the hot days of summer because they're more vulnerable to the heat and often have difficulty breathing at high altitudes. Other airlines ban summer cargo travel across the board.

Inquire about your pet's air-travel environment. Some airlines have special pet areas in their cargo holds. Temperatures are controlled and air quality is on par with that of the passenger cabin. When you've narrowed down your flight options, call the airlines and ask if pets are kept in climate-controlled areas.

Make sure your pet carrier is airline-approved. If it's vetoed at the airport, it could foul up your travel plans big-time. An approved model is leak-proof, ventilated on two sides, and large enough for your pet to stand up, turn around, and lie down in. It's important that your pet be familiar with the carrier and comfortable in it as well. Put the words "live animal" on the outside of the crate, along with your pet's name, your name, your phone number (at home and in your destination), and arrows indicating which end is up. Secure the door, but don't lock the crate—airline personnel may have trouble getting to your pet in an emergency.

Outfit your pet carrier with all the essentials. Include soft bedding and two plastic food and water dishes. Attach a small bag of dry food, and any required medications to the top of the crate along with feeding and medication instructions. Do not keep leashes or toys in carriers, as your pet could injure himself by becoming entangled in the leash or choking on smaller toys. To comfort your pet, include a piece of old clothing or a blanket or towel from home.

Freeze your pet's water bowl. Instead of placing a full bowl of water in the carrier, freeze the water in the bowl the night before departure. As the ice melts, your dog will be able to rehydrate, and you won't have to worry about the water spilling out during the loading process.

Mind that your pet carrier is in tip-top shape. Broken, beat up, or wimpy carriers may not survive the flight. A stressed-out dog or cat may try to chew its way through flimsy plastic or malfunctioning locks, leading to its escape, or worse, its injury or death. Clipping your pet's nails before your trip will also help ensure that your pet doesn't rip its carrier to shreds.

Keep watch at the departure gate. Don't leave the boarding area until you are sure your pet has been loaded onto the plane. As you board, alert the flight crew that you have a pet on board—they'll be more likely to monitor temperature changes in the cargo hold if they're reminded of this.

Check in with your pet at every stop. If you must change planes at a stopover, check with airline personnel again to make sure your pet has made the connection. If there will be a long delay in the second flight departure, claim your pet, take him for a quick walk, and then reboard him.

Choose flight times carefully. You want to be sure your pet travels during the coolest parts of the day in summer (early morning and late evening) and the warmest in winter (midday). The cargo hold itself may be liveable, but wherever your pet is stationed en route to the plane may be another story. In addition, you may be able to avoid restrictions regarding pet travel on very hot days if you travel before or after the sun is at its most powerful.

Keep tabs on ventilation problems. If your plane's stuck on the runway for a long period of time, remind the flight crew that you have a pet on board and ask them to keep an eye on the temperature in the cargo hold. If the delay becomes very long or if you cannot get straight answers from the flight crew, it's worth making some noise—ventilation problems in cargo have killed pets.

CAR TRAVEL WITH PETS

Take short test drives. Most pets only travel when going to the veterinarian, groomer, or kennel. If your pet hasn't traveled much, you should dedicate at least a few weeks before your trip to getting him accustomed to car travel and carrier training. When your pet is calm and relaxed in the carrier at home, you can repeat the training process with the carrier placed in your car. After a few days, take short trips in the car and make the destination a place that will please your pet. Most dogs will learn to love car rides if they believe they will sometimes bring them to play ball in the local park.

Don't get stuck at the border. International borders have special restrictions on animal travel, so check to make sure you're allowed to take your pet on the road before you leave home. The U.S. Department of Agriculture Web site (⊕*www.usda.gov*) has the information you'll need.

WORD OF MOUTH. "It's hit and miss on them asking for a health certificate [at border crossings]. Sometimes they ask, sometimes not. Last time they asked, we said yes and went to get it out of glove compartment, but they said not to bother. Make sure you leave dog food in its original packaging. On our last trip, crossing back into the United States, they asked. Ours wasn't and he said he could confiscate it but didn't." —Ranger

Stop at least every three hours to walk dogs. Your dog will feel less disoriented if he or she is able to interact with the new environments you pass through—and you'll get much-needed breaks during those marathon drives. If possible, avoid high-traffic rest stops, which can translate into high-stress rest stops for your pet.

Strap pets in. A loose pet in the car can make a quick escape if someone opens a door. Also, if you make a short stop or are involved in an accident, the animal could be badly injured or killed, and, in a 30-mi-per-hour collision, an animal becomes a lethal weapon and threat to all passengers. When loose, an animal is also likely to distract you. Options for restraint are a carrier (often seat belt compatible), a pet harness that attaches to a seatbelt (this one's more common for dogs), or a regular leash tied to a stationary part of the car.

Consider crating your dog for the road trip. A crate is helpful for an anxious or jumpy dog. A crate-trained pet might actually be soothed by a snug, familiar environment. Try to use the crate on short drives to a dog park or playground so your pet associates the experience with fun outings instead of only stressful ones like going to the vet. If you choose to use a crate, make sure it is secured so it won't tip over if you make a sharp turn or sudden stop.

Place cat carriers with care. Cats usually aren't enthusiastic about car rides. A carrying case is a must; find a flat, stable place to put it—not on the floor, where road noises are amplified and can terrify your favorite furball.

Don't allow your pet to keep his head out the window when you're driving. Although many dogs love to put their heads out the windows of a moving car, it's not a good idea. The American Veterinary Medical Association (⊕ *www.avma. org*) says it's a great way for your dog to get eye, ear, or nose injuries. Likewise, putting your dog in the bed of a pickup truck can be extremely dangerous.

Combat pet carsickness. Animals are susceptible to motion sickness, which features excessive drooling and vomiting. A carrying crate alleviates this problem for some animals; vets can prescribe drugs for others. Many people have had success with Rescue Remedy, a mix of flower essences sold in pet and health-food stores. It's good to feed your potentially woozy pals small amounts during the day and save most of their food for when everyone's out of the car.

Cool your pet's crate. In warm weather a damp towel draped over the carrier will help to cool the air circulating through the crate while you are in the car with your dog or cat— though it won't do much good in a car that isn't moving.

Keep an eye on drool and stool. The former might just be a sign of motion sickness—unpleasant for everyone, but not dangerous if nominal—or it might be a sign that there's something stuck in your pet's mouth. If it persists, contact a vet. The same vigilance goes for loose stool; call a professional if it persists for more than 24 hours, or immediately if blood or vomit is involved.

RENTAL CARS AND PETS

■ **Research rental-car options thoroughly.** Most major agencies will allow pets in their vehicles, but restrictions—and, at times, additional fees—may apply. And some agencies may have a no-pets policy. Always confirm that pets are allowed, and inquire about cleaning fees and damage deposits.

■ **Take extra precautions to keep your rental car damage-free.** Keep pets in carriers or crates at all times to avoid problems. If your pet can be trusted enough to roam the back seat, cover the upholstery with a sheet or towel. Before you return the car, give the seats a once-over with a vacuum or lint brush to remove excess hair—this may save you a hefty cleaning charge. Inspecting the outside of a vehicle with the rental agent to note prior damage is standard, but if you've got a pet in tow it's a good idea to inspect the interior as well; rips or stains in the upholstery can easily be blamed on your pet if they are not on record before you drive off.

6

HOTEL STAYS WITH PETS

Double-check pet fees and restrictions. Accommodations often have restrictions on the size and age of animals (puppies tend to be discouraged). Fees can range from a nominal daily charge to a refundable damage deposit to a hefty nonrefundable flat fee. Some places hit you with daily fees *and* require a nonrefundable deposit of $100 or more. Make sure you get an itemized list of all additional fees and are clear on which are nonrefundable. Note that daily fees can vary depending on the size or type of pet.

Look for pet extras. Services are especially useful in urban areas where you're more likely to leave your pet behind while sightseeing. Many hotels offer special beds and treats, dog-sitting and dog-walking services, and even spa services and pet-centric activities and events. Before you settle, shop around to see which hotel offers the most support for your pet.

Request a ground-floor room. This is convenient for late-night potty runs, and means little unnecessary schlepping for you at properties that don't have elevators.

Be wary of special "pet rooms." Often pet owners will get stuck in smoking rooms or older rooms with worn furnishings. When booking, ask tough questions about how the pet rooms differ from the rest of the property, and make clear your request for a no-smoking room.

Scope out the surroundings. Looking at a hotel's Web site may not be enough to determine whether the surrounding area is suitable for walking dogs. Chain motels in particular are often along busy roads with no grass in sight. When booking, ask about local green spaces and the safety and general noise level of the area.

WORD OF MOUTH. "As a dog owner, [I'm well aware of the problems associated with] hotels surrounded by blocks and blocks of concrete when it comes to exercising your four-legged friend. In Vancouver, try the Sylvia Hotel (www.sylviahotel.com). It's in the west end, right across from a wonderful walk along English Bay. It's a dog-friendly boutique hotel, with lots of good restaurants nearby. In Victoria there are lots of dog friendly hotels near residential areas or parks. The ferries from both Vancouver and Washington State allow dogs, but you need a car, as they must stay in a vehicle for the voyage." —amygirl

Opt for apartment living. All-suite hotels or serviced apartments will give you the space you need to make sure you and your pet are comfortable. If you're staying in one place for a more than a week, don't underestimate the value of a place that resembles home—with a kitchen in which to arrange food dishes, a bathroom that can comfortably accommodate a litter box, and a bedroom with a door you can shut if anyone needs time out.

Use a crate or carrier when leaving your pet alone in the room. This is for the safety of your pet and of the lodging employees, who might enter the room to clean. Also, be sure he will not disturb other guests while alone. If you must let your pet roam while you're out, it's best to hang the "Do Not Disturb" sign on the door. Note that some establishments won't allow you to leave a dog alone in a room even if it's crated.

Control who comes into contact with your pet. Allowing too many people to say hello to him may add to his stress (and yours). Watch your pet for signs of anxiousness—yawning, excessive panting, avoiding eye contact—and give him a place to relax quietly. Most pets should have no more than one hour of intense meeting and greeting a day.

PET-FRIENDLY U.S. HOTELS

Pet owners represent a growing market, and hoteliers are finally catching on. Options range from the serviceable (ground-floor rooms and a treat or two) to the ridiculous (canine cocktail receptions). Below is a small sampling of the best places to hang your leash.

Several luxury chains pull out all the stops for pets. The best overall is Kimpton Hotels, which has properties in 22 U.S. cities. Dog-walking services, gourmet turndown treats, pet massage services, and employees that are excited to welcome four-legged guests are standard. Some Kimpton properties have special pet events like a complimentary birthday cake and meet-and-greet cocktail hours.

If you stay at any Starwood Group property (Westin, W Hotels, Le Meridien, St. Regis, and Sheraton), you'll get designer dog beds so comfortable you won't have to shoo Spot from your own bed. Westin doggies get a pet bed, dog bowl, and mat; W dogs will be welcomed with a toy and treats. Le Meridien properties have a cute, if pricey, "Feed the Party Animal" pet room-service menu.

As part of their "Loews Loves Pets" program, Loews Hotels provide local information on pet-friendly places, parks, and veterinary and grooming services; if you leave any accoutrements at home, beds, litter boxes, scratching posts, pooper scoopers, and so on can be procured. There are even room-service selections for your pet. Loews also keeps one-time pet fees low—the same can't be said for many luxury hotels.

Affina Hotels, which has properties in New York, Washington, D.C., and Chicago, offers the "Jet Set Pets" program. Upon arrival, your four-legged companion will be greeted with treats, a welcome walk, and plenty of pampering. Pet sitting, walking, grooming, and other services are available, even a pet psychic.

Best Western and Holiday Inn are good mid-range and budget chains. La Quinta also ranks well, though it has stricter size restrictions.

You'll be jealous of your pet's accommodations at D Pet Hotels, a kennel styled as a luxury hotel, in Hollywood, California. We're talking suites with real beds and flat-screen TVs (though standard rooms have the more traditional dog bed), a pet spa, a 6,000 square foot indoor run with different areas for different sizes of dogs, car service (chauffeur, anyone?), and more.

6

WORD OF MOUTH. "You can bring your dog [to the dog cocktail hour at the Liberty Hotel in Boston]. There's snacks for him and you, as well as drinks. It's every summer Wednesday, weather permitting." —cigalechanta

Deal with damaged property immediately. If your pet damages anything, immediately discuss the situation with the manager—don't wait until checkout to resolve such matters.

Find out where Fido can stay. A handful of Web sites out there have hotel recommendations and answers to travel-with-pets related questions. OfficialPetHotels.com features more than 10,000 pet-friendly properties in 35 U.S. cities. Petswelcome.com lets you search by larger dog– or cat-friendly hotels and has international as well as U.S. lodgings. Dogfriendly.com has lists upon lists to help you plan, including those for top hotel chains for pets, off-leash parks, and pet-friendly vacation rentals.

Air Travel

WORD OF MOUTH

"I don't have a lot of holiday time, so I want to minimize jet lag. . . . About a week before departing, I go to bed an hour earlier, get up an hour earlier . . . then two hours earlier, etc. I board the flight ready for a nap—just dinner, no wine or movies, try to sleep/nap. On landing, it's off to the hotel to drop off luggage and then go out (no nap as that just delays your body adjusting). I go for a walk, get some sun (no bus tours), eat at a normal time, and go to bed at normal time. By day two, I'm almost completely adjusted."

—Michel_Paris

Updated
by Alexis
Kelly

Flying was once an occasion that compelled you to dress to impress. Today it can be one of life's more undignified experiences. In the last decade the airline industry has been buffeted by obscenely high fuel prices, terrorism threats, and PR nightmares involving stranded passengers. A couple of heavy hitters have approached the brink of bankruptcy, most have added baggage fees and surcharges of all types, and customer service—and satisfaction—is at an all-time low.

And yet, not all the industry trends are bad: the choice of routes today is dizzying; low-cost airlines abound; and, despite the shrinking leg room and reduced possibility of a free meal, there have been enough innovations to change our idea of "standard amenities." (Only one movie for the entire flight? Please. Where's my personal TV?)

Talk of delays and invasive security screenings have become the stuff of legend, but if you plan well and arm yourself with a few insider tips, you can avoid many air-travel inconveniences and discomforts.

AT THE AIRPORT

SMOOTH DEPARTURES

Minimize the time spent standing in line. Buy an e-ticket, check in at an electronic kiosk, or—even better—check in on your airline's Web site and print your boarding pass before you leave the house. Better yet, look into paperless boarding passes—that is, downloaded into your Smart phone—being offered by increasingly more airlines and airports. If you opt for one of the latter two and pack light (no checked bags), you can bypass the check-in counter entirely; you just proceed to security and head directly to your gate to check in.

Arrive when you need to. Research your airline's check-in policy: It's usually at least an hour before domestic flights and two to three hours before international flights. But airlines at some busy airports have more stringent requirements. If you're traveling with small children, pets, or a lot of luggage, factor in some extra time. Check the Transportation Security Administration's (TSA) Web site (⊕*waittime. tsa.dhs.gov*) for estimated security waiting times at major airports. Flightstats.com is another handy site that helps you check the status of your flight, track delays, and set up automatic notification messages.

If you have an early-morning flight, sleep near the airport. Instead of setting the alarm for 3 AM, get a good night's sleep at an airport hotel. This can be a particularly good deal if you have to pay for long-term airport parking: ParkSleepFly.com can help you book room-and-parking packages at airport-area hotels. For the cost of one night's stay you'll also get at least a week's worth of free parking in the hotel's lot.

Secure a good parking spot ahead of time. Avoid on-site, long-term airport parking lots, which cost much more than off-site lots and fill up fast. To find off-site lots at major U.S., Canadian, and U.K. airports, check out AirportParkingReservations.com. Included in your booking is a free shuttle to all terminals. You may score additional discounts on AviStar/FastTrack Parking's site (⊕*www.avistarparking. com*), which often offers an instant 10% e-coupon on already low rates.

Know when to use a car service to get to the airport. Finding a cab during peak hours and in peak travel seasons (e.g., a Friday afternoon in July in New York City) *or* during off-peak times (say, in the wee hours of the morning for a 5 AM flight) can be hard. To avoid being stranded at such times, book a car service.

Factor rental-car return time into your schedule. If you need to be at the airport two hours before a flight and you're returning a car, get to the agency 45 minutes to an hour before you must be at the terminal. Better yet, phone the rental agency (the actual local office, not the national toll-free number), and ask exactly how far they are from the terminal, how often shuttles run, and how early they suggest you pick up or drop off your car to make your flight.

Factor getting to the gate into your schedule. The distances between the check-in counters and the gate are vast in many of the world's largest airports. The same is true of the distance between domestic and foreign terminals. If you're unfamiliar with an airport, allow plenty of time to go through security and get to your gate. And try not to book connecting flights scheduled too close together.

Check in early so you don't lose your seat. In recent years airlines have started taking more and more chances with overbooking flights. What's worse, getting bumped from a flight in peak season, when most flights are full, means you might have trouble rebooking a flight for the same day. To ensure that you get the seat you paid for, arrive at the airport with time to spare, or take advantage of remote check-in and print your boarding pass at home. If you're making connections, make sure you check in again at the next gate; airlines usually require this, even if you're flying on the same airline for both legs of the journey.

Ask how much it costs to upgrade. If you're not a bigwig or a coveted member of an airline's frequent flyer program, it's unlikely that you'll score a free first-class upgrade without precedent (i.e., being bumped from a flight). Many airlines will, however, let you buy first-class upgrades—if available—when you check in at the airport, particularly if they fear a flight will be oversold. You might get lucky and end up paying only $100–$200 more for first. On longer flights the extra cost could well be worth it. Before you head to the airport, check to see what a first class seat on your flight is going for to ensure that you are getting a good deal.

Consider joining an airline's frequent-flier or VIP program. You may still be riding in coach most of the time, but many airlines offer "elite" customers a few perks: you may get a special (and blissfully short) line to wait in at check-in; you'll probably be allowed to board before the rest of your fellow coach passengers; and you'll get first crack at the better seats and at upgrades. Policies vary from airline to airline, but most push their VIP programs prominently on their Web sites.

WORD OF MOUTH. "Usually with vacation planning, one picks the location, dates and accommodations, and then shops for airfare that fits. When using frequent-flier miles you often have to do it the other way around—see when there are seats available, then build the dates (and accommodations) around that. Flexibility is the key to successful use of mileage programs." —Gardyloo

Make certain your carry-on and its contents comply with airline and security regulations. Size requirements vary from airline to airline, so check when you make your reservation. Also check the TSA Web site (⊕ *www.tsa.gov*) for the most recent restrictions on toiletries, gadgets, and other articles.

Buy a one-day pass to an airline's VIP lounge. If you don't belong to an airport club, you can often get a one-day pass for around $50 (anyone traveling with you will pay between $25 and $35). In exchange, you will get a measure of tranquillity plus free snacks and drinks, magazines and newspapers, and phones—typically with free local calls. Personal computers may be available, or you can hook up your own laptop. And the staff can help with seat assignments and other matters.

Look for kids' play areas in airports. Most major U.S. airports have some amenities for kids. Some airlines have set up simple play areas on their concourses, with playhouses or ball crawls; some airports have more elaborate offerings. There are aviation-themed children's play areas at Seattle's Sea-Tac Airport (Central Terminal), Boston's Logan Airport (Terminal A), Dallas/Fort Worth International Airport (Terminal D and E), Las Vegas's McCarren International (Terminal D), Chicago O'Hare (Kids on the Fly in Terminal 2), and Minneapolis/St. Paul International (Lindbergh and Humphrey terminals).

Be smart about snacks. Packing food from home in your carry-on is still a good idea—it's cheaper than buying fast food at the airport, and it will save you from hunger pangs if you experience long delays on the tarmac. Just keep in mind that these days goodies must comply with the TSA (⊕ *www.tsa.gov*) guidelines, or they'll be confiscated. Don't pack beverages in your carry-on; stick with dry goods like granola bars, mixed nuts, baked goods, or sandwiches. Small containers (less than 3 ounces) of yogurt and pudding are allowed on many flights, too, if they're in a 3-1-1 kit with other liquids. Fruits and veggies might also be okay if you're flying within the lower 48; you may encounter restrictions regarding produce when flying internationally or to Hawaii.

Board as early as is permitted if you have large carry-on bags. There's seldom enough overhead storage space on a filled-to-capacity plane for every passenger. If you're traveling with a carry-on that's too large to fit under your seat, wait near the boarding area, so that you can be one of the first in line when your section of the plane boards. In coach, the rear of the plane always boards first, so if you regularly travel with large carry-ons, book a seat toward the rear of the plane, since you'll be almost assured room in the overhead bins. Just keep in mind that passengers in the rear of the plane board first and debark last.

AIR TRAVEL SECURITY ISSUES

Do your bit to keep the skies safe. Never allow a stranger to pack your bags for you or agree to pack an item given to you by someone you don't know. Don't carry a bag for another person onto an airplane, and report any unattended bags.

Keep cool during security screenings. No passenger is immune from what may seem like annoyingly invasive screenings, at the ticket counter and the gate as well as at airport security checkpoints. Grin and bear it—asking why you've been chosen or appearing grumpy just gives the security staff reason to be suspicious and to spend more time checking through your bags. Keep in mind that passengers who pay for a ticket with cash or buy a one-way ticket are more likely to be taken aside for questioning; try not to take it personally.

Rid yourself of items that set off metal detectors. All kinds of items that seem unassuming can set off the detectors and cause delays—and possibly inconvenient or embarrassing searches. Items to be aware of: keys, belt buckles, loose change, pens, watches, jewelry, aluminum foil, and cigarette cases.

Charge your electronic devices. You may be asked at security to turn on a laptop computer, iPod or MP3 player, Kindle or iPad, video camera, or other gadget to prove that it is what it seems.

Pack carry-on luggage neatly. If you're traveling with a laptop or other electronics that must be X-rayed separately, make sure you can easily remove such items from your bag without having to pull everything else out, too. Packing neatly—and not overstuffing bags—also decreases the time it takes for personnel to inspect your carry-on's X-ray image. And finally, having your bags searched at a security checkpoint will be quicker and much more tolerable if your bag is tidy.

Organize liquids. TSA regulations change regularly, but at this writing, small (no larger than 3-ounce) bottles containing liquids such as contact-lens solution, hand cream, mouthwash, and the like are allowed on most flights. You must, however, place all such containers in a clear 1-quart resealable plastic bag that you must remove from your carry-on before everything goes down the conveyor belt. Organize liquids before you reach the airport: Fussing with toiletries on the security line causes delays and invites much ire from security personnel and fellow travelers. Note that liquids such as baby formula and prescription medications are allowed in reasonable amounts exceeding 3 ounces, but you must declare them as you go through security and be prepared for them to be inspected.

Check wine and liquors. You won't make it through security with those big bottles no matter how tightly they're sealed—you'll either have to give them up or go back to the check-in counter to surrender them to your checked bag. You can carry on small bottles of no more than 3 ounces if you need a tiny tipple to get you through a long flight.

Don't take souvenirs for granted. Some seemingly innocuous souvenirs—snow globes, for example—aren't allowed in carry-ons. Many sporting goods, as well as weaponry (even if it's decorative items like collectible swords or antique firearms) won't be allowed as carry-on. If something's too expensive or fragile to risk stowing in checked baggage, consider shipping it home.

Don't wrap gifts. If TSA personnel need to inspect your packages, they will unwrap them.

Take extra care with your computer if an airport has outdated equipment. Although state-of-the-art scanners won't harm computers, an outmoded scanner in some small overseas airport—using old technology—might have an effect. Request hand inspection if in doubt.

7

WORD OF MOUTH. "In U.S. airports (and many others) you're required to take your laptop out of your bag and send it through in a separate bin. At other airports (those in Brazil, for example) you won't be required to. There are usually signs about this, or you can just ask the security attendant when you walk up." —laurie_ann

Wear slip-on shoes when flying. Most airports still require you to remove your shoes at security. Even at airports that don't require shoe removal, you may be delayed and asked to remove your shoes if they're big or high enough to potentially conceal a weapon. Simple sneakers, shoes you can slip off easily (mules, loafers, etc.), or dress shoes are your best bet. Flip-flops seem even better, but keep in mind that you'll end up walking around barefoot on dirty floors.

Say good-bye to long security lines. If you're a frequent international traveler, the U.S. Customs & Border Protection recently launched its Trusted Traveler Programs (⊕ *www. cbp.gov/xp/cgov/travel*), which help expedite reentry for Americans traveling internationally. The Global Entry program is designed for people traveling outside of the Northern Hemisphere. The NEXUS card is used for travel between the United States and Canada, and the SENTRI pass is used for U.S.–Mexico border crossings. You can avoid the longer normal lines by using kiosks and specially designated lines.

Don't leave home without a government-issued photo ID. Airlines strictly enforce the requirement that every traveler have one. A driver's license works for domestic trips; a passport is mandatory for all foreign trips by air, even for travel between Canada, Mexico, and non-U.S. territories in the Caribbean. Some travelers feel more secure always using a passport, even if all their travels are domestic. As solid identification, you can do no better. If you are in the United States on a green card or long-term visa, make sure all your paperwork is in order (you might need a reentry permit) and up-to-date before you travel abroad; reentering the United States can be a nightmare if you're missing any documentation or if your visa is about to expire.

Book your ticket using the name on your ID. Just married? If you were ticketed using your spouse's last name but your ID remains in your maiden name, bring your marriage license to back up your explanation. Does the name on your ID differ from a nickname or middle name you prefer to be called? Avoid hassles and make sure that the ID matches the name on your ticket or e-ticket confirmation.

Make sure you have the proper boarding pass. If you're taking advantage of remote check-in, which allows you to print boarding passes at home, or e-ticket systems that require you to print your boarding pass at a kiosk, make sure that what you're holding is a real boarding pass and not just a receipt or an e-ticket that must be validated at a check-in counter. Boarding passes include gate information and time of boarding but not personal info (address or credit-card info) other than your name. When in doubt, ask an airline employee.

Prepare the whole family for the security checkpoint. Even a child's backpack can be subject to a hand inspection. Make certain your kids' bags don't contain any liquids or materials that may be confiscated. Before going through security, avoid tears by explaining the process to small kids

WORD OF MOUTH: FLYING FEARS

"Read up on how a plane gets to fly in the first place. Knowing the mechanics can help. Also, you can find out all the data about accident rates—it's incredibly low." —rkkwan

"Usually fear of flying is a control issue. When you are flying, someone else is very definitely in control. Cognitive therapy helped me deal with this. Knowledge of the noises planes make and when and why you are likely to experience bumps (turbulence) helped me cope." —Ackislander

"Even with the fear of heights, I prefer window seats and being able to see the ground. Something about seeing that the ground is so far from me, makes crashing seem less likely in my crazy flying logic." —Rachelanneb

"I always get a seat where I can see the wing of the plane outside the window. Seeing the wing comforts my brain— illogical as it seems, the wing tells me there's something I can stand on outside of the plane." —Toedtoes

"Google 'fear of flight class,' this is how I dealt with fears. I printed out some pages (which also had breathing exercises) and read them at bedtime." —FainaAgain

7

so that they know they will get their belongings back. Be aware that you'll be asked to send all your gear, including strollers, diaper bags, carriers, and car seats, through the X-ray machine; items that are too big for the X-ray will be inspected by security personnel.

Know your rights. If you're pulled aside for a pat-down, you're supposed to be provided with a screener of the same gender. Many airports have partitioned screening areas for bag inspections; a TSA employee should conduct the search there, not in front of fellow travelers. Unfortunately, if you feel you've been the victim of discrimination or profiling, there's not much you can do at the checkpoint, but you should file a complaint with the TSA (note the name of the employee and the time and date of the incident). You should also file a claim if something goes missing from a checked bag, especially one that has been opened by TSA screeners (bags might have special tape across them and/or a printed card inside alerting you that your bag was opened). Note that it takes time to process a claim, and if yours isn't denied outright, the average payout hovers around $200.

AIRPORT DELAYS, CANCELLATIONS, AND BUMPING

Check in with the insiders. Who could possibly know more about avoiding flight delays and airport congestion than the National Air Traffic Controllers Association? Their easy-to-use Web site for travelers, Avoid Delays (⊕ *www.avoiddelays.com*), has information on everything from the best time of day to fly out of a specific airport to the best airports to connect through, plus up-to-the-minute flight delay data.

Find out the cause of a delay. Knowing the cause of the problem can help you decide how to respond. If the problem is at your departure or arrival airport—say, local weather or air-traffic problems—there's not much that anyone can do to speed up your departure. If the problem is at an airport where you're making a connection, you could look into the possibility of getting rerouted through another hub, even on another airline. You could also investigate switching to another flight if the cause of the delay is an airline-specific problem—say, the plane and crew to be used for your flight are late coming in because of a mechanical problem or bad weather in its originating city.

Read your airline's contract of carriage. You know that *very* small print on your ticket and that text that's buried deep inside an airline's Web site? This contract is what protects you from being stranded if a flight is canceled. It used to be that the magical Rule 240 protected U.S. passengers by stipulating that in the event of a cancellation the airline was required to do everything in its power to get you to your destination the same day—including booking you into first class if that's all that was available or booking you on a competitor's flight. Some airlines have become lax in their adherence to Rule 240; many will only put you in coach seats or refuse to book you on a competitor's airline. Know what your airline is responsible for, and keep a copy of the contract of carriage in case anyone balks should you invoke Rule 240.

Dread the "force majeure" event. That's airline speak for "act of God." If delays or cancellations are caused by weather, security shutdowns, strikes, or other events outside the control of an airline, the force majeure clause can absolve the airline from providing you with alternatives or reimbursements. The best way to safeguard against this is to shell out more money for refundable tickets. You have virtually no flexibility or rights when you've bought the lowest, "special deal" ticket off an airline's Web site. On the other hand, with a refundable or transferable ticket you'll at least be reimbursed for your loss.

Know your rights if you're bumped. Around 12 in 10,000 passengers with reservations are bumped. The U.S. DOT has rules about compensation in such situations. You're entitled to nothing if the replacement flight will get you to your destination within one hour of your original arrival time; you'll get $200 (maximum, or the one-way fare), if you'll arrive between one and two hours later domestically and one to four hours internationally; and you'll receive $400 (maximum, or twice the one-way fare), if you'll be more than two hours later domestically or four hours later internationally. You always get to keep your original ticket for use on, or credit toward, a future flight. If the bumping is caused by the airline's substituting a smaller plane for the one it originally planned to use, it isn't required to pay you anything.

Before you volunteer your seat, do the math. If you're traveling during peak times (e.g., Thanksgiving or Christmas), when nobody wants to give up his or her seat, you may get a true payout—a voucher approaching $1,000 in addition to complimentary dinner and a hotel room if you have to stay overnight. Most of the time, however, vouchers rarely exceed $200, they're usually nontransferable, and they must be used within one year. Before you let your seat go, ask the airline and yourself a few questions: When is the next flight on which the airline can book me a seat? Will I be flying on standby status for that next flight, and if so, am I willing to wait around for yet another flight if necessary? If the airline can't fly me out until the following day, will it pay for meals, hotel, necessary phone calls, and ground transportation during the interim? If not, can I afford to do so?

Opt for a voucher instead of a round-trip ticket when bumped. Free round-trip tickets usually come with many restrictions and usually only apply to domestic destinations. It's a far better deal to get a voucher of several hundred dollars that can be used toward any future flight. Of course, nothing's that simple, so if you're offered a travel voucher, ask the following questions: Is it "positive space"—that is, you'll be able to get a reservation in advance? Or "space available," which means you will have to fly on standby? Is it subject to blackout dates or other restrictions? Can it be used in the United States as well as abroad?

Always try to negotiate when being bumped. How much the airlines are willing to offer travelers who volunteer to get bumped depends on how oversold the flight is and how desperate they are to free up seats. Before passengers are denied boarding on an involuntary basis, the airlines usually up the ante considerably to get more volunteers. (It really does generate bad publicity to deny boarding to confirmed, ticket-holding passengers.) Exactly how much you can get depends on the circumstances, but even if you agree to get bumped for the initial offer, ask for an upgrade to first or business class as well.

Act quickly if your flight is canceled. Ask a gate agent about flying on another carrier. Your airline might have canceled all its flights and say its hands are tied due to weather, etc., but carriers have ticket-sharing arrangements and can put you on another airline's flight if they're running and there's room. Better yet, don't wait for a gate agent to help. If you're a member, go to the airline club or call your travel agent and/or the airline's 800 telephone number. The airline can be more helpful with weather conditions or equipment updates, and your travel agent will probably be faster making reservations on your scheduled carrier, or another carrier.

Understand what it means to fly "standby." Airlines no longer offer standby fares. You fly standby not to save money but when your flight is canceled, when you miss your flight, or when you arrive early enough to try to get on an earlier flight. Standby, in other words, is a status, not a fare. Technically, it's a waiting list—and not a very democratic one. Your place on it depends on what fare you paid or your frequent-flier status. Always ask how many people there are ahead of you on the list and what your chances are of clearing it. If you really need to be somewhere and can make a good case for it—family emergency, important meeting, sick child at home—let the gate agent know and hope for sympathy.

If you miss your flight, be patient and try to relax. The gate agents' first responsibility is to get the flight off safely and on time. If you're bumped because you were late, they'll get around to helping you after the plane has departed from the gate.

Call your hotel if your flight is delayed. It's one of the last things you may think of when faced with the chaos and uncertainty of a delay, but your failure to do this could result in your reservation's being dropped because your hotel believes you to be a no-show.

Leave enough time between connections. If you have to make a connection, leave ample time between flights. If there's less than an hour between the time you're supposed to land and the time you're expected to board your connection, you're taking a gamble. If you miss a connection because of a delay, the airline of the first leg will usually try to rectify the situation; however, if you're flying on a busy day or if many of your fellow passengers have missed the same connection, you may have to wait hours—or even overnight—to get a new connecting flight.

ON THE PLANE

Dress comfortably. Smart but casual, loose-fitting clothing is best for the air, especially for long-haul flights. Avoid wearing tight clothing. Also, the temperature on a plane fluctuates, so be sure to layer. Wear short sleeves, even in winter, and pack a sweater or light jacket in your carry-on even in summer.

Grab a pillow and blanket as you board. It can be difficult to find these once the plane has taken off, so even if you don't anticipate needing them, it's a good idea to snag them before sitting down.

Stow big bags overhead. Even if a bag technically fits under the seat in front of you, it may be big enough to restrict your leg room—and create another obstacle for fellow passengers to climb over. Throw essentials in the seat pocket and stow bigger bags above: your legs and back will thank you for the extra few inches of foot room.

Use a children's car seat on flights. Although most airlines allow children under two to fly free or for reduced rates if they sit on an adult's lap and do not occupy their own seat, children are safest in FAA-approved car seats aboard planes. Some airlines offer up to a 50% discount on the extra seat needed for car seats, which you should ask about when booking.

Be courteous about reclining your seat. Some passengers feel it's their absolute right to throw their seat back into a reclining position the minute they're allowed to, while others consider even the occasional and polite use of a seat recliner to be rude and invasive. At the very least, recline

FIGHTING JET LAG

Most travelers try to make the most of their limited time overseas, yet fail to take into account the leap in time zones they make in a matter of hours. It can take your body's internal clock several days to catch up to that leap, and in the meantime you're likely to experience the disruption of your sleeping and waking cycle known as jet lag. Symptoms of jet lag include sleepiness during the day, insomnia at night, poor concentration, confusion, hunger at inappropriate times or lack of appetite, and general malaise and irritability.

■ **Adjust your internal clock.** Several days (at least four) before departure, gradually shift your sleeping and eating times to coincide with those at your destination. Once you arrive, adopt the local time for your daily routine.

■ **Opt for overnight flights.** You'll have dinner at a normal time and be much more likely to sleep than on an afternoon flight. Depending on the length of the flight and the number of time zones you cross, you'll arrive at your destination in the morning or afternoon. This is the best way to replicate your normal schedule, and it'll be easier for you to reset your clock.

■ **Curtail coffee.** For 12 hours before, as well as during, your flight, avoid overeating and caffeine. Although caffeine can help keep you awake longer, it makes you wake up more often once you do fall asleep and so reduces total sleep time.

■ **Stay hydrated.** Drink at least 8 ounces of water for every hour you're in the air—even if you don't feel thirsty. If you wear contact lenses, clean them thoroughly before your flight, use eye drops in the air, and consider removing your lenses if you nap. In your carry-on pack a bottle of moisturizing lotion, lip balm, and a hydrating spray with essential oils (not just water) to spritz your face with occasionally. Just be sure all toiletries are TSA compliant.

■ **Avoid or limit alcohol inflight.** Cabin air dehydrates passengers, and altitude changes can quicken the effects of alcohol (the rule of thumb is one drink in the air is the same as two or three on the ground). A cocktail may relax you, but it's also apt to dry you out, and even worsen symptoms of jet lag.

Try to sleep on the plane. This is especially important when you're traveling overnight or flying west to east. Travel is extremely tiring, and the more rest your body gets en route the more prepared you'll be to deal with the stresses of jet lag. If you're taking a very long flight—United States to Asia, for example—consider saving up enough dollars or frequent-flier miles to fly business or first class, as it's a lot easier to sleep when your seat reclines all the way back. If you can't avoid coach, opt for a window seat and bring enough padding (pillows or something that can act as such) to prop yourself up against the wall.

■ **Use sleeping pills wisely.** A pill with a short cycle may be helpful on overnight flights. Make sure, however, that you time the dosage correctly or you may be very groggy when you land. Also, an airplane is not the place to try out a pill for the first time, so only take medications you are already familiar with.

■ **See if melatonin is for you.** Consider taking the non-prescription drug melatonin. Research suggests that the body uses this hormone to set its time clock. Because melatonin seems to control when we go to sleep and when we wake up, a number of scientists advocate supplements to alleviate jet lag. Some (but not all) studies suggest that taking 3 milligrams of fast-release melatonin prior to bedtime for several days after arrival in a new time zone can ease the transition.

■ **Get outside.** After arrival, spend a lot of time out in the sunlight, which will help your body reset its natural time clock to coincide with your new surroundings.

■ **Don't drift off too early.** Unless you arrive at your destination at night, and reasonably close to a normal bedtime, don't go to sleep as soon as you reach your hotel. Unless you're used to taking regular short naps at home, you're better off staying up until bedtime: If you're really exhausted from travel, a 20-minute nap could easily become a three-hour nap, which will disrupt your sleep schedule even more—you might find yourself wide awake at 4 AM.

7

your seat back gently and slowly, so the person seated behind you is prepared. You should also avoid reclining during meals, when seat trays are in use. Also, if the person behind you is on a laptop, give them some warning before you slam the seat back.

Share your armrest. There's no getting around it—those tiny armrests, especially in coach, are simply too narrow for two adults to fully rest their arms simultaneously. But you'll have a more pleasant trip if you try to avoid hogging too much of the armrest, and politely remind your neighbor to do the same, if it comes to that. Making a pleasant request generally beats sitting and fuming throughout the duration of your flight. Surrender the inside armrest if you have the aisle or window seat on a three-seat (or more) row. It's a giving gesture to the person crammed between you and some other stranger.

WORD OF MOUTH. **"If someone asks me to trade seats, I always ask to see their boarding pass to make sure they do indeed have the seat they want to trade me. In general, I think trades need to be 'like for like.' If I have an exit row, I'll trade for an exit row. If I have an aisle, I'll trade for an aisle. If the trade is a result of a parent needing to sit with young children, that's a call you have to make. If I board and someone is already in my seat under the assumption that I'll trade, definitely no trades. Ask me. Don't assume." —Jeff_Costa_Rica**

Remove your shoes once your plane takes off. Your body swells at high altitudes, so you'll be much more comfortable if you slip out of your shoes and loosen belts or tight-fitting clothing. (But be considerate of the passengers around you—stinky shoes are better left on—you can always untie or loosen them instead of removing them completely.)

Don't go hungry. Find out whether food is being served on the plane and plan accordingly. If your airline offers snacks, find out if they'll cost you—it might be better just to pack a few snacks from home. If your airline does offer meal service, be sure you make special requests for vegetarian or kosher meals ahead of time. Also, ask whether the food contains things to which you're allergic.

Bring your own headphones. The headphones provided by the airline are usually subpar and ill-fitting, which means you have to crank up the volume to hear anything over

IN-SEAT WORKOUTS

Isometric tightening of your muscles is the simplest and least obvious way to exercise during a flight. Focus on a muscle or group of muscles—say, your stomach. Sit up straight, and take a deep breath. As you exhale, tighten your muscles and hold for a count of 10. Release and breathe in. Repeat 5 to 10 times. Do this every 20 minutes or so, choosing a different muscle or set of muscles each time.

To exercise your legs, sit up straight with your feet flat on the floor. Keeping knees bent, raise one leg a few inches. Rotate your ankle around five times, lower your leg, and switch to the other leg. Repeat five times with each leg. Then, keeping your knees bent, raise one leg, pulling your knee up to your chest. Lower your leg and repeat on the other side. Go back and forth between legs 10 times. To relax tension in your shoulders, pull them up toward your ears and hold for 10 seconds while breathing in. Breathe out and release. Repeat five times.

Stretching keeps blood flowing and muscles limber. If you can get up, hold onto the back of your seat or a wall for balance. Place one leg behind you with the toes 12 inches from your front heel.

Shift weight to the back leg and slightly bend the knee, then slowly lean forward over the front foot to stretch. Switch legs and repeat this calf stretch. If you can't leave your seat, put your hands on your hips and twist your shoulders and your torso from side to side (being careful not to bump your seatmate). Next, slowly straighten your arms and pull your shoulder blades together until you feel a stretch. Hold for a count of 10.

If you suffer from back pain, don't lock your knees while you're standing in all those lines; this causes bad posture and puts pressure on the lower back. Bend your knees slightly, and keep your pelvis tucked in. Utilize luggage carts for big checked bags, and don't overload yourself with heavy or unwieldy carry-ons—you'll be dragging and hoisting them a lot. If you experience sharp, stabbing back pain or spasms en route, apply ice; massaging the feet may also help, as reflexologists say that the instep has correlations to the spine, and working your thumbs up and down the area may ease some back pain.

7

engine noise and passenger chatter. Plus, some airlines are charging a small fee for them. Most airplanes have jacks that can accommodate standard headphone sets. Noise-canceling headphones are even better, as they block out engine noise while providing superior sound quality.

Bring a sleep mask and earplugs. Nothing says DO NOT DISTURB more effectively than wearing a sleep mask while flying. Most fellow travelers will leave you alone, and you may even sleep more effectively. Engine noise can be unnerving after several hours; earplugs will help block out that and other cabin noise. Alternatives to earplugs are noise-canceling headphones.

Be proactive if you have a cold or sinus problems. The cabin air dries out already aching sinuses and sore throats, and the pressure changes during takeoff and landing can cause severe ear pain. Consider investing in EarPlanes, earplugs designed to keep the pressure in your ears consistent. They really do work, and their semihollow design also helps to block out engine noise while still allowing you to hear what the flight attendant is saying. And over-the-counter nasal sprays work wonders on congested sinuses. Give each nostril a spritz well before takeoff, so that the stuff has time to work before you ascend.

Avoid deep-vein thrombosis. On flights of four hours or more, the dry atmosphere combined with the immobility can lead to the rare but very serious condition of deep-vein thrombosis (DVT). When blood flow is restricted, clots can form in the legs. These can then break free and travel to the lungs, where they block the flow of blood. To prevent this, periodically massage your calves and thighs in a circular motion, get up and move around every hour or so, and do in-seat stretches. Try to keep legs slightly elevated when the plane reaches its maximum altitude; prop them up on footrests or carry-on baggage. Walking around the terminal before boarding may also help. Certain people are at higher risks for DVT; check out the Web site www.dvt.net for more information about the condition.

ON ARRIVAL

Always save your boarding pass. If you're not properly credited for frequent-flier miles for a trip, or if some other dispute arises following a flight, your only true proof that you actually traveled someplace is your original boarding pass. This document can come in handy months after you've completed your travel—it's a good idea to keep your boarding pass indefinitely.

Be careful opening your toiletries. Ever open a bottle of hair gel or shaving cream after a flight only to have the contents shoot out all over you and the bathroom? Changes in air pressure during flight can cause all kinds of things to become unsettled. Always open any pressurized or airtight canister or container gently after you've just flown. Keeping shampoo, hand lotion, and similar items in a resealable plastic bag can limit messes.

Know your rights as a passenger. There are rules concerning liability for lost luggage, compensation for delays, airline security, and other issues. The DOT's Aviation Consumer Protection and Enforcement office's Web site (⊕ *airconsumer.ost.dot.gov*) details such rules.

Resolve lost baggage issues immediately. If your luggage isn't on the flight, don't leave without speaking with the appropriate airline staff and getting written acknowledgement of the lost luggage. Get the name and direct phone number of the person who takes your report, and make sure they're legible, if handwritten.

Know that sometimes the best transport from the airport is a rental car. Especially in cities like Denver and Los Angeles, where the airport is a 30-minute drive from downtown, it can be cheaper to rent an economy car than to take a cab or even shuttle bus into town—and you may get frequent-flyer miles this way. And using your car instead of a cab for trips during your visit may increase your savings. When pricing this option, be sure to factor in the cost of parking the rental at your hotel.

Know that sometimes the best transport from the airport is a taxi. In San Francisco, New York, and other cities, cabs to the center of town cost about $40, not including tip, or more, and shared-van and bus services could cost from $10 to $25. But if you're splitting expenses with a traveling companion, the cost of a taxi might be only a tad more than the cost of the alternatives (which usually take longer and can be less comfortable).

Car Travel

WORD OF MOUTH

"I use trains when going from big city to big city, but for [places like] rural Italy, a car is a big plus in my opinion."

—J62

"Take things slow. Plan ahead. Keep tummies full. Be flexible. Don't try to do too much. Have fun!"

—BKP

www.fodors.com/forums

Updated
by Alexis
Kelly

Road trips appeal to our sense of wonder, our yearning to know what lies just around the bend, and what happens if we choose one tine of the road's fork over another. Whereas trains, planes, and buses are captained by others, we take our automobiles where we want to go. Other forms of travel limit our luggage allowances, force us to follow somebody else's schedule, and cramp our style. Car trips allow us the ultimate freedom and flexibility.

Perhaps the biggest decision you'll make when planning a road trip is whether to get to where you're going quickly or to make a leisurely journey part of the vacation. Superhighways are great for fast, efficient trips, but die-hard road-trippers argue that the best way to understand a destination—its contours and climates, architecture and history, inhabitants and customs—is to stick to narrow, two-lane roads through the countryside.

Regardless of your route, hopping into your car and gliding down a twisting road, windows down, feels totally empowering. There really is no better way to see the world around you.

ROAD-TRIP PLANNING

Join the American Automobile Association (AAA). If you need emergency road repair, or even help with a dead battery in your own driveway, it pays to belong to AAA (⊕ *www.aaa. com*). In addition to roadside assistance, the association has other great services, such as discounts on rental cars and hotel rooms. Memorize the number for long trips: 800/ AAA–HELP (800/222–4357).

If you lease a car, look into a rental car for your trip. If you lease your car, or have some other reason to avoid putting a lot of miles on your own vehicle, you may want to consider using a rental car for long road trips. A rental car with unlimited miles can pay for itself if you drive it for a couple of thousand miles instead of using your own vehicle.

Consider renting an RV instead of a car. RV travel has become increasingly popular. Certain circumstances—visiting parks and/or areas with campgrounds, traveling with a large group—make this form of getting around more enjoyable and potentially more economical than traveling by car. The Recreation Vehicle Rental Association (⊕ *www.rvra. org*) has lots of tips as well as information on the different types of RVs. Cruise America (⊕ *www.cruiseamerica.com*)

and El Monte (⊕ *www.elmonterv.com*) have rental locations across North America.

Don't rule out RV camping abroad. You can rent an RV and explore the French countryside with the help of FrancePassion.com, which lists 1,500 sites that include vineyards and farms throughout France. With the purchase of the French Passion Invitation booklet ($42 including shipping), motor home guests can stay on participating properties for up to 24 hours, free of charge, with no commercial obligation.

WORD OF MOUTH. "In France there are over 2,500 free sites, 1,500 French Passion sites and 3,500 paid sites [to camp with an RV]. In Germany there are even more. The funny part is that the free sites in France are limited to motorized RVs, not trailers or tents. In most cases the free sites are maintained by the local municipality and have electrical/water hookup and dump stations. Sites are literally everywhere. From paid camping areas inside Paris to little free sites on the banks of the Danube to free downtown sites in Rome on the Tiber." —daveesl

Make a list of attractions along your route. Use a regional travel guide—such as *Fodor's National Parks of the West* or *Fodor's Essential USA*—to research the attractions along your route. You might not plan on seeing the world's largest collection of kangaroos outside Australia in Dahlonega, Georgia, but it's a fun pit stop on a rainy day or if the kids just won't settle down.

Get the best mapping resources. A state map won't have all the local roads, and a city map won't guide you to that B&B that sits a few miles outside of town. Make sure to get maps you're comfortable using, whether they're the fold-up, spiral-bound, or laminated kind. Road atlases are favorites of long-distance travelers, but might be too bulky for short trips. Flag the relevant pages with Post-it notes, and consider highlighting your route or important landmarks along the way. Better yet, invest in a Global Positioning System (GPS), a satellite-based navigation tool that really takes the guesswork out of getting there.

WORD OF MOUTH. "I got the Garmin 775T with Europe and North America pre-installed for $350. It's worth every penny as far as I'm concerned. The best feature is the ability to hook it up to my PC and program in all my upcoming hotels, restaurants, sights and shops in advance of the trip. The traffic reports are a godsend. [Note that] no GPS anywhere is 100% accurate, nor is any map. New roads, new signage, repairs and detours, and traffic change constantly. Part of the fun of travel is dealing with the unexpected." —Otzi

Find the cheapest gas. Gas prices are greatly influenced by state gas taxes. A Web site operated by the U.S. Environmental Protection Agency, www.fueleconomy.gov, gives national and regional average prices. More helpful are sites like Gas Buddy (⊕ *www.gasbuddy.com*) and Gas Price Watch (⊕ *www.gaspricewatch.com*), which use tips from consumers to rank the lowest and highest gas prices in a particular area. Note, though, that the information on these sites can be outdated, so it's best to use them as a general guideline.

Look into hotel coupons. Roomsaver.com prints hotel-coupon books on every region in the United States, and they reprint them seasonally. These are available free at many highway rest stops and fast-food restaurants and in some visitor information centers, but you can also log onto the Web site and print out the coupons from home. These coupons often provide the lowest hotel rates around (even better than what you'll find on Expedia.com or Priceline.com), are good only for walk-ins, and are subject to availability. They aren't honored for guaranteed reservations. You can hedge your bets by calling a hotel a day or even a few hours ahead of time and asking if they're likely to have availability that night, and confirming that they'll be accepting coupons.

If you drive an unusual car, get a list of repair shops. Mechanics who specialize in Saabs, Volvos, Audis, Mercedes, Jaguars, and similar luxury cars are hard to find outside major urban and suburban areas. Keep a list of repair shops around the country in your glove compartment (most car dealers can supply you with a free directory), and avoid taking a truly exotic car on trips to remote areas.

Be sure you have a roadside assistance plan. Check to see if your car's warranty is still in effect and that it includes emergency roadside assistance, which typically covers towing, changing flat tires, and retrieving keys locked inside cars. If you don't have such a plan, definitely join AAA, which offers this service.

GREAT ROAD-TRIP MOVIES

There are loads of great movies out there that involve road trips, and it can be great fun renting one before you embark on a journey. A few favorites, of varying artistic merit, are listed here in alphabetical order.

■ *The Adventures of Priscilla, Queen of the Desert*. Three drag queens head across the Australian outback. (Trust us, it's hilarious.)

■ *Boys on the Side*. Friends Drew Barrymore, Mary Louise Parker, and Whoopi Goldberg are three unhappy women searching for different things on a cross-country journey.

■ *Elizabethtown*. Orlando Bloom is headed home for his father's funeral, and along the way learns important lessons about life from Kirsten Dunst.

■ *Easy Rider*. Jack Nicholson joins two motorcyclists on their way from California to Louisiana and becomes a major movie star along the way.

■ *Little Miss Sunshine*. A dysfunctional family travels across the country in a VW bus to enter their young daughter in a beauty pageant.

■ *The Motorcycle Diaries*. In this Spanish-language Oscar winner, Gael García Bernal is prerevolutionary Ché Guevara on a trip across South America.

■ *Rain Man*. In this Oscar winner Tom Cruise takes Dustin Hoffman, his autistic savant brother, on a cross-country road trip.

■ *Sideways*. Paul Giamatti takes a soon-to-be-married friend on a trip through the Napa Valley, meeting a lot of women along the way.

■ *Thelma and Louise*. Susan Sarandon and Gena Davis are two women running from the law—and running into the arms of an impossibly young Brad Pitt.

■ *Y Tu Mamá También*. In this film from Mexico two young men see their friendship threatened by their attraction to the same older woman.

Get a passport for trips to Mexico and Canada. Due to security measures, anyone crossing between the United States and Canada or Mexico will be asked to supply a valid passport. A driver's license typically sufficed in the past. Note that people who live near the borders of these countries can get license-size passport cards, which are a little cheaper and more convenient to carry. They're only good for crossings by land or sea.

Have the right insurance for trips to Mexico and Canada. Your U.S. car insurance will cover you during your car trip into Canada, but the State Department recommends getting a Canadian insurance card from your insurer in advance of your trip. Your car insurance will not cover you in Mexico, so you need to purchase supplemental insurance from a Mexico-based firm.

Obtain an international driving permit. Your driver's license may not be recognized abroad. If needed, international driving permits (IDPs) are available from the American and Canadian automobile associations and, in the United Kingdom, from the Automobile Association and Royal Automobile Club. These international permits, valid only in conjunction with your regular driver's license, are recognized in 150 countries, and are printed in 10 different languages; having one may save you a problem with local authorities. In the event of an accident, local police could confiscate your paperwork, and it's far better to surrender this temporary permit than your actual driver's license.

WORD OF MOUTH. "An IDP (International Driver's Permit) is like insurance. You don't need it 99% of the time. The one time you do need it, you're in deep you-know-what if you don't [have it]. For instance, your car insurance would be voided since you'd be driving illegally." —janisj

Put your car-insurance card in your wallet. It's okay to keep a copy in your glove compartment, although some drivers prefer not to for the simple reason that if the car is stolen, the illegitimate driver will have a much tougher time talking his or her way out of a traffic stop without an insurance card. But definitely keep one in your wallet at all times, so you'll always have it handy should yours provide coverage for cars you rent or borrow.

Copy important documents. Before you leave, make copies not just of your passport and credit cards, but also of your driver's license, itineraries, contacts, insurance papers, and other car documents. Store one set at home or with a friend or relative, and the other set in your luggage. Better yet, scan the set into a computer and e-mail the documents to a friend and yourself.

RENTAL-CAR RECOMMENDATIONS

Inspect the rental car before you leave. Always check for damage, and take the time to point out anything you notice to an agency staffer—otherwise you could be charged for damage. Look for dings on the windshield, dents and scrapes, torn upholstery, missing ashtrays, etc. Don't forget to check the trunk, interior roof, and floor. Pop in a CD and see if the CD player works. Test the ignition, horn, headlights, blinkers, and windshield wipers. Check the trunk for spare and jack. Locate the gas tank; make sure the gas cap is on and can be opened.

Jot down details about your rental car. Want to be able to remember which unfamiliar car is yours? Always carry with you a slip of paper on which you've noted the model, make, color, and license plate number of your rental car.

Ask for a car with GPS. GPS is widely available in the United States and Europe, less so in other parts of the world. You'll pay extra for it, unless you're renting a luxury car. Ask about GPS when you book; if a device isn't available, you might want to invest in one manufactured by Garmin (⊕*www.garmin.com*), Magellan (⊕*www.magellangps.com*), or Tom Tom (⊕*www.tomtom.com*), available at electronics stores.

Know the local traffic laws. Rules of the road can vary considerably from country to country (especially with regard to right-of-way and right turns on red). The U.S. State Department Web site (⊕*travel.state.gov/travel*) has safety tips for driving abroad, although the information isn't country specific and the Web sites it recommends aren't always in English. Alternatively, try the Association for Safe International Road Travel (⊕*www.asirt.org*), a nonprofit that gives the rules of the road abroad, the meaning of road signs, information on road conditions, and how locals feel about their laws (in Peru, drivers "usually ignore the few traffic signals that exist"). You can order detailed descriptions of transportation issues worldwide for $30.

WORD OF MOUTH. "It might surprise you to learn a couple of other laws about driving in Spain: if you wear prescription glasses, you need to have an extra pair with you, and you must carry an emergency kit with you in the car with flares and other stuff (likely your rental will come with this, but it sure won't come with extra glasses)." —StCirq

WORD OF MOUTH: RENTAL CARS

"Most rental agencies won't allow their vehicles to be taken off paved roads. And if you do, they'll void your insurance. In that case—since you haven't obeyed the rules of the agency—your own insurance (either personal car insurance or that provided by a credit card) will be voided as well. So any damages to the vehicle or towing or anything will have to come directly out of your pocket. If you'd like to explore off-road, see if you can find a rental agency that will allow to do so, and be sure this is specified in the agreement." —nytraveler

"Find a local company that rents four-wheel-drive cars for the days you actually need such a vehicle, and save yourself the money of having one for the whole trip." —TheWeasel

"We just picked up a car in Genoa center at Europcar.

We rented it using ⊕ *www.autoeurope.com* and had no problems at all." —jamikins

"If you are renting a stick, learn exactly how to get it in and out of *reverse* before you drive off the lot. I suppose it sounds stupid but this "problem" occurred when we rented a Megane in Bordeaux…it was not intuitive in terms of that one gear. Once we were shown how, it was no problem. And, don't panic if it takes a while for your GPS to acquire the satellites; the invisible coating on some car windshields can hamper that process." —Dukey

"I'd recommend checking and double-checking what type of fuel the car takes. [I have] many stories about using the wrong one. Note that in France, *gazole* means "diesel," which can be confusing." —BikerScott

Rent a cell phone from your car-rental agency. Some agencies rent cell phones, which can be handy and even cost-effective in countries where your own cell phone doesn't work.

Fuel your rental car a few miles from the airport. Gas stations nearest airports and car-rental agencies charge the highest rates. You can save several dollars on a full tank of gas by filling up well away from the airport. But make sure you're not so far away that you'll have less than a full tank of gas when you return your vehicle.

PREPARING FOR YOUR ROAD TRIP

Make a spare set of car keys. Be sure your traveling companion has a set or, if you're going solo, pack an extra set in your luggage in case yours are stolen or misplaced. Maybe stash a copy of the door key in your wallet, in the event you lock yourself out. As an added backup, it's not a bad idea to leave an additional set with a friend or relative back home who can send them via overnight mail.

Invest in an electricity power inverter. These adapters, which plug into your cigarette lighter and cost about $30 to $60, depending on wattage, can power virtually any appliance that runs on electricity—cell-phone chargers, mini-refrigerators, TVs, hot pots, and so on. You can also buy an adapter that allows you to plug two items into your cigarette lighter, or use a dual-plug attachment to power multiple appliances. Just remember that you can run power appliances only when your engine is running, and that you need to be careful not to overload the adapter.

Prevent dampness in the trunk. Car trunks are highly prone to dampness—wetness from one big storm can remain in your trunk for long periods and then creep into luggage and other goods that you store there during long car trips. Either line the bottom of your trunk with a waterproof tarp or, better yet, with some kind of slightly elevated platform, which allows air to circulate between the base of your trunk and the goods stored in it.

Consider a roof rack. If you have skis, surfboards, or other special sports gear that takes up lots of space, think about a roof rack. They aren't as expensive as you might think—the cheapest ones start at about $30—though racks built for specific pieces of equipment, such as bicycles, can be quite a bit more.

Leave big suitcases at home. There are few things less pleasant than having to haul a giant suitcase around when traveling. If you're driving long distances and staying in several places for just a night or two, pack only a carry-on-size suitcase with two or three nights' worth of clothing. Keep the bulk of your clean clothing in a laundry basket in the trunk of your car, and repack your carry-on suitcase every few days as needed, storing your dirty laundry in a separate bag.

Separate your "getting there" and "there" clothes. If you're planning the kind of trip that involves a stay at some place bracketed by a long drive there and back, keep the clothing you plan to use once you arrive in one piece of luggage, and store this at the back of the trunk or under other bags. Fill lighter and smaller duffel bags or luggage with the clothing you'll be using during your drive, and keep these in an easier-to-reach place by loading them last.

Leave essentials within reach. Leave the emergency kit out until after you load all your bags, and then find a corner where it will be easily accessible. Be sure that every passenger has an extra shirt or a jacket for a pillow and for darting in and out of the car, as well as his or her own book or iPod or MP3 player. Keep the car cell-phone charger handy.

Invest in a set of bungee cords. You can wrap these sturdy elastic cords around boxes and luggage and keep the contents of your trunk from sliding around. They're also perfect for securing any items you might need to transport on the roof of your car.

Travel with a soft, collapsible cooler. Collapsible coolers are ideal for car trips, and because they fold up compactly and can fit inside your suitcase, they're also worth taking with you when you fly somewhere and rent a car.

Get some folding chairs. You can guarantee yourself a comfortable front-row seat wherever you are by packing collapsible nylon chairs (they resemble director's chairs) in your trunk. Even if you fly somewhere and rent a car, consider buying a couple of cheap folding or beach chairs for your rental car—they're very inexpensive at most discount department stores. And at the end of your trip you can give the chairs to fellow travelers.

Organize with plastic drawers. You can buy cheap, stackable plastic drawers at most department stores. Put a few of these in your trunk, filling one with books and maps and another with toiletries, and you'll have an efficient system for even the longest trip from home.

Stock up on road supplies at warehouse shopping clubs. By far the most expensive places to buy snacks and toiletries when traveling are the convenience stores attached to roadside gas stations. Try to buy groceries at discount department or grocery stores before you leave. Members of warehouse superstores like Costco and Sam's Club can save a huge amount by stocking up on bulk foods and even toiletries at these places. Best bets include bottled water, crackers, cookies, chips, trail mix, sports bars, nuts, and

ROAD SAFETY

■ **Have your car checked out before the big trip.** How long has that red engine light been flashing? Are your windshield wipers smearing the glass instead of clearing it? When's the last time you had your oil changed? The last place you want little irritations to turn into major headaches is far from home. So take your car in for a checkup before you leave.

■ **Make sure your spare tire is in good shape.** Routinely check on the condition and pressure of your spare tire, as well as your vehicle's four primary tires. If you're not used to changing a tire, do a test run before you leave home. Be sure the lug nuts can easily be removed (mechanics often overtighten them). Keep a pair of work gloves near your spare, as changing a tire is a messy job.

■ **Pack flares or reflectors.** These are invaluable in the case of a breakdown or accident. Store them under the front seat if you have room; otherwise, keep them in the trunk in a waterproof container. But be sure flares are kept away from children.

■ **Invest in a first-aid kit.** You can buy an inexpensive, prepackaged kit at many drug stores, or you can create your own. Some items to consider: topical cream for cuts, scrapes, and bug bites; sunburn lotion; car-sickness medication; heartburn medication; necessary prescription and over-the-counter drugs and allergy remedies; contact lens solution; ointment; tweezers; bandages and bandage tape; pain relievers; and scissors or a pocket knife. Periodically check that medications are current.

■ **Stock up on important car parts and fluids.** For long trips to unfamiliar places, keep extra coolant, windshield-washer fluid, hose tape, jumper cables, oil and transmission fluid, fan belts, and fuses. These items are particularly useful if you drive a car that's relatively exotic or uncommon.

■ **Prepare for bad weather.** An umbrella, poncho or waterproof windbreaker, cap, and sturdy gloves are indispensable if you need to check under the hood or change a tire during a rainstorm. In winter warm gloves, a de-icing spray, an ice scraper, a small shovel, and antifreeze are invaluable. Keeping a bag of sand or rock salt in the trunk is useful for traction if your car gets stuck, and the added weight will help to negotiate slick roads and snow-covered hills.

breath mints, as well as aspirin and pain relievers, antacid tablets, laundry detergent, and film. These shopping clubs also usually have the cheapest gas prices around, and many are just off major interstates or along other well-traveled roads; before you hit the road, research the locations of some on your route.

STAYING HASSLE-FREE ON THE ROAD

Look into audiobooks. Your local library is always a great source for them. The chain restaurant Cracker Barrel has a program where you rent a book-on-tape for a small fee and then return it to any of the more than 500 Cracker Barrel locations. Online services such as Simply Audiobooks (⊕ *www.simplyaudiobooks.com*) send you CDs of your favorite books, from classics to new releases. When you're finished, just drop them in any mailbox. You can also download more than 10,000 titles to your MP3, and there's a free downloadable book each month. The Audio Bookstore (⊕ *www.theaudiobookstore.com*) has a similar service, except they have more than 75,000 titles you can download and more than 10,000 titles you can rent. iTunes (⊕ *www.itunes.com*) is in on the act, as are Barnes and Noble (⊕ *www.barnesandnoble.ebooks*), Amazon.com, and Audible (⊕ *www.audible.com*), among others,

Bring an e-reader. Bringing a Kindle on a road trip will save lots of space in an already packed vehicle. They retail for less than $200, download titles in less than 60 seconds, and can hold about 1,500 books. Kindle isn't the only reader out there. Barnes and Noble now offers the Nook, Sony and other companies have their own products, and, of course, there's the iPad from Apple.

Upgrade to satellite radio. Hate tuning in to your favorite song on the radio only to have it crackle and fade as you're driving along? To receive a satellite radio signal, you need to pay for a subscription service and install a satellite radio receiver (which adapts to any existing car stereo), but it enables you to tune into dozens of music, news, and sports channels with few or no commercials. The reception is good nationwide, no matter how remote your location.

Buy a hands-free cell-phone adapter. Hundreds of U.S. cities and regions have banned driving while talking on a cell phone, and it's looking likely that this practice will be banned virtually everywhere before too long. However, using a phone with a hands-free adapter, which allows you to keep both hands on the steering wheel while you talk, is legal, and these adapters are generally small and inexpensive.

Don't drive on an empty stomach. Crackers, sports bars, and other easy-to-digest and mild foods are good snacks for long car rides, as motion sickness is much more likely to occur when you have an empty stomach. Keeping hydrated with water or juice also helps to ward off carsickness. Eating rich or spicy foods can exacerbate the problem, as can smoking.

Keep your eyes on the horizon. If you suffer from queasiness during car rides, try to get as much fresh air as possible, sit in the front seat, and avoid reading or looking out the window at nearby objects as you pass them. It's much better to fix your eyes on the horizon or a distant object.

Rest often during long road trips. It may sound counter-intuitive, but you're more likely to make better driving time—and to arrive safely—if you take frequent breaks when traveling long distances. Pull off the road, get out of your car, and stretch every two to three hours; you'll actually increase your alertness and endurance. On the other hand, if you drive four or five hours without stopping, you're more likely to become fatigued and unable to continue safely without stopping for a long break or even an overnight. Breaks are also important when traveling with kids—stopping to toss a ball around or play a game helps to stave off boredom and restlessness.

Have spare change at the ready. A bag or cup of change is useful for tolls, parking meters, and other small expenses. Just be sure to keep it in a discreet place, maybe the glove compartment, the ashtray, or under a seat. Thieves have been known to break into cars just to steal a few nickels and dimes.

Keep extra toiletries handy. Anybody who travels regularly by car knows how frustrating it is to run out of tooth-paste, razor blades, or pain relievers on the road. Hotel gift shops and convenience stores charge exorbitant prices for replacements. Keep a bag containing spares of your most important toiletries handy, and replenish your supplies when it's convenient, ideally between trips.

Keep clean. How many times have you used the lavatory at a roadside gas station only to learn that it's out of soap or toilet paper? Or have you eaten a messy meal in your car

WORD OF MOUTH: KIDS IN THE CAR

"When my kids were young, and we went on long trips (400 miles+), I gave them 'Mile Bags.' Every 75 miles they got a bag with something in it (candy necklace, new movie, crayons and paper, a few dollars, a book, etc). It was some work preparing it, but, boy, did they behave—the alternative was waiting a good few miles for the next one." —mei

"If traveling with kids, give them their spending money (in singles) before leaving on the trip. Each time they ask 'are we there yet?' or they fight, take back a dollar. Believe me this works! Also, if they have all their dollars when they get where you're going, give them a $5 or $10 bonus." —suebeoh

"For really long distance trips, my son and I always take along a list of license plates. We're pretty cut-throat about trying to spot plates from more states than the other person!" —CAPH52

with no place to wash up? Baby wipes are great for cleaning up your hands, and they're also perfect if you're traveling with children or babies who need a quick cleanup. Liquid hand sanitizer such as Purell requires no water, kills germs, and dries without a towel. And given the dreary state of many restrooms, it's not a bad idea to keep a supply of toilet paper or pocket packs of tissues handy. It's also good to bring along a box of trash bags and roll of paper towels.

Avoid driving into big cities by parking at commuter bus or train stations. Driving in cities like Boston, New York, and Washington can be intimidating, and parking can cost $20, $30, or even $40 per day in some areas. If you're using a car to get from city to city, save yourself hassles and money by parking just outside the city limits. Instead of driving into Manhattan, for instance, you could park at the secure and covered garage at the Metro North train station in Stamford, Connecticut, for just $10 per day, paying about $9 to $12 (one-way) for the one-hour train ride into the city. If you buy your ticket on board, you can expect to tack on another $5–$6; if you buy your ticket online you save 5% and shipping is free and takes 2–3 days.

Remain with your car if you break down or are in an accident. If you're in an accident, no matter how seemingly minor, wait with your car until authorities arrive, even if the other driver insists on leaving or offers to cover the damages. In the end, your insurance company is going to care about only one thing in determining the fault in an accident: the police report. Never admit fault to another driver, and avoid confrontation. It's best to remain calm and wait patiently for a police officer.

Never leave luggage or valuables visible. Even if thieves aren't interested in the exact contents left on your backseat, a car with luggage or bags is a much more likely target. Even loose change, music tapes or CDs, and snack food should be stowed in the glove compartment or the trunk.

Conserve gasoline. The way you drive greatly affects your car's gas mileage. Making sudden stops and starts, driving with the air-conditioning on or with all the windows down, using underinflated tires, and idling unnecessarily—such as while you eat at a fast-food restaurant or talk on your cell phone—waste gas and pollute the environment.

Look for clusters of gas stations when refueling. If you're driving down the interstate looking for a place to refill your gas tank, avoid the exits that have just one or two stations. You'll save money at exits with three or more stations, as competition helps drive down prices.

Gas up when you're down to a quarter tank. It can be tempting to go as long as possible between refills, but it's a great idea to get used to refueling your car whenever it's down to about a quarter tank. Particularly when you're traveling in unfamiliar territory, you never know exactly how far you are from the nearest gas station—waiting until the indicator is on empty (or below) puts you at great risk of running out of fuel before you can find a gas station. Also, engines run more efficiently when there's more than a couple of gallons in the tank.

Try the pump at a station that appears closed. Next time you're rolling down the highway on fumes, don't fret if the first gas station you pass appears to be closed. Many gas stations with automated pumps, which you activate using your credit or debit card, remain open 24 hours.

Train and Bus Travel

WORD OF MOUTH

"Roads along the Cote d'Azur get jammed in summer. If you want to visit Nice, Cannes, Antibes, Monaco, take the train, it's less hassle, quicker and no parking worries."

—Man_in_seat_61

"Traveling by train in China during daylight hours is one of the best ways to see the countryside where there are mountains, hills, and small villages near the route. Definitely bring toilet paper, soap, a small hand towel, perhaps hand wipes."

—JohnCa

Updated
by Alexis
Kelly

Travel by train—and even its pokier cousin, bus—might just be the most relaxing way to get where you're going. You get to sit back and enjoy not only the scenery but also the relaxed pace without enduring a long check-in or other airport shenanigans. And there's far greater chance that you'll make new friends during your trip than when you're flying or driving; these forms of travel seem to foster camaraderie.

So which mode of transport should you choose? In some places it boils down to issues of time and money. Especially for very long routes in the United States and Canada, train travel can be more expensive, sometimes even more so than flying. Bus travel usually costs much less, but it also tends to be cramped and take far longer.

When you're traveling abroad, the whole equation changes. In Europe, train travel can be economical, especially when you consider the exorbitant price of gas. Buying a rail pass in advance increases your savings significantly in some regions. In Latin America, buses are often the preferred—or only—means of long-distance public transportation; in Mexico, intercity buses marked *gran lujo* (top luxury) have comfy seats with lots of legroom. You may even get a smiling attendant offering you a complimentary beverage.

Often overlooked by today's harried traveler, trains and buses are nevertheless great options. This chapter has plenty of ideas for making your trip as enjoyable as possible.

SMOOTH TRAIN AND BUS RIDES

Travel midweek to avoid crowds. For most rail and bus service, especially intercity and international travel, you'll find less crowded trains and buses if you travel midweek. The exceptions tend to be commuter-oriented buses and trains, which get the most traffic during the week.

Travel by day when possible. Part of the joy of busing or training across country is enjoying the magnificent scenery out your window. If this is the main purpose of your trip, consider traveling only during the day and staying in motels or hotels at different stops along the way for your overnights.

Allow enough time for connections. Trains, particularly during the busy summer months, are highly susceptible to delays. If your trip involves a connection, try to allow a few hours from the time of your arrival to the time of your connecting train's departure.

Get written directions when signage is in another language. In places where even the alphabet is unfamiliar, such as Eastern Europe and Asia, using buses, trains, or subways can prove extra difficult for foreigners. Get written directions from your hotel clerk or other local and show them to the driver.

Get to the station well before departure. You remember that timeless bit of advice about arriving early to get a good seat, right?

Bring only what you need on board. Put the rest in luggage compartments to maximize your legroom and general comfort. Better yet, pack a carry-on with trip essentials and have the rest of your luggage sent ahead to your destination. This way, you're really free to get out and explore at each stop without worrying about all your bags.

Don't forget the creature comforts. Earplugs are your best assurance of a restful nap. A small pillow can also help. You might want to consider buying an inflatable pillow, which can be easier to store.

For kids, pack noiseless toys and games. Fill your toy tote with items that won't make a lot of noise and bother other passengers: pencil and crayon sets, stickers, colored paper, and other crafts-oriented goods. Magnetic travel board games and puzzles are also ideal.

Be smart about belongings. Use a small bicycle lock or padlock to secure your travel bags, and never leave baggage unattended in stations. Even if you plan to step a few feet away for only a few minutes, don't ever lose hold of your bags. Put money, credit cards, and other valuables in a money belt or a concealed clothing pocket—any spot that's difficult to access while you're napping.

WORD OF MOUTH. "Rather than locking individual bags, I've used a cable lock through the handles of several bags. Not that this would prevent a determined thief, but the opportunist who wants to grab and run will be deterred from taking this bundle from a train cabin, rental-car trunk, or loosely attended station baggage room." —kayd

Watch what you eat. You'll feel much better when you arrive at your destination having eaten well. Bottled water and

BY TRAIN OR BY BUS?

■ **Compare routes.** Spend some time on the Web to determine whether the train or bus will put you close to your destination. In some areas a bus will go express and/or will drop you closer to your actual stop than a train station.

■ **Factor in your nature.** If you're the restless type or you require extra space, go by train. Train seating areas are usually less cramped than those on buses (unless you're in a place where legroom on buses is the norm, like some parts of Latin America), and it's much easier to get up and move about. Best of all there's often a dining car.

■ **Weigh your needs.** With room for fidgety kids to roam in, trains are a great alternative to buses or even cars. Snack bars, restrooms, water fountains, reclining seats, overhead luggage racks, and even sleeping compartments on long-distance routes make things relatively comfortable. If you have at least 25 people (30 to 40 is even more ideal), chartering a bus may be cheaper than buying individual bus or bus-tour tickets, and it's a great way to bond with friends and family.

snacks such as grapes, cheese, and crackers are a refreshing way to offset the sodas and packaged sandwiches and chips sold in dining cars and at rest stops. Choose items that aren't sticky (peeling oranges can be a mess) or overwhelmingly saucy, making sure to include some protein. Also, forgo richer and aromatic foods, which are a better eaten in a stationary position so as to minimize indigestion.

TRAIN TRAVEL

Book in advance. Many people cling to the romantic notion that they can hop aboard any train as it pulls out of the station. The truth is that, at best, you'll be hit with a surcharge for buying a ticket on the train. At worst, you'll find that the train is full, and you'll have to stand the entire way—if you can get on at all. Do yourself a favor and buy a ticket in advance, either at the station, by phone, or online.

Do your research. If the train you're taking travels through a beautiful landscape or past some interesting buildings, you'll want to be sitting on the side with the best views. For example, traveling from San Francisco to Los Angeles, you should sit on the right to take advantage of the ocean views.

On the train to Machu Picchu, only those on the left see spectacular ruins. (Those on the right often only see rocks.)

Ride the rails, then rent a car. Traveling long distances by train and renting cars at different destinations along the way can be both more economical and more relaxing than driving your own car the entire trip. Many rail stations have on-site car-rental agencies, and other car-rental companies will deliver cars to you at the station.

Consider a sleeper. Does a sleeper car seem like an extravagance? Think again. Compared with the price of a hotel room, a sleeper car is often a good deal. You'll travel through the night and arrive the next day relaxed and refreshed (barring any snore-prone cabinmates).

TRAIN TRAVEL IN NORTH AMERICA

Go online. Amtrak's (⊕ *www.amtrak.com*) Web site has lots of bells and whistles, making it a valuable resource for anyone considering U.S. rail travel. Click on the interactive route map to see where you can ride. Check out weekly specials, rail passes, and vacation deals. Canada's rail carrier, VIA Rail Canada (⊕ *www.viarail.ca*), has an even better site that gives you a peek into all the types of cars you might consider. Check out TrainWeb.com if you're a rail enthusiast. It has the lowdown on North American tourist and scenic railways, dinner trains, private railcar excursions, and train museums.

Look into Amtrak's USA Rail Pass. Looking to see the Wild West, New England, the Deep South, and the West Coast? Amtrak's USA Rail Pass will take you here, there, and everywhere in the continental United States. Available in three time frames—15 days, 30 days, and 45 days—each time frame has an allotted number of "segments" or trips available; a segment is the equivalent of one one-way trip. Some trips may count for more than one segment. Travel must begin within 180 days of the purchase date. Tickets can be purchased online or through an Amtrak affiliated travel agent. The pass does not work on any Canada-bound trains.

Check out VIA Rail Canada's discount passes. VIA Rail Canada's Canrailpass–System allows for 7 economy-class trips anywhere in Canada within a 21-day period. In addition, VIA Rail offers the Canrailpass–Corridor, good for 7 days of travel during a 10-day period within southern Québec

RAIL-PASS REALITIES

■ **Take a pass.** Almost every rail line offers several different types of discount passes. Some are available only abroad, so look into these well before your trip.

■ **Calculate point-to-point fares before buying discount passes.** Depending on where you're going and how much train travel you have planned, it may be cheaper to buy individual tickets than to pay for a discount pass.

■ **Have your rail pass validated before you board.** For some trains, both in the United States and internationally, you'll pay a service fee (about $5 to $30) if you wait to have your pass validated onboard. Never write anything on the pass itself—this could void it. Instead, go to the ticket office of the first station you're traveling from and have the pass validated there.

■ **Keep your rail pass safe.** These passes aren't refundable or replaceable if lost or stolen, so keep yours in a safe place. For some passes you can buy rail-pass insurance, which will get you a refund for the unused portion of your pass; just be sure to report the pass as missing as soon as something happens to it.

■ **Read the fine print for rail passes.** This pass will get you onto a train, but it won't guarantee you a seat. Also, some high-speed trains cost extra, so you may have to pay a supplement for using your pass with these services.

and southern Ontario. It can be bought by anyone, but must be bought at least three days in advance.

Ask for discounts. Children between 2 and 15 ride for half fare on Amtrak when accompanied by an adult paying full fare. One child under 2 rides free per full paying adult. Senior citizens (62 and older) get 15% off the lowest available fare on most trains. Students with the Student Advantage Discount Card or the International Student ID card save 15%. Active-duty military personnel and their families get 10% off most fares with their military ID. Veterans get 15% off, but they have to apply for the Veterans Advantage card. To take advantage of most of these discounts, tickets must be purchased three days in advance, and restrictions are always possible, so be sure to ask. Similar discounts may be available on commuter trains.

Mention AAA membership when booking. Always mention your membership when booking train tickets; you'll get a 10% discount on Amtrak.

Ask about the quiet car. What started as an option on just one route out of Philadelphia in 2000 has become the norm. On many Amtrak trains there's now one car where music players, cell phones, and loud conversations are banned. Even the lights are dimmed, allowing for a more peaceful journey. Announcements are made in stations and onboard trains indicating the Quiet Car's location.

Book an excursion train ride. In many parts of the country—such as Durango, Colorado; Napa Valley, California; and Newport, Rhode Island—sightseeing trains provide passengers with a chance to take in magnificent scenery. Many excursion trains offer meals, and most of them are leisurely round-trip journeys that aren't intended to be the quickest or most practical way to get between two points.

Investigate commuter trains. Amtrak may be the most popular service for intercity travel in the United States, but many regions also have more extensive and less pricey commuter rail service—especially New England and the Mid-Atlantic states. Commuter rail service is a great way to get from New York City to some of the great getaways on Long Island and in the Hudson River Valley.

TRAIN TRAVEL ELSEWHERE IN THE WORLD

Travel Europe high-speed. Some national high-speed train systems, which see trains traveling at an average speed of 125 mph, have begun to link up to form the nucleus of a pan-European system. On a long journey you still have to change trains a couple of times, as the national railways jealously guard their prerogatives. France, Switzerland, Italy, Belgium, the Netherlands, and Germany are among the nations offering this service. Remember that this service requires reservations, and doesn't come as cheaply as conventional rail service.

European rail passes may be the way to go. Eurail Passes can be purchased online or from your home country. There are many types of passes with different time frames and geared to different groups; think carefully before picking one. Note, too, that even with a pass, you'll pay a supplement for riding high-speed trains. If you plan to rack up miles, get a Global Pass, which includes travel to 21 coun-

WORD OF MOUTH: TRAINS

"Some trains in Europe require reservations, even for pass holders. These are the premium trains, TGV, Thalys, etc. For some routes (e.g., Brussels to Paris), those are the only trains on the route. Never make a reservation in the United States; wait until you get to Europe. Schedules will show a capital R in a rectangle if a reservation is required." —hopscotch

"I traveled with three others, and we learned we needed reservations. We tried without and at every stop, someone with a reservation would come and boot us out of the seat we were in. Because the luggage thing at the end of the train car was full, we were putting luggage above our heads on the rack so each time we moved we needed to also move our stuff." —queener

"The real difference [between first and second class] is there are three seats across [in first class] instead of four and you get a beverage." —kybourbon

"Hang on to your tickets [in China], as you'll need them to exit the train station. A few people misplaced their tickets and had to buy another ticket." —annieO

tries. The Select Pass has the three-, four-, or five-country option. The Regional Pass covers popular countries such as Belgium, the Netherlands, and Germany or France and Italy. There's even the One Country Pass. The EurailDrive Pass, valid for two months, combines a two-day car rental (additional days are available) with 4 or 10 days of train travel. It's valid in 21 countries, including Austria, France, Germany, Greece, the Netherlands, Hungary, and Ireland.

Francophiles rejoice! If you're planning to visit multiple destinations in France, the Anywhere Anytime France pass, a prepaid electronic ticketing system, is the perfect option. You can book trips an hour before departure, print tickets at kiosks in the stations, and travel on any train type—including the TGV. The initial trip is $169, any additional trips you add at that time are $50. Each time you log back in to add a trip, it's just $70. All trips must be used within a month of your original departure date.

Learn Europe's "class" system. Virtually all European rail carriers, including the high-speed ones, operate a two-class system. First class costs substantially more, and is usually a luxury rather than a necessity. Some of the poorer European countries retain a third class, but avoid it unless you're an adventure-minded budget traveler.

Talk to the machine. Automated ticket machines in Europe's larger towns and cities can switch back and forth between any number of languages. The humans behind the counter may or may not be able to do the same.

Stand in the right place. In Europe, train platforms in larger towns and cities are divided into sections designated by letters of the alphabet. The sign announcing the next train will often tell you where the first- and second-class carriages will stop, letting you stand in the most convenient part of the platform.

Look up rail routes online. In many countries maps are not customarily provided to passengers. You may do best to consult a map on the Internet first or obtain one from a travel agent in your home country.

BUS TRAVEL

Ask what a "direct" or "nonstop" bus trip means. Even when a bus is supposedly a "direct nonstop" there's usually a quick stop if the ride is more than three or four hours. Sometimes passengers have time to dart into a convenience store or truck stop to buy food or use the bathroom. Sometimes not. If you smoke, though, and the thought of seven hours without lighting up makes you edgy, call a ticket agent and ask if the "nonstop" bus actually will stop somewhere along the way. You'll have enough time to suck down a cigarette or two.

9

Find out whether food is allowed aboard the bus. You might have to eat before you travel on some small, regional coach lines, which prohibit snacking.

Choose the right side of the bus. Figure out from the direction you are headed which side of the bus is likely to get the most sun, then choose a seat on the other side. The sunnier side is often blindingly bright, making it hard to read a book or watch a movie.

Try to travel by bus with a friend. The affordable yet somewhat cramped seats come in pairs, so the person beside you might as well have personal boundaries, social skills, and eating habits that you know you can stand.

WORD OF MOUTH: SCENIC ROUTES

"The [trip] between New York and Boston is scenic for certain stretches in Connecticut where the train tracks run along the shore of Long Island Sound." —ellenem

"If you like fall foliage colors, the train from Atlanta to D.C. passes through some beautiful forests in the Carolinas and Virginia." —boom_boom

"The train from Denver to Reno is pretty scenic, especially in winter. I think the train from Emeryville to Los Angeles passes through some of the most outstanding coast views available." —Wellvis

"The train to Mittenwald via Garmisch is scenic. Take the mountain train up the Zugspitze; it's probably the most scenic line. All are rather scenic south of Munich however." —PalenQ

"Our journey from Porto [in Portugal] was marked with tunnels cut from the mountainsIdes and wonderful views of vineyards, small villages nestled into the valley sides, and the blue Douro River. Unfortunately my journey came to an end at Régua; next time I'd go further." —Matt_from_England

"The train ride from Interlaken to Lucerne is one of the most scenic in Switzerland. From Interlaken-Ost you board the narrow-gauge Brunig Pass train that putzes first along the shores of idyllic Lake Brienz to Meiringen, where it reverses to begin the climb up and over the Brunig Pass. The line is so steep at points that the train has to use cogs to climb and then later descend at safe speeds. After the pass you pass some large Alpine lakes." —PalenqueBob

Make cell-phone calls before you board the bus. Some buses ban all nonessential cell-phone conversations, so make that call while you're still in the station. Otherwise, you might be asked to comply with increased no-chitchat regulations designed to give all passengers a quiet ride.

Don't sit in the back of the bus. It's where the bathroom is, so there will be an unmistakable odor, and it's over the rear wheels, so the ride can be bumpy.

Choose a good movie-watching seat. Many buses show movies en route. If you're really interested in seeing one, don't sit in a seat with a screen directly overhead; sit a row or two back from one.

BUS TRAVEL IN NORTH AMERICA

Don't worry about reserving for Greyhound. Generally, no reservations are needed for shorter trips on Greyhound (⊕ *www.greyhound.com*), but as a good rule of thumb, plan to buy your ticket an hour before boarding time. No reservations means no seat assignments, so this extra time will allow you to find a seat and get settled.

Consider the Greyhound Discovery Pass. The Greyhound Discovery Pass, a one-price ticket for up to 60 consecutive days of travel in the U.S. and Canada, can be used by both U.S. citizens and foreigners. You can buy it online, at bus stations, and at travel agencies throughout the United States.

Ask about discounts. Greyhound and other large companies offer discounts for children, students, senior citizens, active-duty military personnel, and veterans. Ask before you purchase your ticket.

Book bus travel online and in advance. Like the airlines, Greyhound and other bus companies often have special Web-only fares. That said, make sure to check the regular fare, as sometimes these "specials" aren't special at all. Also, for Greyhound you can save as much as 25% off regular ticket prices when you book at least 14 days in advance, 10% when you book 7 days in advance.

Consider regional alternatives. Greyhound isn't the only game in town. If you're in the northeast, for example, also check out the rates for Peter Pan Bus Lines (⊕ *www.peterpanbus.com*), a Greyhound affiliate, or Trailways (⊕ *www.trailways.com*). NeOn (⊕ *www.neonbus.com*), another Greyhound affiliate, offers service between NYC and Toronto and stops in between. In the Pacific Northwest, Quick Shuttle (⊕ *www.quickcoach.com*) goes between Seattle and Vancouver, B.C.

9

Take the "Chinatown Express." One of the cheapest ways to get between many major cities is what is colorfully called the "Chinatown Express." These small bus companies shuttle a largely Chinese crowd between cities, often from one Chinatown to another. The buses are usually clean and comfortable, and often show movies (although they are often martial-arts flicks in Mandarin or Cantonese). One-way tickets are usually $20 or less. Chinatown-bus.org has a comprehensive list of all the companies across the country that offer "Chinatown Express" service. GoToBus.com also has listings for many companies.

Check out budget buses. Bus tickets for $1? Yes, please. To get this rate you do have to be one of the first to reserve a seat; for the rest, ticket prices average $25. MegaBus (⊕*us. megabus.com*) travels to 28 cities in the Northeast, Midwest, and Canada. BoltBus (⊕*www.boltbus.com*) travels the East Coast with stops in Boston, New York, and D.C. These discount alternatives also offer more legroom, free Wi-Fi, and power plug-ins at your seat.

WORD OF MOUTH. "Stick with Megabus or Boltbus. If you're firm with your travel date, buy your ticket ASAP. The earlier you buy, the cheaper it is. I've taken Megabus Boston–New York round-trip twice, and my brother has taken Boltbus once. We have no complaints. Both Boltbus and Megabus depart from Penn Station in New York." —yk

Pick bus travel days carefully. Fares are often cheaper, and buses less crowded, if you travel Monday to Thursday. If you want to see lines around the block, show up at a bus station on a holiday weekend.

BUS TRAVEL ELSEWHERE IN THE WORLD

Ask about bus passes. When you arrive in a new town or city, ask at the local tourism office about bus passes. You might even get a pass good for free travel on local transportation. If you're in a tourist-friendly destination, such as Switzerland, your hotel might have government-issued bus passes to give you.

Know that a bus isn't always a bus. In many places, such as some regions in Latin America, buses have been replaced by minivans. They work exactly the same way as a bus, except for the fact that there's a person standing in the door announcing the destination and collecting the money. Fares and destinations are usually written on the windshield.

Choose the right class. Many countries outside North America have classes of buses. Buses range from huge, modern, air-conditioned beasts with plush seats, bathrooms, and an occasional movie to something a little less new and a whole lot sweatier and more crowded. Ask the tourist board or a hotel staffer for the recommended tourist-class bus.

Comparison shop. Wherever you have a tourist bus headed to a local landmark, you can be sure there is another, much cheaper bus used by locals to get to the same place. In

Prague, for example, the tourist bus to the medieval town of Český Krumlov costs about $8. The local bus is closer to $1.

Prepare for delays at borders. Even if the bus company has a tried-and-true international route, long lines at borders can happen due to traffic—or, as is usually the case, if each bus passenger must show a passport and pay an entry tax (carry a bit of local currency or small bills in U.S. currency).

Expect a squeeze on local buses. In many countries local buses are crowded and cramped. In Central America this means three occupying a seat meant for two on a retired U.S. school bus. Sometimes a bus won't depart until it's completely filled with passengers, both sitting and standing in the aisle. It's also common for vendors to hop on, shove their way down the aisle as they sell snacks or newspapers, and jump out the emergency exit at the back.

Double-check your destination. The names of towns and cities often look alike to newcomers, so pay attention. If you're headed to the Mexican city of Xalapa, don't get on the first bus whose destination starts with an X. You might end up miles away in the tiny village of Xico.

WORD OF MOUTH. **"I quite liked finding the local buses and buying a ticket just like anybody else, and it was reasonably priced. I had a particularly lovely trip from Campbeltown to Carradale [in England] on a bus with all the school children and a trip thru blooming fields and hedgerows from Wells to Bath with an elderly lady who showed me all the sites of her childhood. If you like that sort of travel it's a great way to go." —CharlotteK**

9

Ask about return buses. If you're traveling by bus to an unfamiliar destination, always ask the driver where and when the return buses depart.

Cruises

10

Updated
by Doug
Stallings

Cruising has evolved from an elite leisure pursuit into one of the world's most popular and accessible forms of travel. There are still ultraposh ships sailing the seas that charge top dollar and provide plush staterooms and fancy food, but others offer almost unbeatably affordable opportunities to tour parts of the world you might never otherwise see.

Megaships are like small cities, complete with shopping arcades, numerous restaurants, spas and health clubs, multiple swimming pools, and snazzy casinos and nightclubs. Other vessels emphasize education, offer a more intimate ambience and easy pace, or focus more on ports of call than leisure time at sea. Smaller ships often access ports and scenery that larger ships could never hope to navigate.

Whether you're a first-timer or an inveterate cruiser, it pays to spend a little time researching your cruise options. Better yet, find a knowledgeable travel agency that specializes in cruises. Reading this chapter and doing a bit of legwork will ensure a relaxing, exhilarating vacation at sea.

BOOKING YOUR CRUISE

Test the waters. If you're new to cruising, try booking a short trip—maybe a three- or four-day sail to the Bahamas out of Florida, or to Cozumel out of New Orleans or Mobile, or even a four-day cruise down the Southern California coast to Baja. Short itineraries may include stops at one or two ports of call, or none at all.

Consider a cruise to nowhere. If you're a first-time cruiser unsure about committing to a longer trip, ask your travel agent about a short "cruise to nowhere." There are no ports of call and no real itinerary. You set sail, float at sea, and return home. That's it. These cruises last between two and four days, usually over a weekend, and they cost just a few hundred dollars. If you are concerned about seasickness, look for a single-night cruise from New York, Miami, or Fort Lauderdale so you can test your sea legs.

Arrange your own flight to your port of embarkation. If you are going on a round-trip cruise, you may be able to find a better airfare—or simply a more convenient flight—than that offered by your cruise line's air-and-sea department. Just be certain to book an early enough flight to ensure that you'll have ample time to get from the airport to the ship, and keep in mind that you'll be responsible for your own transportation between the airport and the cruise

10

terminal. It often pays to arrive in the port the day before your cruise starts.

For peace of mind, book your flight to your embarkation point through the cruise line. There's a chance you'll pay more by booking your flight through the cruise line, but you'll also be guaranteed to make your cruise. If your flight is canceled or delayed, the cruise line will make the necessary arrangements to get you to the ship as soon as possible, even if it means flying you to the next port of call.

Know the single-supplement charge to go it alone. Some ships are better geared toward single travelers than others (*Norwegian Epic,* for example, which has a large selection of excellent single cabins), but almost all ships charge single supplements—a higher surcharge for a single traveler who books one cabin. The single supplement will have you paying anywhere from 125% to 200% of the published cabin rate based on double occupancy. On request, some lines will pair a single traveler with another, so that you can each avoid the single supplement, and if there's no one to pair you with, you get the double cabin to yourself for no additional charge.

Cruise through your honeymoon. Most cruise lines offer special perks for honeymooning couples, from breakfast in bed to a special cake to free champagne. You may also be given a credit for dinner in an extra-charge specialty restaurant, a complimentary massage in the ship's spa, or some other upgrade or perk. Always let your cruise line or agent know that this will be a honeymoon cruise (or even a major anniversary or other important celebration).

With a reluctant first-timer? Cruise Alaska. Trying to get a spouse, friend, or family member to enjoy a cruise with you? Certain destinations have more appeal to first-timers than others. Alaska often appeals to folks who aren't wild about the tropics, or who want to mix education with relaxation on their travels. Cruise ships offer access to parts of Alaska's Inside Passage that you simply cannot reach via other transportation. And these ships often attract a more adventuresome and cerebral crowd than party-oriented cruises to the Caribbean or up and down the Mexican Riviera.

Know your prospective fellow passengers. You've found what appears to be the perfect-size ship and a dazzling itinerary, but what about the crowd that will be sharing

WORD OF MOUTH: CRUISES NORTH

"We were on the Zuiderdam 2 years ago, and thought it was great. We had a verandah and I wouldn't want to cruise otherwise. Consider the inland tour to Fairbanks." —Aristotle

"We are in our 60's and we like HAL (www.hollandamerica.com). Their midsize ships cruise from Vancouver and Seattle to Alaska, and they have rail/land tours as add-ons." —jimingso

"We did many tours on our own, booked well in advance of leaving home. Whale watching in Juneau; helicopter to a glacier in Juneau ($$$ but worth it) and seaplane to Anan Creek to see the bears feed on Salmon. Oh, took the train in Skagway as well." —rncheryl

your vacation? It's worth finding out who they are: Some ships and itineraries draw certain age groups and styles. A good cruise-travel agent can tell help you to figure this out. The ship brochure is another clue. If the people pictured look like people you'd like to know, you may well find sympatico fellow cruisers.

Plan a cruise for your whole tribe. Cruises are ideal for multigenerational trips because they generally provide activities for all ages in a self-contained setting and a variety of accommodations to suit varied budgets. Most ships offer kids' programs, which free up time for the adults in the group to pursue their own interests. Other activities—such as poolside games and shore excursions—are often perfect ways for kids and adults to spend time together.

Negotiate a group discount. Planning a cruise for a large group of friends or family members? Work with your travel agent or directly with the cruise line's group sales department for a perk—if you book at least 16 passengers in 8 cabins (third and fourth passengers in the same cabin don't count), you should be able to score a substantial discount or even a free cabin. Other discounts, such as shipboard credit or free parties, are also sometimes given.

10

For the best group discount, approach more than one cruise line. Let each line know that you're negotiating with the competition, and have each group sales department provide a written offer.

Ask about discounts for senior citizens. Several cruise lines offer reduced rates for senior citizens (sometimes only on certain sailings), and seniors may be able to take advantage of local discounts ashore.

Be flexible on dates. Some sailing dates are more popular than others. If a sailing is "soft"—that is, not all cabins are booked—cruise lines lower the price in order to fill the ship. So leaving just a week earlier or later can get you the same cruise—same ship, same itinerary—for a lower price.

Consider booking an off-season cruise. Many itineraries are based on seasons—Alaskan cruises are typically offered from May to September, while European cruises are usually from April through November. Off-season sailings always cost less, but even within the off-season, prices for different departure dates can differ considerably. Sailings early and late in the season are typically cheaper.

Figure out whether your cruise line is a good citizen. A cruise-ship brochure can help you figure out whether your cruise line is a good corporate citizen. Some lines trumpet their respect for the environment and charity to environmental causes. Others have very high-profile recycling programs. Of course, it's not just altruism that drives the cruise lines. They believe it's good business, because many passengers care about a cruise line's environmental record.

Take advantage of your cruise line's Web site. Many cruise lines now offer multimedia features on their Web sites, not to mention detailed ship diagrams, pictures of cabins, and lists of services and amenities. Take advantage of these features by going online; or ask the cruise line to send you a promotional DVD about their ships.

Watch the weather. The Caribbean hurricane season begins on June 1 and continues through November 30, with greatest risk for a storm from August through October. Ships will still sail unless a hurricane is bearing down on their port of embarkation, but they could skip ports or change itineraries entirely in case of bad weather. You don't want to end up on a New England fall foliage cruise suddenly when you were expecting to head to the warm Caribbean.

Consider trip-cancellation insurance. Weather, technical problems, and financial difficulties—unfortunately, each of these can lead to the cancellation of a cruise, as can an unexpected illness or a death in the family. If you've purchased an insurance policy that covers cancellation, you're covered. If you didn't buy insurance, then you will have to live with your line's cancellation penalty, which can be as much as 100% of the cost of the fare if you cancel within a month of your scheduled cruise.

Be a frequent cruiser. After your first cruise, you will be made a member of the past passengers' club and offered discounts and special treatment on your next cruise with that line. The more cruises you take with one line, the better the perks.

Know the line's policy on late passenger arrivals. Whether you book your own flight or book it through the cruise line's air-and-sea department, read your cruise line's policy carefully to find out what your responsibilities and entitlements are if a flight delay or cancellation forces you to miss your sailing.

Consider booking a pre- or post-cruise tour. These short trips in or near the city from which your cruise originates and/or terminates will allow you to bypass the throngs of passengers racing from the airport to the cruise terminal on the day of departure. Best of all, however, these trips extend your vacation and give you a sense of enjoying two trips in one—it's especially nice if somebody in your party is more of a landlubber than a seafarer.

WORKING WITH A TRAVEL AGENT

Use a travel agent who's an expert in the field. Just as there are all kinds of doctors with finite specialties, there are travel agents specializing in virtually every style of travel—and many of them are cruise specialists. A specialist not only knows the ins and outs of the industry, he or she can often get you cabin upgrades and provide 24-hour service in case of travel snags.

Know how to pick a cruise specialist. A reliable travel agent with experience booking cruises can be your best friend: One who works regularly with few cruise lines may be able to negotiate a more favorable deal for you on several carriers than travel agents who work closely with one cruise line, who often know the inside scoop down to the floorplan, but can't offer deals on others. It's always good to ask whether your agency has partnerships with certain cruise lines, and to keep clear of agents who seem to steer you persistently toward these in hopes of netting a big commission.

10

Look for a CLIA-endorsed travel agent. Travel agents who are members of the Cruise Lines International Association (CLIA) can become Accredited Cruise Counsellors (ACC), Master Cruise Counsellors, or Elite Cruise Counsellors (ECC). These agents have completed demanding training programs including touring or sailing on a specific number of ships. They make it their business to know all they can to serve their clients' needs.

Favor agents who ask you questions. A good cruise agent will ask you many detailed questions about your past vacations, your lifestyle, and even your friends and hobbies. Never book a cruise with an agent who asks only a few cursory questions before handing you a brochure.

Get help when choosing a cabin. With some lines it's hard to get cabin assignments in advance, and if you've never sailed on a particular ship before, it can be difficult to know ahead of time whether your cabin is in a convenient and less noisy location. This is where booking through an agent with extensive cruise experience, especially one working with the line you're interested in, can be invaluable. He or she is also better able to contact the cruise line directly and get you moved to a better cabin in the event that you've been assigned an undesirable one.

Be loyal. With luck, after you've taken a couple of cruises and maybe dealt with a couple of travel agencies, you'll find one you like. If you become a frequent customer, many agencies, especially larger ones, will keep you informed of special deals and last-minute discounts. Notification may be by newsletter or maybe even e-mail, so get on the list.

Choose an agency with a 24-hour client hot line. All kinds of things can happen just before or during a cruise that could require assistance from your travel agent. Agencies that have 24-hour hot lines can be invaluable when crises arise.

Never consider unsolicited over-the-phone or e-mail offers. Occasionally, con artists will buy a direct-marketing list and call people blindly or send out a mass spam e-mail offering a "special deal" on a cruise. If anybody you don't know contacts you directly to discuss a deal on a cruise, don't listen, or don't read the e-mail.

Don't let yourself feel rushed. Even if you're nearly certain that you've found the perfect cruise, or your agent has sold you on a great trip, resist the temptation to book immediately. Cool off, go back home and go over your brochures

WORD OF MOUTH: CRUISES

"Nowadays, in our fast-paced world, only the *Queen Mary 2* offers this lost and mostly-forgotten tradition via its regular transatlantic crossings. For those of you who the idea of crossing the Atlantic by ocean liner appeals, my advice is not to let yourself get intimidated or embarrassed by those of your acquaintances who say, 'Why don't you just fly? It's faster and cheaper!' Go for it and I think you'll be onto a relaxing, elegant secret that only those who bite the bullet get to find out." —Daniel_Williams

"I did a crossing on the *QM2*, and it was one of the great-est experiences of my life. If I could afford it, I would never ever fly across again but ALWAYS do a crossing. It's truly wonderful!!!" —LEANNA

"With over 2,000 passengers on board you're bound to find some agreeable companions. We did a transatlantic on the *QE2* and certainly didn't find it stuffy. (And had the hangovers to prove it!)" —grandma

"The secret is getting out $$ for $$ the best bargains are transatlantic cruises!! You can fly to Europe, stay a few days at a reasonable hotel and tour that city, whether it's Rome, Barcelona, or Venice. And then cruise back to Florida." —ParrotMom

and other research materials one last time, and sleep on it. Any agent who pressures you to act immediately shouldn't be trusted.

Consider booking your cruise online. In addition to local travel agencies, there are many hard-working, dedicated travel professionals working for Web sites. Both big-name travel sellers and mom-and-pop agencies compete for the attention of cyber-savvy clients, and it never hurts to compare prices from a variety of these sources. In addition to cruise specialists, the large online agencies like Expedia and Travelocity also offer cruise bookings and special deals of their own. And some cruise lines now let you book directly through their Web sites, though this doesn't mean you'll always get the best price.

CHOOSING A SHIP AND ITINERARY

Above all other factors, choose the right ship. Some say the most important aspect of a cruise is the destination or itinerary. Others say it's the cruise line. But they're wrong. The most important choice you'll make when booking a cruise is the ship—this will be your home for seven days or more. The ship you choose will determine the comfort of your sleeping quarters, the quality of your food, the quality of your entertainment, and the ports you'll visit. Also, each ship attracts a certain crowd. If you don't like your ship, you won't like your cruise.

Do your homework. Check cruise-lines' Web sites, and, to get other points of view, check out cruise guidebooks that include ship portraits; you might also read travel articles about the ships you're considering. Also see what cruisers are saying about the ships and lines in reader forums on such Web sites as Fodors.com and CruiseCritic.com. There's a wealth of information out there on most cruise ships, and a little research can go a long way toward helping you choose the voyage that's right for you.

Choose a cruise line with varied dining options. It used to be the standard rule on cruise ships that you were seated at the same dinner table at a set time with the same waiters and guests every night of your cruise. Well, no more. Almost every ship these days has one or more specialty restaurants. You may have to pay a supplement (usually $10 to $25 per person) to dine in these restaurants, but they almost always offer made-to-order meals just as in a shoreside restaurant. Many cruise lines now offer much less structured dining. Norwegian Cruise Line, for example, allows you to dine wherever and whenever you wish; helpful electronic screens in many public rooms and outside each restaurant give you the average waiting time for every restaurant on the ship. And on their purpose-built, "Freestyle" ships there may be over a dozen different restaurants to choose from.

Make a list of your favorite activities and interests. Narrowing down which cruise suits you best is much easier if you, and any friends or family members you will be traveling with, compile a list of the things you enjoy doing. Are you seeking a full slate of onboard activities or hoping for privacy and relaxation? Will you want to go on organized sightseeing tours while on shore, or laze away at the beach? Is evening entertainment a high priority? Haute cuisine or informal dining? Fancy staterooms you'll want to spend time in or simple cabins you're using only as a place to sleep?

If you're a nightlife maven, consider a larger ship. On most smaller ships evening entertainment is decidedly low-key, but today's modern megaships often have myriad bars, pulsing discos, over-the-top Las Vegas–style shows, cavernous casinos, and other after-dark diversions. But look at the line's reputation; Carnival, Royal Caribbean, and Norwegian Cruise Line ships are known for their varied nightlife options; Holland America is not.

If you have mobility concerns, book a cabin near an elevator. A traveler who uses a wheelchair or faces any other challenges related to getting around easily might be most comfortable on a ship whose public rooms are clustered on one deck. Ideally, choose a cabin that's midship and relatively close not only to the elevator but also to public areas. And be sure not to book a cabin with upper and lower berths (where one bed folds out from the wall above the lower one, sort of like bunk beds). Many ships these days have specially designed wheelchair-accessible cabins with wider doors and bigger bathrooms.

Avoid older ships if you have disabilities. Generally speaking, the older, smaller ships cause the most problems for people with limited mobility. Older ships have more raised lips between the doorways, for example, and fewer flat-to-level entrances to go on decks.

Single? Look for special singles sailings. Cruise ships are generally a great place to meet people, and many single travelers have found cruise vacations well suited to their lifestyle. Making the choice between a large or small ship depends on your exact needs. Larger ships have more people on board, more singles, and more activities, while a smaller ship may sail to a remote and exclusive island where champagne parties are held in the surf. Companies such as RSVP Vacations and Atlantis Events charter ships for gay- and/or lesbian-themed cruises that can be fun for singles hoping to meet others of the same sex.

Consider a ship's size. The biggest ships, registering 70,000 tons to as many as 200,000 tons with as many as 5,400 passengers, are cities at sea. They have the best amenities and can feel less crowded than smaller vessels, but they're also prone to long lines waiting to disembark or to eat at the buffet. If that's not your style, consider a midsize ship, carrying 1,000 people or so and registering 30,000 to 50,000 tons, or an even smaller, yachtlike ship that carries just a few hundred passengers and registers 10,000 to 25,000 tons (sometimes even less). They're cozier, and what they lack in facilities they make up for in intimacy—although seasickness is more likely on these.

10

Get the best cabin you can afford. People often want to save money, so they book the cheapest available inside cabin thinking they won't spend much time there. Don't make the same mistake. Although all cabins are designed to be as comfortable and functional as possible, you can't get around the fact that cruise-ship cabins are still much smaller than the typical hotel room, and further, you'll end up spending more time there than you think. If you intend to do nothing more than sleep in your cabin, book the cheapest option. But if comfort is important to you, book the best cabin you can afford. On newer ships more and more cabins have balconies, and the chance to sit outside on your balcony to have breakfast or just to relax and look at the stars is an unbeatable luxury.

Avoid cabin fever by picking a cruise with interesting ports of call. The real reason to choose a cruise over a land-based vacation is the opportunity to see more than one place on your vacation. If you pick an itinerary with many interesting ports of call, you will maximize your vacation experiences and have more opportunities to get off the ship and explore.

If you're an adventurous traveler, consider a small ship. Small ships can go to places big ships can't. With a small-ship cruise you'll have many more interesting opportunities to explore. You'll visit quieter beaches on smaller islands in tropical climates. You might have the chance to kayak with whales directly from your ship in Alaska. You might tie up in a smaller port closer to interesting attractions in Europe. Plus, disembarking is faster when you get to port, and shore excursions are done with smaller groups. And small ships are also better if you don't like structured activities, which are legion on the megaships.

Consider a ship's pools and deck layout. Most ships have a pool, but the quality and size of the pool can make or break a sunshine cruise. Avoid large ships with small pools, where on a hot day the pool can seem like an overcrowded bathtub. Make sure there are enough pools and hot tubs on deck to accommodate your and your family's needs. Look for kid-friendly designs such as slides and water parks. And if you aren't traveling with family, look for a ship that has an adults-only pool deck. The newest Royal Caribbean ships even have Surfriders, with which you can practice catching the perfect wave.

Study a deck plan to decide on a cabin. Most cruise-line Web sites these days have detailed deck plans you can study to decide which cabin is best for you. The least desirable cabins are those on lower decks, particularly those far aft, which can be plagued by mechanical noises and vibration. But also beware of cabins immediately below pools and nightspots, especially if you want to sleep early. Finally, take note of where lifeboats are located; views from some outside cabins can be partially or entirely obstructed by the boats.

To avoid motion sickness, choose a cabin near the ship's middle. Upper-deck cabins, as well as those far forward or aft, are much more susceptible to motion than midship cabins on a middle deck. The closer your cabin is to the ship's center of gravity, the less rocking you're likely to experience.

Consider your cabin's proximity to public areas. If noise isn't important to you but convenience to dining rooms or nightclubs is, then go ahead and book a cabin near the public areas. But keep in mind that cabins near dining rooms, nightclubs, theaters, and casinos—as well as cabins near stairwells and engine-room bulkheads—tend to be the noisiest.

Honeymooning? Don't plan on leaving the day after. Cruises may be the perfect honeymoon getaway, but keep in mind that most seven-day cruises depart on Saturday or Sunday (almost never on Monday), so you may need to plan for a departure the day of or after your wedding.

PREPARING FOR YOUR TRIP

Anticipate the extra costs. Most cruises are not all-inclusive, so extras—such as beverages (alcoholic or not), shore excursions, specialty restaurants, spa treatments, onboard video games, laundry and dry cleaning, and Internet-use—can add up. Cruising is still an excellent value, but be sure to factor in all related costs. The cheaper the cruise and the bigger the ship, the more likely you are to have to pay for extras.

Budget for tips. Most ships these days automatically add a gratuities surcharge of $10 to $15 per person per day to your account at the end of the cruise. Staff members are rarely tipped in cash, as in the past, and you aren't expected, for example, to tip the person who brings your bags to the cabin (especially because they are usually brought by your cabin steward). You can usually adjust the gratuity charge up or down before disembarkation. Room-service waiters are usually tipped in cash (a dollar or two is sufficient), and some cruise lines request that you give a separate tip

10

to waitstaff in specialty restaurants. But be sure to budget for the gratuities; the salaries of the hard-working crew members depend on it.

Don't overpack. The average cruise-ship cabin is about 170 to 200 square feet, about half the size of the average hotel room. Although you can get away with a lot, you'll be much more comfortable in a cabin this size if you pack as lightly as possible, with just enough clothing—and variety of clothing—to get by.

Consider a ship's dress code. Not all ships require you to dress up for dinner anymore. On Norwegian Cruise Line ships you can now even wear jeans to the main dining room at night. Other ships, such as Celebrity and Holland America, have more formal nights. During the day, all ships are universally casual.

Know the ship's electrical specifications. Most of the large cruise lines provide U.S.-style current and plugs, but some international ships, particularly those sailing in Europe and Asia, may have other electrical standards. Be sure to verify that before you cruise. Almost every ship provides a hair dryer, so there's rarely a need to pack one.

Find out what toiletries and amenities are in cabins. Almost all cruise ships provide shampoo and soap (though it may be liquid shower gel), beach towels, and hair dryers; some provide conditioner and other toiletries, but if you need something specific, always ask. Almost no cruise line allows irons in cabins (they are considered a fire hazard), but some lines have coin laundries with irons or separate ironing rooms (on a few lines the use of self-service laundry is free). Royal Caribbean and Norwegian Cruise Line ships (and those of several other lines) do not have self-service laundry rooms. More upscale cruise lines typically provide a much more extensive array of amenities.

Make a list of important items to pack. It can be expensive or difficult to buy seemingly common household products at sea, or if you can buy them the prices are exorbitant. Some often-forgotten, useful items include: an alarm clock (few cabins have them), batteries, feminine hygiene products, insect repellent, sunscreen, over-the-counter cold remedies, sandals, sports gear, sunglasses, and a light windbreaker.

Bring along some cash. There are circumstances that will warrant it, even on an all-inclusive trip. And although some ships have ATMs, they often have huge surcharges. You'll need cash for the casino on board, and you will also need some cash on shore. Though ATMs are common in most ports, they can still be hard to find in some places.

Look into details about your cabin's beds. Bed configuration is key. On most newer ships cabins come with two twin-size beds that are usually pushed together to create a king (though your cabin steward can separate them). On some older ships the beds are nailed to the floor and may be laid out in an L-shape configuration. Sometimes you can figure this out from cruise-line brochures, but it's safest to ask your cruise line or travel agent to confirm this information before you book.

Get a passport or passport card. If your cruise calls in a foreign port (even Canada or a Caribbean destination other than the U.S. Virgin Islands or Puerto Rico), you must have proof of citizenship (either a passport, a passport card, or in some cases a so-called "enhanced" driver's license). Taking a passport is always a good idea—even if you're cruising to Alaska. Many people don't consider what might happen if they had to leave the ship and come home early. If you are in a foreign destination (even Canada), you'll need your passport (not a passport card) to fly back home. But if you don't plan to fly to or from a foreign destination, a passport card works for all cruises originating in and return to the U.S. and costs half as much as a full passport.

Check your documents. With luck, you've been so busy preparing for your cruise that you haven't had time to worry about your tickets and your cruise documents. Then a couple of weeks before your departure, they arrive. When they do, make sure to check your tickets over immediately and carefully. Usually they're perfect. But mistakes do occur. If you've bought an air-and-sea package, check your airline tickets. Make sure you're ticketed for the right dates, from the right airport, and to the right destination.

10

ON BOARD YOUR SHIP

Make sure your cabin works. Run the water in the sink and shower, flush the toilet, and turn on lights to make sure that everything works. Report problems right away.

Learn about your ship as soon as you check into your cabin. When you arrive in your cabin, you'll find a folder of information about your ship either on the bed or on the desk. This will be your bible for the cruise. It's full of information on everything from ordering room service and using the shipboard telephone system to channel surfing on the TV.

Tour your ship. On arrival, you'll normally find a deck plan of your ship in your cabin or with your welcome folder (or one may be handed to you as you board). Tuck this in your pocket and set a course for ship exploration. Begin by taking the nearest elevator to the top deck. Go to the front of the ship (the bow) and walk toward the back (the stern). Once you've reached the stern, take the stairs or elevator down to the next deck and walk all the way to the bow, passing through all of the corridors and public rooms. Continue this front-to-back, back-to-front exploration until you've covered all the public decks.

Make appointments and reservations early. As soon as you're settled onto your ship, consider booking a massage in the spa, shore excursions, a reservation for a special show, or dinner reservations at some of the specialty restaurants that are common on many newer ships. These types of activities and meals fill up quickly.

Check your dinner assignment. One of the first things you should do on boarding the ship is find the maître d', who typically sets up shop in one of the ship's public rooms (usually not the dining room). If you have a set dining time, now is the time to double-check your dining-room assignment and to change it if you didn't get the seating you want. The maître d' will have a layout of the ship's dining room showing the location and configuration of every table. He or she can tell you where in the dining room your table is and how many people will join you for dinner. Make sure you get what you want, whether it's a table for two or a no-smoking table. If you don't have a set time for dinner, you can usually make reservations at this table.

Make the most of days at sea. On almost every cruise there are days at sea, when the ship doesn't stop in any port of call. Cruise ships, with their expansive outdoor facilities, have plenty of ways to keep you entertained (including sundecks that stretch three football fields long and multiple swimming pools). You'll find that days at sea also are perfect for enjoying the great indoors. Your ship undoubtedly has many indoor attractions in addition to the spa, restaurants, and shops you saw on your initial tour—some have video arcades, shopping boulevards, and caviar-and-wine bars.

Beat the rainy-day blues. Life on a cruise ship when it rains doesn't have to be a drag. It's a vacation, after all, and sometimes it's nice to have a day to play couch potato. Even a standard cabin can be a cozy place to pass some time. Recently released movies are run continuously on TV; many ships have a movie theater on board where recent releases are shown several times a day. Some ships have a collection of DVDs you can borrow, as well as onboard libraries filled with books. There's also the card room, where you'll find decks of cards and board games. Games and books are usually free to borrow, but you often have to pay for DVDs. And you can order room service for free on most ships.

Know where to find privacy. Cruise ships can feel crowded. If you want privacy, both on and off the ship, consider booking a cabin with a private veranda and booking a table for two in the dining room. When the outdoor buffets are in full swing, eat inside—the indoor restaurants are often half empty.

Try a midnight whirlpool. At least once during your sailing, slip into your bathing suit and head to the upper deck in the middle of the night. Ease into the whirlpool and enjoy the bubbles under the stars. You've just turned a 2,000-passenger megaship into your own private yacht.

Get teed off on deck. Besides putting greens, miniature golf courses, and golf simulators, some ships carry onboard pros. And virtually every major line has a shore excursion program for golfers, who can tee up while everyone else is on a bus.

Bring the running shoes. It's easy to feel cramped on board even the largest ships, especially if you're at sea for a few days. However, you can usually find a place to stretch your legs. For jogging there are generally two options. Most ships have a wraparound promenade deck, which is also ideal for a light stroll. On other ships there are specially designed and dedicated tracks, sometimes covered with a high-tech cushioned surface. Keep in mind that some smaller ships may have no place to jog at all. Other fitness facilities may come with fitness instructors. There may be aerobics classes, stretch classes, and group jogs (though there is often a charge). Some fitness programs run all day.

Enjoy a dinner in your cabin. Most cruise ships offer complimentary 24-hour room service, which ranges from light

10

snacks and breakfast to full meals on some luxury ships. Some passengers who prefer informal attire order room service during a cruise's formal nights. It's also a good option if you've enjoyed a large, late lunch during your shore visit and only need a light snack at dinner. If you have a private veranda, you can eat outdoors.

To contact home, send an e-mail or text. Improved technology has made it easier than ever to phone home during a cruise, even using your own cell phone. But calling is expensive. Even if you use your own cell phone, you will pay a huge surcharge of up to $2 to $5 per minute; ship-to-shore calls are even more expensive—up to $18 per minute. E-mail can be much more cost-effective, if still pricey. Internet service can be up to $1 per minute, but some ships offer Internet packages for unlimited use during a cruise; and more ships than ever have Wi-Fi service, allowing you to bring and use your own laptop (or rent one from the ship during your cruise). Text messages are always cheaper than calls, and although they can cost up to 50¢ with surcharges, that's still much cheaper than the cost of using the Internet on most ships.

HEALTH AND SAFETY

Know your ship's medical facilities. Information about medical care aboard ship is usually buried in the fine print in the back of brochures. No government body or international treaty governs medical care aboard cruise ships. Each cruise line is left to its own devices, and some lines are better known than others for the quality of their medical care. If you have any concerns, book a cruise line that has a reputation for medical readiness at sea—and buy travel insurance that includes coverage for preexisting conditions. But this care is not free; if you see the doctor or nurse on your cruise ship, there will be a fee, and it may not be covered by your insurance.

Don't forget a sufficient supply of medication. Bring a supply of prescription drugs and medications extensive enough to last a few days longer than your trip and return home. Place all medications in your carry-on—never in checked baggage. Carry a written list of medications and their dosages on your cruise. And be sure to bring along the phone number of your home physician. The ship's small pharmacy will carry some drugs, but it will not be comprehensive.

Ask about a cruise line's health standards. If you have concerns about whether you'll contract a virus on a cruise, ask your cruise line how they rank and how you're protected. The Centers for Disease Control (CDC) Web site (⊕ *www. cdc.gov*) posts many details about sanitation standards and the latest news on the topic of vessel sanitation.

Protect yourself on the ship. No one wants to get sick during a highly anticipated vacation. The best way to avoid illness is to wash your hands thoroughly and often. Most ships place dispensers for hand-sanitizer near dining rooms. Use them. If you become sick, always follow the doctor's recommendations for quarantine so you don't infect other passengers.

SHORE THINGS

Book shore excursions early. Many cruise lines now allow you to book your shore excursions in advance, but many people still wait until they board. That's a mistake. The longer you wait, the more likely it is that you will not be able to take the excursion of your choice. If there's a trip you want to take, book it as soon as possible. Just don't book anything you're unsure of: Shore excursions are usually nonrefundable.

If you're independent, avoid organized excursions. You can usually visit the same places and attractions offered through your ship's shore-excursion programs for less money on your own, especially if you gather up a group of like-minded passengers to split the cost of transportation. But you may need to plan ahead of time. Take along a travel guide to your port of call; once there, you can hire a local driver to take you around to the attractions that interest you—and the flexibility can make your exploring more pleasurable. Just be certain to get back to your ship on time.

10

Book an excursion to unfamiliar ports. Shore excursions offer plenty of advantages over simply wandering around a port by yourself. You'll usually be led by an experienced guide, you'll have the opportunity to mingle with other passengers, and you're guaranteed to make it back to the ship on time (in the very unlikely event that your group is delayed and misses the ship, the cruise line will make arrangements to get you as quickly as possible to the next port of call).

Remember that itineraries may change. Cruise lines reserve the right to change their itineraries for virtually any reason—often this happens because of weather conditions. You may end up calling at the same ports as planned but on different days, a port may be dropped at the last minute, or a new one may be substituted. If you're making your own private arrangements for shore activities, such as a personal tour or a trip to a local spa, make sure you call and cancel or change your reservation if the ship changes its itinerary.

KIDS' STUFF

Ask about children's discounts. Most cruise lines charge children under age 12 third- and fourth-passenger rates or children's fares when they're traveling with two adults in the same cabin. These rates tend to be about half—or sometimes even less than half—the lowest adult fare. On certain off-peak sailings children may be permitted to travel free if they stay in their parents' cabin.

Sailing without mom or dad? Get a letter. Cruise ships require that children sailing without one or both parents carry a notarized letter of permission from the absent parent(s). This is the case even when the kids are sailing with grandma or grandpa.

If you're traveling with your family, start small. No matter how enthusiastic you are, don't book your entire brood on one of the megaships the first time out. Massive ships like *Oasis of the Seas, Norwegian Epic,* and *Carnival Conquest* can seem irresistible on paper, but the behemoths run only weeklong excursions, and seven days can be an eternity if you discover halfway through that the adventure isn't for you. If you haven't been at sea before, consider a three- or four-day jaunt to start; Disney Cruise Line, which is especially family-friendly, offers these sorts of short cruises. If you love it, you can always go back.

Go when other families will be on board. Whether you're traveling with teens or young children, it's important to make sure that other kids will be on board. You don't want to be the only family with kids on a couples-only cruise. Search the brochures and videos for images of children. Timing is also a factor—summer cruises, holiday cruises, and cruises during major school holiday periods (Christmas, Easter–spring break) will have more children on board and, it's likely, more children's activities planned. Even lines that do not ordinarily cater to children may have organized kids' programs during busy school and holiday breaks.

Look for separate programs for each age group. Younger groups may have a clubhouse, a pirate ship, storytelling, or arts and crafts. Older children may be able to access science and educational programs and computers and undertake detailed art projects. Programs for teens might revolve around movies, sports activities, or dances; some ships even have teen-only areas, where parents aren't permitted.

Check out the children's programs' staff-to-child ratio. Especially if you have very young kids, it's best to find a children's program where this ratio is no greater than 1 to 3.

Evaluate the supervision and activities. The best programs have supervised activities throughout the day and include meals. Some ships provide facilities for children and child care but no organized activities.

Ask about baby-sitting and day care. Some ships provide day care and group baby-sitting for younger children at no extra charge, although most charge an hourly rate. On many ships private baby-sitting is by arrangement with crew members (at a negotiated price).

With younger kids, get the first dinner seating. If your ship offers assigned dinner seatings, an earlier time is preferable for families with younger children (in fact, some cruise ships always assign guests with children to the earlier seatings). Some lines will not permit children to eat alone in the dining room. If your kids are picky eaters, choose a line that offers special children's menus. And if you'll be needing a high chair, request it in advance.

Find out about age requirements. Some cruise ships don't allow infants aboard, period; others require a minimum age, anywhere from 4 to 18 months.

Pregnant? Make sure you can cruise. Most lines do not allow pregnant women to cruise in their third trimester. Some lines are more strict; some even require a note from your doctor certifying your expected due date.

10

Know the requirements on toilet training. Many cruise lines require that kids be fully toilet trained before taking part in supervised activities. Other lines issue beepers to parents so they can come to change diapers. Of the major cruise lines, only Carnival and Disney will change diapers for toddlers.

Check facilities. If your ship does allow toddlers and infants, find out exactly what the cruise line provides (few provide formula and baby food) and plan accordingly. Parents should also know that most cruise lines will not allow kids who are not fully toilet trained to swim in even the children's pool (not even in swim diapers). Only a few lines have ships with specially filtered pools to accommodate tots in swim diapers.

Got a baby? Get a cabin big enough for a crib. Many cruise-ship cabins are tiny, and you'll need one large enough to accommodate your child's crib comfortably. Make your request well in advance.

Book an outside cabin opposite an inside cabin for your family. Side-by-side outside cabins cost more than a combination of an outside cabin across from an inside one. Sure, those occupying the inside cabin won't enjoy a view, but this can be an ideal compromise if you're traveling with kids, or even with another couple, and you wish to save money. Plan to congregate more as a group in the larger, more pleasant outside cabin. Some ships have family suites; though expensive, these can be ideal, because they often include a separate bathroom and sleeping area for the kids.

Look for a ship with a no-adults teen club. A cruise is an ideal vacation for families with teens. Parents can rest assured that the kids are in a safe environment on board, and yet the teens can roam independently and find plenty of cool things to do. Look for a cruise ship that has an exclusive program for teens—ideally, this includes a private club room where no children or adults are allowed.

Got teens? Know the drinking ages. Most large cruise lines do not allow anyone under 21 to drink, though some lines (particularly those based in countries with lower legal drinking ages) have different minimums. If you want—or don't want—your under-age teen to drink, be sure to do your homework. Most ships allow anyone 18 and over to gamble.

Sightseeing

WORD OF MOUTH

"I prefer to visit a site without having to reread a guide book while doing so.in other words full frontal entertainment with eyes wide open to the sights at hand."

—rhkkmk

"Carry a compass with you. I can't tell you the number of times I have come out of subway thinking I knew which way was north only to be completely turned around."

—nonstop

Updated
by Alexis
Kelly

Vacationing isn't a competition or a scavenger hunt—it's not especially fulfilling to arrive with a checklist of "must-see" sites and knock them off one by one. Sure you can make a list of places you hope to see and activities you'd like to pursue. But the list really should include the things that interest you, not the things you've been told are most popular.

It really is OK to visit Paris and never ascend the Eiffel Tower or to visit Washington, D.C., without setting foot in a Smithsonian museum. And don't be afraid to hop in a car, rent a bike, or set out on foot to wander and see what comes your way. Venture down roads and lanes that look intriguing. Allow yourself to get sidetracked, or jot down the name of an interesting shop or attraction you stumble upon but would rather spend more time visiting another day.

This chapter is filled with tips on how to make the most of your time during your travels—choosing activities and a pace that fit your needs, getting around with ease, and staying safe and healthy along the way

GETTING ORIENTED

Stop by the tourist office when you arrive. It never hurts to see what maps, brochures, and other resources are available at the tourist board. Staffers can answer any lingering questions you have about getting around, tours, places to eat, and the like. And many tourist boards have discount passes, coupon books, or other package deals good for several or possibly even all the main attractions.

WORD OF MOUTH. "In Kyoto at the tourist office they will be able to give you all kinds of info on tea ceremony, bunraku, kabuki, etc." —gertie3751

Get advice on safety issues before starting to sightsee. Ask hotel or tourist-board staffers about where to go and how best to get there. Also find out where the bad parts of town are, including areas that are safe by day and become less friendly at night. The same goes for places that may take kindly to locals but not to visitors. If you know where you're going ahead of time, you can walk with an air of confidence and purpose that deters bad guys.

Familiarize yourself with a general-overview tour. It can be very helpful to take a guided bus or walking tour as soon as possible after you arrive. This will not only give you the lay of the land but will also help you to decide what activities and attractions interest you most and where they are in relation to one another.

Hire an English-speaking driver or private guide. If you're not a fan of big tour groups, try this option. You'll get the guide's expertise in English—and his or her companionship. In some destinations, this request is par for the course and will be quite standard. And, depending upon where you're traveling, you may end up safer, too.

Include classes or special-interest tours in your sightseeing plan. Consider participating in a cooking class in southern France, a rock-climbing course in a Utah park, an architecture tour in Chicago, or a tea-ceremony demonstration in Tokyo. Look for activities and tours that tickle your fancy while exposing you to an important aspect of your destination. In the process, you might see spots that would be difficult to reach on your own, and you might meet other travelers—or even locals—with similar interests.

Consider your transportation options. Study subway and bus maps, and check your Fodor's guide to find out how the public transit system works, fares and methods of payment, and discounts. Find out how cabs work (metered or not) and how to get one (hail one on the street, grab one at a taxi stand, call for one). Decide whether you can readily drive yourself to that out-of-town sight or whether it makes more sense to take a bus or commuter train or go on a tour.

WORD OF MOUTH. "If you're going to be in Rome for 3 days or more, buy the Roma pass. You must plan how to use it to save money. We went to the Colosseum–Forum–Palentino the first day and the Villa Borghese the next morning. With all the buses we jumped on and off, we had already paid off the card and more by then. The rest of the places we went had discounts (sometimes 50%) and all the transportation was free—including the train to Ostia Antica. I figure that we saved about 30 euros each by using the card." —Taltul

When given directions, ask for specifics. Ask about distances and landmarks along the way. Don't accept an answer such as "Oh, it's only three blocks away." The length of a block can vary greatly from one city to another—or even from crosstown to uptown—and what might be a charm-

TRAVEL PHOTOGRAPHY

Whether it's the trip of a lifetime or the place that you return to year after year, the photos you take while on vacation will end up being your best travel souvenirs. It's quite possible today to just point, shoot, and let your digital camera sort out all the details. But there are still some things that your camera can't do automatically. It can't tell you the best time of day to get the best exposure, it can't override shaky hands, and it certainly can't compose memorable photos. So, here are a few tips on how to get the best shots.

■ **Know the Golden Hours:** The best photos are taken when most of us are either happily snoozing or relaxing over dinner—an hour before and shortly after sunset and one hour on either side of full dawn. That's when the light is gentle and golden, and when your photos are less likely to be overexposed and filled with harsh shadows or squinting people. If you want the most beautiful shots, start snapping early and stick around for sundown.

■ **Divide to Conquer:** You can't go wrong with the Rule of Thirds, the classic photographer's tip for creating interesting images. When you're setting up a shot, mentally divide your LCD screen or viewfinder into nine squares.

Place the primary subject where two of those squares intersect. If all this talk of imaginary lines makes your head spin, just remember not to plop your primary focal point in the center of your photos. Set up the shot so the prime point of interest is a bit to the left or right of the midpoint.

■ **Lock Your Focus:** When your digital camera is in automatic mode, it focuses when you depress the shutter button (the button you press to take a photo) halfway down. To get a properly focused photo, press the shutter down halfway and wait a few seconds. Most cameras emit a cheery beep when an image is focused, or a light will go on near the viewfinder or on the LCD screen. Once the image is in focus, press the shutter completely down. If you don't give the camera a few seconds to focus, your photos won't be as sharp as they could be.

■ **Circumvent Auto Focus:** Your camera may not focus on what you consider the correct focal point of a particular photo. So center the primary subject smack in the middle of the frame, depress the shutter button halfway and allow the camera to focus. Then, while still holding the shutter button down, compose your photo properly and press the shutter button all the way down. This procedure ensures that your selected focal point is in proper focus.

■ **Jettison the Jitters:** Shaky hands are the most common cause of photos that are out of focus. If your hands aren't steady, invest in a tripod or put the camera on something steady: a wall, a bench, a table, a rock—anything that's not going to move. If all else fails, lean against something sturdy like a building, a tree or a stable friend to avoid the wobbles that ruin photos.

■ **Mind the Flash:** Photos taken in less than ideal light conditions take longer to capture because the camera needs time to grab whatever light is present. During that waiting period there's a chance that your hands will shake or someone will move, resulting in a blurry image. Deal with the dark by following the jitter tips above to stabilize yourself and your camera. The absolute best solution for managing odd light situations is to get a digital camera that offers super-high ISO speeds, like Fujifilm's FinePix F30, which shoots full resolution at ISO 3200; you can capture great images in dim light or even in motion with this camera.

■ **Have a Purpose:** Before you press that shutter but-

ton, take a moment or two to consider why you're shooting what you're shooting. Why do you want to take this picture? What's important here? What do you want to remember? How can you photograph this scene so that you capture the mood? After you've thought a bit, start setting up your photo. Look for interesting lines that curve into your image, a path, the shoreline, a fence—use these lines to create the impression of dimension. Photographing people with their bodies or faces positioned at an angle to your camera, rather than looking directly at you, also adds a sense of depth to photos.

■ **Ignore All the Rules:** Sure, thoughtful contemplation and careful technique are likely to produce brilliant images, but there are times when you just need to capture the moment. If you see something wonderful, grab your camera and get the photo—don't think about it. If the photo turns out to be blurry, over- or underexposed, or everyone in the picture chose that exact moment to grimace and blink, oh well. Nothing ventured, nothing gained.

ing stroll on a summer's eve becomes an unbearable trek on a subzero winter's day. Also find out whether the route includes challenges like steep hills or bridges.

Drop everything for an unforeseen adventure opportunity. Even after you've logged lots of time laying out plans and possible itineraries, it's important to honor your whims and recognize a once-in-a-lifetime opportunity, should one come your way.

GETTING OUT AND ABOUT

SIGHTSEEING BY DAY

Don't over-schedule your vacation. Think back to your last vacation—did you overextend yourself or visit so many attractions that you ended up not liking some of them? Resist succumbing to the fear that you may never return and so must see everything a destination has to offer, and instead focus on those activities and attractions that truly appeal to you. Take it easy—this is your time off.

Vary your vacation activities from day to day. Visiting large art museums back-to-back can be taxing for even the most ardent culture vulture, just as shopping for six straight hours can wear out inveterate browsers. If you're someone who simply must pack a lot into every day of your trip, try to mix and match your activities. Spend a morning at a museum, and follow with a light hike or garden tour in the afternoon. Save a second museum for a different day, when you might also take a bus or boat tour.

Reconfirm hours and admission. No matter how much you trust your guidebook, or how recently you've checked an attraction's Web page, call the day of your visit to make sure the place is open. Some museums open or close late or early at a whim, or may close unexpectedly because of a staff shortage, a local holiday you're not aware of, a change in the budget, or for renovations.

Carry a bit of change in local currency with you. You might find that little unexpected payments are required in order to gain admission to sights, like public parks, or in order to use illumination devices in churches (timed lights on certain parts of the interior or artwork).

Bring bottled water. There's probably no travel accessory more underestimated than bottled water. Drinking a bottle (or even two or three) is sometimes the difference between conking out halfway through a hike and trekking 2 mi farther than you thought you ever could. It's also a must at theme parks, for city strolls, and just about any place that gets lots of sun. And although you can often buy bottled water at convenience stores or museum or attractions shops, you'll pay dearly—if you're traveling by car, buy a case of bottled water at a discount store and keep it in your trunk.

Put your feet first. Sightseeing can be hard on your tootsies. Let go of your high-heel-shoe fetish if you have a day of walking or exploring planned, and wear lightweight, breathable shoes with good arch support. Carry a small bottle of foot spray and/or a small tube of foot cream or gel and fresh socks. Then, during a bathroom break in the middle of sightseeing, give yourself a five-minute foot treatment and change your socks. When your feet are invigorated and refreshed (read: cool), so is the rest of you.

Bring along just one bag for sightseeing. Fill your day pack with only a day's worth of necessities—guidebook, maps, cell phone, bottled water, IDs, sunscreen, portable umbrella, etc.—and take turns carrying it. There's no reason for everyone in the group to haul around a separate bag.

Don't forget your cell phone or phone card when touring the town. Carry your phone with you, even if you don't plan to use it. Turn it off and use it only when you want or need to, but do keep it close at hand. It can be a lifesaver when you're trying to confirm a museum's hours, directions, or admission; need to make or change a dinner reservation for later in the day; or if you become lost or disoriented. If your cell phone doesn't work where you're going, you can rent one or get a prepaid phone card to make calls home.

Write down your hotel name and address on a slip of paper. In places where you don't speak the language, jot down the name, address, and phone number of your hotel on several pieces of paper, along with the same information for any restaurants, attractions, or other sites you're planning to visit, and present these to cab or bus drivers as you travel. Be sure, if appropriate, to write this information in both the local alphabet and your own.

Avoid unlicensed taxis. So-called "gypsy" cab drivers are sometimes legit, but you generally have no way of knowing this before you hop into the vehicle. And if you are overcharged or mistreated, you have little chance of disputing the incident. Use authorized cabs. And if you're unsure, check your guidebook or ask at your hotel or the tourist board for information about which cab companies are reputable.

Find out when museums offer free admission. Many large museums offer free or "pay-as-you-wish" admission one or two days per week, often for just part of the day (the first couple of hours in the morning, or a few hours late in the evening). Thursday and Friday evenings are common for this practice, but exact days can vary greatly—you might be able to plan your museum visits to get into several places free. Keep in mind, however, that most museums are nonprofit. If you are in a financial position to make a donation, it's always appreciated.

On vacation plan a late-night museum jaunt. Quite a few major museums extend their usual opening times by two or three hours one night a week. This can be a great time to visit a museum, perhaps combining your tour with dinner afterward at a nearby restaurant. Sometimes museums offer special evening programs, such as lectures, wine-and-cheese socials, exhibit openings, or films.

Traveling with a group? Consider a theme park. Most parks have been planned specifically to appeal to a broad range of interests, so apart from wild rides there are gentle ones that please young children, older travelers, and more sedate types. Plus, many attractions in many theme parks are completely accessible to people who use wheelchairs or who have other disabilities.

Check for theme-park discounts. Local tourism boards almost always have coupons for the big theme parks—and many people are eligible for corporate deals through their company, school, or credit-card company. If you go after 4 PM, many parks charge almost half price; if you go in the off-season, your discounts will be even better. Check around for deals before you fork over your money.

Save money at theme parks with a multiday park pass. Theme-park admission can be pricey, but multiday packages are always available, and these often include additional benefits, such as accommodations, transportation, or even some meals. Some packages include early entry to the park.

WORD OF MOUTH: SCRAPBOOKS

"I haven't made one, but a friend did make one with Shutterfly and it was very nice—beautiful, actually, and very good quality. I have also seen their cards which are very nice." —vjpblovesitaly

"Blurb.com is the company I'm using for my parent's anniversary book. A friend brought several different books and I really liked the paper and book quality. If you have a Mac, iPhoto is easy to use as well." —BeachGirl247

"Smilebooks.com really is one of the better online photo book companies. Smilebooks puts a huge focus on paper and printing so your photo books look professional and high quality." —sarahanne26

"I made one of wedding pictures from my son's wedding. I used Walgreen's. It turned out great. I only spent $35 on it. I was afraid that it might turn out cheesy, so I didn't want to spend a lot on it. What a wonderful surprise when I received it. Almost as nice as the $400 one I purchased from the photographer at my daughter's wedding. Live and learn." —DebInTN

"I have used Picaboo (www.picaboo.com) several times. Very good quality and very user friendly." —CKE2512

"I recommend visiting Smilebooks.com. Not only do they have very easy to use in-browser software, you can also download their software if you prefer. The quality of their finished product is incredible, and they are quite affordable." —Stwo

"The trick to getting the exact mix of photos on the page that you want (along with whatever captions, etc) is to make a 'digital scrapbook.' Essentially, you choose the picture layout that is one picture that fills the entire page, but that picture is a 'collage' of your pictures and captions. It is somewhat advanced—you need something like Photoshop Elements—but once you learn, you won't want to go back to the templates." —fb

SHOPPING

Research local prices for items that interest you. Do a bit of Web research before you go so that you'll be able to spot a good deal when you see one. Also, if you're planning to visit a notable shop during your vacation, especially one with a brisk mail-order business, check the company's Web site before you arrive. There may be online coupons that you can print out and present when you shop or there may be Web-only offers or ads for upcoming sales.

Don't get tied up in chain stores. Unless you live in a rural area and have little access to national chain shops when you're at home, on your vacation try to avoid districts and malls packed with the chains. Seek out neighborhoods, often downtown arts and/or entertainment districts that cultivate a local retail scene with plenty of independent shops. You're more likely to find places that stock locally made arts and crafts, too.

Look beyond outlet shops to find the best deals. What began as a way for shops to unload last season's fashions; discontinued merchandise; and less popular colors, sizes, styles, and models—at cut-rate prices—has blossomed into a lucrative side industry. Most outlet stores do offer some deep-discounted items and great deals, but they also frequently sell merchandise designed expressly for outlet shops, and they sell items that are no cheaper than those in regular shops.

Don't assume you'll save at duty-free shops. Sure, it's tempting to buy anything that piques your interest in a duty-free shop, especially if you're trying to dump currency that you won't be able to use back home, or if you're bored and killing time at an airport or on a cruise ship. But avoid buying easy-to-find goods—liquor, candy, some jewelry, electronics—unless you're really sure how a duty-free shop's prices compare with those at home.

Find out about tax refunds when making purchases abroad. In many countries the local or national taxes you pay on certain goods will be refunded to you at customs, as long as you fill out the proper forms, save your receipts, and document your purchases. Check with the tourist board, and for major purchases, double-check with the merchant you're dealing with.

Shop where locals shop. Sometimes items are sold to tourists that locals, who know better, would never touch. In an unfamiliar place it can be hard to spot a markup unless you shop where locals do. When buying edible souvenirs, like coffee, for example, go to grocery stores and see which brands of coffee locals really drink—and you'll get the lower price they'd pay.

Travel globally, buy locally. Be sure the items you want to purchase were made in your destination by carefully reading the tag or asking the salesperson. How sad will you be to discover the Moroccan slippers you've purchased in Marrakech were actually made in Taiwan?

When possible, pay with a credit card. It's easier to dispute charges, to be credited in the event that you must return an item, and to document any case of unfair business practices or consumer fraud, if you paid with a credit card. This is less important on minor purchases, and you may actually get a better price if you offer to pay cash on smaller items.

Know when to haggle. In some cultures you're expected to haggle over the price of goods, in other cultures it's an insult to offer anything less than the asking price. Sometimes it depends simply on what you're shopping for. Find out, by consulting a guidebook or even checking with your concierge or local tourism office, when and to what degree haggling is appropriate. And no matter how aggressive the seller is, always set a fixed price in your head and stick to it.

Make sure it's legal to bring your purchases home. Many countries ban the exportation of antiquities, products made from endangered species, and other items. And your home country may also ban the import of some products and impose a hefty duty on some others.

Consider shipping purchases home. Many merchants have special volume deals with certain shippers, and places that specialize in antiques, art, crafts, and other delicate items usually know best how to pack your goods carefully. Not having to lug around pottery or artwork can easily justify the shipping costs. And if the merchant in question doesn't usually ship items, ask for the name of a good shipping service.

SIGHTSEEING AT NIGHT

As soon as you get to town, find a coffeehouse. If you're keen on nightlife, theater, concerts, and other evening activities, the local coffeehouse is like a de facto resource center. Here you'll typically find local alternative newsweeklies with events and entertainment listings, and you're likely to see postings for upcoming shows. Furthermore, coffeehouses are often in arts or gallery districts, near college campuses, or in lively shopping areas. And they can be a great social alternative to bars.

Check the college scene for nightlife. Whether you're visiting a big city or a small town, if there's a college or university around, even a little one, find out what's happening on campus—either call, look for a college newspaper, or visit the school's Web site. Universities often have performing-arts venues that produce or host both local and sometimes professional plays and musical events. The commercial strips near college campuses often buzz with coffeehouses, bars, and eateries, too.

Look for half-price, same-day theater- and concert tickets. Many cities have booths or agencies that specialize in sell-ing concert and theater tickets to performances that day. If you're flexible and open-minded about what you may see that evening, these can be a bargain and a fun way to experience a performance you might never have thought you were interested in. You may end up paying half the ticket price (or less) for a top show.

Catch a matinee. Taking in a show or concert during the afternoon can be a nice change of pace, and it's an excel-lent way to see a performance if you're traveling with kids. Matinee shows are often less likely to be sold out, and are less pricey, too.

Drink downscale. If you're looking for the best or funki-est or offbeat happenings at night, ask around at smaller watering holes, as the people there are probably locals who know what's really hot.

Visit a bar or club on an "off" night. If you're a die-hard disco bunny, hitting a nightclub on the weekend might be your best bet. But if your goal is more to meet others, people-watch, and get a feel for the local vibe, you may end up having a better time on a weeknight. Monday and Tuesday tend to be quiet in most cities, but on Wednesday, Thursday, and sometimes Sunday, bars and clubs often have special theme nights and draw sizeable but manageable crowds.

Take your fashion cues from the queue. If you're interested in getting into the bar of the moment, pass by the night before you want to go and note how people in line are dressed. Or stop by a chic local boutique, ask advice, and buy appropriate (read: local) club wear. Once you achieve the right look—and anybody can with a little effort—expect your appearance to be scrutinized. Only those on the A-list escape this.

Don't let velvet ropes ruin your night. Is gaining admission so important that it's worth waiting an hour in line or subjecting yourself to the whims of the fashion police? If it is, then plan to arrive late enough to look cool but early enough so the line's not too long. Also plan to smile at the bouncers, conduct yourself with aplomb (whining or acting desperate will likely be met with dismal results), and possibly grease palms. A $20 subtly pressed into the hand of a bouncer might be just the thing that gets you on the other side of the velvet rope.

Look for free-admission and open-bar teasers. Many nightlife promoters try to fill their clubs up early by offering free admission or one- to two-hour open bars early in the evening—usually around 9 or 10 PM. This can be a good way to check out a place before having to commit to an exorbitant cover charge. You can often find out about these deals in local alternative newsweeklies and other nightlife-oriented papers.

STAYING SAFE

GENERAL SAFETY

Check in regularly with someone at home. Tell friends when they can expect your calls and give them a copy of your itinerary. And don't forget to call.

Take extra steps in destinations where safety is a concern. If you're traveling to a foreign destination that has recently suffered from political instability or civil strife or one that is prone to natural disasters, register online with the State Department (⊕ *travelregistration.state.gov/ibrs/*). Having your trip information on record will enable the State Department to readily locate and help you in the event of a crisis.

When traveling abroad, have emergency phone numbers at the ready. Program emergency numbers into your cell or jot them down in a small notebook. Be sure to include numbers for local police and/or ambulances as well as the nearest American consulate or embassy (⊕ *usembassy.state. gov/*). Although local officials are your best bet for immediate assistance, consular or embassy officials can help with things like replacing a passport or finding a local English-speaking lawyer or doctor. (Note that the State Department's emergency assistance numbers—888/407–4747 or 202/647–5225—only work at home, and are more useful to your loved ones gathering information on your behalf.)

In foreign destinations keep your passport with you. Many hotels ask for it upon check-in; however, all they may really need are foreigners' passport numbers and/or a copy of the passport document page. Make photocopies of your passport in advance for this purpose, and give another to your family at home (or scan the page and e-mail it to someone at home and/or yourself), and keep a third copy with you, separate from the original in case it gets lost or taken.

Be savvy about accessories. Don't wear earphones. It gives someone a chance to catch you with your guard down. Do wear sunglasses. The ability to stare someone down can go a long way toward making you less of a target. Waist packs signal to everyone that you're a tourist and, hence, more of a magnet for thieves. If you don't want to be taken for a rich American, use a day pack that's something a local would carry. Your fancy American backpack will stand out among, say, the handwoven bags and canvas totes of Central America.

Don't flash those funds. Waving your money around or blatantly fishing for it in a money belt that you're wearing lets everyone know you're a sitting duck, er, tourist. Access money only as needed and don't keep it all in one place. Put some money in your hotel safe, stash some "walking around" money in a wallet in your front left pocket (crooks tend to go for the right one), and put a little more in your bag or a money belt. (Women have the option of using a money pouch that hooks to bra straps and hangs down inside the front of a shirt.)

Be cautious in remote places. Some destinations contain open roads and beautiful scenery but few well-traveled places to stop and enjoy the view. You'll be tempted to stop and look while driving, which is dangerous. Always lock your doors, even in small towns where nothing seems likely to go wrong. And never leave your belongings in plain sight in the backseat.

SAFETY AT NIGHT

Always carry a local cab company's phone number. Whether you're headed to a bar or a show, always have a cab company's phone number handy. One of the best things about having a night on the town is potentially one of the worst: You never know quite what's going to happen. Be prepared in case your original transportation plans fall through—and make sure you have enough money with you for cab fare.

Alternate alcoholic drinks with nonalcoholic ones when out on the town. A lot of club goers end up consuming more booze than they'd intended simply because they drink quickly or feel most comfortable always having a drink in hand. If you're planning a big night out, you can go easier on your body and even save money by ordering one nonalcoholic drink, or even two or three, for every one that contains alcohol.

Don't accept drinks in bars from strangers. Unless you see the bartender make the drink, follow this simple, common-sense variation on the advice your parents probably gave you as a kid: Don't take candy from strangers. If you're in unfamiliar territory, around people you don't know, it's important to keep your wits. Scam artists and other ne'er-do-wells are often extremely charming.

SAFETY FOR WOMEN

Follow the women-and-children rule. If you see women around, especially women with children, you've less to worry about. This is critical at night. If all you see is men, men, men, high-heel it out of there.

Don't speak to creeps—in any language. If you're dealing with an unsavory guy who speaks English, don't say hello back. Shake your head or shrug your shoulders and say "No English." If he says "Speak Italian?" say "French, no." If he says "Speak French?" say "German, yes." However, do learn such key phrases as "Help" and "Get lost" in the language of the country you're visiting.

Make like you're hitched. Whether you're married or not, straight or not, consider wearing a wedding band. If a man bothers you, say you're meeting your husband soon, or pat your belly to indicate you're pregnant.

Consider going first class on trains. If you're nervous or simply want to relax, stick with first class, sit in a corner, and don't meet anyone's eye—keep your stuff on the seat next to you and scowl a lot.

Women should trail other women in bazaars. They don't even have to know. One Fodor's editor, tired of being stared at in Calcutta, walked closely behind a woman with kids, which quickly put an end to the stares. Another time she asked a middle-aged woman if she could walk with her. The lady graciously obliged, and even bought her an orange.

AVOIDING SCAMS

No matter how smart you are at home, you can be an easy mark for small-time scammers when traveling. Here are a few of the common tourist rip-offs, along with some tips on how to avoid canny connivers.

■ **Pickpockets:** Be wary if you're bumped or jostled in a crowd, if someone points out that you have something on your back, or if people in front of you drop to the sidewalk in a faint or approach you with a flower, a map, or a baby. While they're catching your attention, they're also getting into your pockets. If you're in a crowd, keep your hands on your valuables. Don't worry that it will alert thieves to your cash's location—they already know. But being hands-on with your belongings makes it clear that you'll notice if anyone tries to lift your cash.

■ **Taxis:** Most taxi scams revolve around overcharging. Check the meter when you first get into the cab to make sure it's at the zero rate, make sure the driver turns it on when you head off, and then watch to ensure that the meter total corresponds with the posted per-kilometer or per-minute rate. If you notice the meter is "broken," speak up right away and agree on a set fare to your destination, but remember to make this agreement before you're too far away from a place where you can easily grab another cab.

You also may encounter taxi drivers who insist that the place you want to go is closed due to some sudden calamity or is overpriced, filthy, or overbooked. But no worries, *he can bring you to some place far nicer and less expensive.* Just say no— chances are good that your driver is getting a commission from the place he's trying to take you to, and its prices will be inflated. If a driver tells you he wants to stop somewhere to call and confirm your hotel booking, tell him you did this at the airport.

■ **The Big Switch:** If you're buying a local specialty item—Oriental rug, jewelry, artwork—do your research and know what the item should cost and how to determine whether it's real or a fake. Then check your guidebook or the local tourist board for reputable dealers. The most commonly reported scams concern the sale of fake gemstones (Southeast Asia), antiques (the Middle East, particularly Egypt), and bogus designer products like handbags, leather coats, and scarves (in flea markets and sidewalk vendors everywhere, but particularly in big U.S. and European cites).

11

■ **Shipping Scams:** It's a good idea to ship heavy or fragile items home, except that sometimes the item sent to you isn't the one you paid for. Pay for all shipped goods with a credit card, and hang onto your receipts so you can file a claim with your card issuer if your purchases don't show up. Check your credit-card issuer's rules on filing claims; you may need to file within a specified time to get a chargeback. And take pictures of your purchase before leaving the store. If the shop owner knows you snapped photos, he or she will be less likely to ship you another item.

■ **Counterfeit Cops:** If police officers stop you on the street and ask to check your wallet for counterfeit bills or "drug money," ask them to take you to the police station where you'll be happy to let them do so. Tourists in South America and Mexico have reported being ripped off by bogus cops who palm a couple of bills while searching wallets.

■ **Altered ATMs:** Before inserting your card, check out an ATM to see if there's a thin piece of plastic hanging out of the slot that a thief could use to extract your card after the machine eats it. There have even been reports of ATMs with false fronts designed deliberately to collect cards. Use ATMs in banks and big hotels, where it's unlikely that a thief can modify the machine. Be cautious everywhere when using an ATM, but especially in the Caribbean, South America, and Mexico.

■ **Sacred Scams:** At some temples and religious festivals people may offer to perform a ritual for you and then demand a sizeable donation. Be prepared to donate some money when you visit such sites, but don't be intimidated to ask "how much?" before agreeing to participate in any ritual or blessing.

■ **Money for Nothing:** Internet forums are full of the sad tales of travelers to Southeast Asia who agreed to bring gemstones to someone's business partner in the States for a cut of the profits, and left a deposit with the stone's owner as a goodwill gesture. The stones turn out to be cut glass, and the travelers are out their good-faith money. This scam is played out in Africa and the Middle East and occasionally in Europe with local crafts and other items.

WORD OF MOUTH. **You are less likely to attract attention if you have another female companion, and even less likely if you have a male to vouch for you. I think the most protection is offered by a companion who is obviously a local (male or female)." —Femi**

Sit next to older women or a couple. To avoid unwanted propositions, put yourself "in the orbit" of an older woman or a couple. Their presence may help deter sleazy offers and comments.

Use high- and low-tech protection. A cell phone can be invaluable for calling—or threatening to call—the police. But a whistle can be just as effective at warding off trouble.

SPORTS AND THE OUTDOORS

Research your sports interests in advance. Whether you want to use a health club or play a round of golf, call ahead and ask about any deals such as reduced fees for certain days or times of day. You may save a bundle.

Rent sports gear rather than carrying your own. If you're an avid golfer or skier, the idea of renting equipment may simply be beyond comprehension. But at least consider renting—sports gear is readily available at many golf, ski, and other sports venues, and equipment is often reasonably priced and in very good condition. It can even be a chance to test a brand or type of equipment you've always wanted to try. Then you will enjoy the freedom of not having to haul a giant golf or ski bag with you through airports, on shuttle buses, and in taxis.

Hire an expert to guide your outdoor activities. Are you an avid fly-fishing enthusiast who's visiting a place for the first time? Have you always wanted to hike a particular national park but know nothing about local trails? You might be surprised how inexpensive it is to hire a guide, especially if there are several people in your party. Guides can usually help you to custom-design your itinerary, and they can be available for as little as a few hours or for as long as several days. Their expertise in a given field may end up saving you time and frustration—just be certain to find someone with excellent credentials in the activity you're planning to pursue.

In busy national parks, bypass the busiest areas midday. Take this time to explore the park's more peaceful areas.

Don't rule out 18 holes at a private golf course. Many of the world's top courses are closed to all but members and their guests, but depending on when you hope to play and how you couch your request, you might be fortunate enough to gain entry to what's normally an off-limits club. Many private clubs allow members of other private clubs to visit, and others will honor guests of certain hotels or passengers of certain cruise ships. Also some companies (yours?) have corporate affiliations. Avoid being heavy-handed or pulling rank—just ask politely, and try asking whether you can play on a Monday or during the late afternoon on another weekday, when courses are least busy.

Visit a farm. Agricultural tourism is a rapidly growing industry, and visits to farms can be great fun for kids and adults. Many farms invite customers to pick their own produce, cut down their own Christmas tree, or enjoy fresh food made with locally grown or produced ingredients (from ice cream to apple cider). Hayrides and petting zoos are other popular activities. In addition to checking with tourist boards for names of farms open to the public, also consult the department of the environment or agriculture wherever you're visiting.

Catch a minor-league game. You might think of attending a football, baseball, basketball, or other game only when visiting a big city with a major-league team, but hundreds of smaller municipalities across North America offer lively minor-league games. Tickets are cheaper, stadiums are often more intimate, and many minor-league clubs throw fun or outlandish promotions, such as concerts and giveaways. Minor-league players are generally friendlier and more approachable than their big-league counterparts, and you might just catch a glimpse of the next superstar while he's still working his way through the farm system.

HEALTHY ACTIVITY

Don't skimp on scuba-diving training. Resorts often offer guests introductory scuba instruction in a pool, followed by a shallow dive; some hotels have on-site dive shops. All shops or resorts should offer instruction and certification according to the standards set by either the National Association of Underwater Instructors (NAUI) or the Professional Association of Diving Instructors (PADI). Prices will vary from place to place, but the quality of a program should not.

Don't fly within 24 hours after scuba diving. Find out where the closest decompression chambers are ahead of time, just in case.

Don't swim alone in unfamiliar waters. Similarly, never swim too far offshore; most beaches, except for the big, public U.S. ones, have no lifeguards.

Anticipate getting seasick. Look out at the horizon, take Dramamine, or use pulse-point bracelets, which some travelers swear by.

Climb carefully. Altitude mountain sickness—which causes shortness of breath, nausea, and splitting headaches—may be a problem when you visit Andean, Himalayan, and other high-altitude countries. The best way to prevent it is to ascend slowly. Spend a few nights at 6,000 feet–9,000 feet before you head higher. If you must fly straight in, plan on doing next to nothing for your first few days. If you begin to feel ill, local traditional remedies are a good way to go—in Chile, for example, there's an herbal tea made from coca leaves. Over-the-counter analgesics and napping also help. If symptoms persist, return to lower elevations. Note that if you have high blood pressure and/or a history of heart trouble, check with your doctor before traveling to the mountains.

In warm weather wear a hat, long but lightweight clothing, and sunscreen. These really do help your body to cope with high temperatures. Choose a hat with a broad brim, and wear loose, lightweight, and light-color clothing. Don't assume that shorts and sleeveless shirts are the way to go—take a look at what the locals are wearing. It's likely they're wearing long pants or skirts and long-sleeve shirts to protect themselves from the sun. Whatever you wear, slather all exposed skin with a good high-number sunscreen—a sunburn will hamper your skin's ability to perspire and keep you cool.

Avoid becoming overheated or dehydrated. To avoid losing too much water and salts from excessive perspiration, allow your body to get used to hot weather slowly by gradually boosting the amount of time you spend in the hot outdoors each day and planning outdoor activities and tours in the morning or evening when it's not so hot. Don't rely on thirst to tell you when to drink; people often don't feel thirsty until they're a little dehydrated. If you're exerting yourself, drink about a quart an hour. Also, refrain from drinking alcoholic beverages, which cause you to lose more fluid.

Know the telltale signs of dehydration. These include crying without tears, a dry tongue or mouth, no pooling of saliva under the tongue, sunken eyes, no sweat under the armpits during a fever, dizziness, lightheadedness, or headaches. Especially look out for signs of dehydration in children—vomiting and diarrhea can quickly reduce their body fluids to dangerously low levels.

Avoid heat cramps. Heat cramps stem from a low salt level due to excessive sweating. These muscle pains usually occur in the abdomen, arms, or legs. When children say they can't take another step, determine whether they have cramps—sometimes they really mean it. If you have heart problems or are on a low-sodium diet, get medical attention for heat cramps. Otherwise, stop all activity, and sit quietly in a cool place and drink clear juice or a sports beverage. Then don't do anything strenuous for a few hours after the cramps subside. See a doctor if heat cramps persist more than an hour.

Watch out for heat exhaustion. Your body's response to an excessive loss of both water and salt is to emit warning signs, which may include heavy sweating, pallor, muscle cramps, tiredness, weakness, dizziness, headache, nausea or vomiting, fainting, fast and shallow breathing, and a fast and weak pulse. Heat exhaustion can progress to heat stroke, which can be deadly. Seek medical attention immediately if your symptoms are severe or last longer than an hour, or if you have heart problems or high blood pressure. In the meantime, be sure to rest, drink cool fluids, and, if possible, take a cold shower or recover in an air-conditioned site.

Watch out for heat stroke. Heat stroke occurs when all your body's means of coping with heat shut down, allowing your body temperature to quickly soar. Heat stroke can kill or cause permanent disability if not dealt with immediately; watch for signs of heat stroke in yourself and your companions. These may include high body temperature (above 103°F or 39°C); red, hot, and dry skin (no sweating); rapid, strong pulse; throbbing headache; uncontrollable muscle twitches; dizziness; nausea; confusion; and unconsciousness. These signs warrant immediate emergency medical attention. Until such medical care arrives, cool the victim rapidly with shade, cold water from a hose, a fan, ice cubes, or air-conditioning. Give fluids to the conscious victim, and prevent choking during vomiting by turning the victim on his or her side.

Know the myths and facts of hypothermia. A potentially fatal decrease in body temperature can occur even in relatively mild weather. Symptoms are chilliness and fatigue, followed by shivering and mental confusion. The minute these signs are spotted, get the victim to shelter of some kind and wrap him or her in warm blankets or a sleeping bag. Ideally, another member of the party should climb into the sleeping bag, too. If practical, it's best for both people to be unclothed, but if clothing remains on, it must be dry. High-energy food and hot drinks also aid recovery. Always carry warm, dry clothing, avoid immersion or exposure to cold water or rain, and keep energy levels up by eating high-calorie foods like trail mix.

Avoid frostbite. Frostbite is caused by exposure to extreme cold for a prolonged period of time. Symptoms include the numbing of ears, nose, fingers, or toes; white or grayish-yellow skin is a sure sign. Frostbite victims should be taken into a warm place as soon as possible, and wet clothing should be removed. The affected area should then be immersed in warm—not hot—water or wrapped in a warm blanket. Do not rub the frostbitten area, as this may cause permanent damage to the tissues. When the area begins to thaw, the victim should exercise the area, to stimulate blood circulation. If bleeding or other complications develop, get to a doctor as soon as possible.

Ask about which animals are threats in your destination. Some animals, especially rodents, carry dangerous diseases. If you are bitten by a wild animal, it's important to see a doctor as soon as possible. Many animal bites require a tetanus shot and, if the animal could be rabid, a rabies shot. In other places, wildcats, bears, or monkeys can cause serious property and personal damage. Take all warnings seriously, including two big ones. Don't feed wild animals (they can confuse you for the food or become less able to fend for themselves), and use bear boxes where they're provided.

Know how to avoid and treat snakebites. Snakes will do everything to avoid you, but in the event you have a run-in and are bitten, act quickly. If it's a harmless snake, ordinary first aid for puncture wounds should be given. If the snake is poisonous, remain as still as possible so as not to spread the venom through the body; lie down, keeping the wound area below the rest of the body, and have another person seek medical help immediately. The Brazos River Rattlesnake Ranch offers step-by-step emergency instructions at ⊕ *www.wf.net/~snake/firstaid.htm.*

Take care in deer-infested areas. Lyme disease is a potentially debilitating illness caused by a virus carried by deer ticks, which thrive in dry, brush-covered areas. When walking in woods, brush, or through fields in areas where ticks may be found, wear tick repellent and long pants tucked into socks. When you undress, search your body for deer ticks—which are no bigger than a pencil point—and remove them with tweezers and rubbing alcohol. If you find a tick, save it if possible and watch the area for several weeks. Some people develop a bull's-eye-like rash or flulike symptoms; if this happens, see your physician immediately. Lyme disease can be treated with antibiotics if caught early enough. If you are traveling with pets, be sure to check them as well: people have been known to catch the disease by coming into contact with ticks from pets.

Familiarize yourself with poisonous plants. Knowing how to recognize poisonous plants is half the battle. In new places, ask about which plants to avoid and never eat unfamiliar berries or leaves unless a local guide can confirm they're safe. If you touch poisonous plants (poison ivy, poison oak, or poison sumac), wash the area immediately with soap and water. A variety of ointments, such as calamine lotion and cortisone cream, may relieve itching. The American Academy of Dermatologists (⊕ *www.aad.org*) has produced a pamphlet (under the public tab, click on conditions/diseases, then pamphlets) that includes pictures of said plants, gruesome photos of plant-poison sufferers, and prevention and treatment tips.

Eating Out

WORD OF MOUTH

"In most cases, calling ahead by a few hours is more than enough time to reserve a table. And it lets me relax, knowing I'm not going to waste my time, calories, and money on the luck of the draw. If there's someplace I *really* want to go, I reserve a couple of days ahead."

—shellio

"We (a group of 6) went to Italy for 10 days . . . [We looked] down the smaller streets for business looking people and went where they were going for lunch."

—pantelia

Updated by Alexis Kelly

Through the simple act of eating a meal on a trip, you're actually participating in the cultural landscape of a place. Ingredients, flavor combinations, and cooking methods are essential elements: Particular dishes and preparation techniques, like spices, tell us something about who settled there—or who tried and failed—and who lives there now.

12

Eating on vacation is part of the adventure—at times delicious, exhilarating, and challenging. Sometimes those tactile, sensory memories of eating pad thai noodles from a street cart in Thailand or enjoying an eight-course meal in Paris are the most engaging of all. "I can almost taste it," you may find yourself saying years later.

Here we've provided tips to help you navigate the fascinating world of food and restaurants. We hope it helps you eat your way around the world. *Bon appétit.*

SAVING MONEY ON FOOD

Eat at the counter. Note that in cafés, bars, and some restaurants in certain parts of the world (Paris, for example), it's less expensive to eat or drink standing at the counter than it is to sit at a table. Some other destinations honor this practice, too.

Get a cheap meal at happy hour. You might be surprised just how much free food is out there. Not only do bars frequently offer great drinks discounts at happy hour, they sometimes set up hors-d'oeuvres buffets, dole out pizza and sandwiches, and pass around big bowls of nuts and snacks.

Don't pay for an expensive hotel breakfast. Of course, if it's included, by all means, indulge. However, hotel restaurants can be expensive and mediocre; ask the concierge or staff about the neighborhood's bagel shops, cafés, and coffee places.

Check out the local supermarket. That's especially advisable if you're staying put for a while or have a hotel room with kitchenette. You'll get better prices here than at hotel shops, and you'll get a good look at cultural habits by seeing what the locals purchase.

WORD OF MOUTH. "I always seek out department stores in Europe for two things: the basement deli/groceries and cheap souvenirs. I've never experienced bad take out from a department store." —jahlie

Have a picnic. The proliferation of inviting prepared-food shops, chichi delis, boulangeries, and the like mean that you can cobble together a veritable feast without forking over a tip. Find a special sanctuary—a bench overlooking a canal, a low stone wall in a park, a shady and grassy spot under blossoming trees—and bring your Leatherman or other multipurpose slicing-and-bottle-opening tool.

Don't assume you can use your credit card at restaurants. Some countries don't have the phone lines required to run a credit-card processing machine or prefer not to wait for reimbursement from credit-card companies—although invariably some of the top-notch places or hotel restaurants do. If you must use credit, call ahead or have your hotel investigate on your behalf which restaurants take cards.

Plan a whole day around sampling food. Rather than having an entire meal at any one restaurant, move around and snack. The idea isn't to get uncomfortably full, but to expose yourself to different kinds of restaurants, gourmet shops, markets, and even snack stands. For obvious reasons, you might want to incorporate a bit of walking into this plan. You should also try doing this on a weekday, as restaurants are less crowded and more willing to let you drop in for just an appetizer or dessert.

Ask about special dinner prices. If you can be flexible about when you dine, you can take advantage of early-bird specials or pre- or post-theater special menus.

Don't treat roadside food everywhere with scorn. There are definitely some places where you should avoid it entirely and other places where it's perfectly fine. Just make sure you've done some basic research, read your travel guide, and know the difference.

HOW TO BE A SAVVY DINER

Do your foodie research. Plan to take in a really good restaurant or two. A trip is a time to kick back and savor the pleasures of the palate. Read up on the culinary scene before you leave home. If you have a business colleague based in your travel destination or friends who just returned from a trip there themselves, ask them for their firsthand advice on where to go and where not to go. It's always a good idea to consult a travel guide for recommendations. Note that some local publications may have "pay-to-play" reviews based on advertising. It's better to consult an independent source.

Investigate whether your destination is vegetarian-friendly.
Vegetarians traveling to Vietnam will find it easy to a good meal, as the country's largely Buddhist, a religion that shuns eating living things. On the other hand, some countries have yet to really figure out what counts as vegetarian. On a trip to Peru, a veggie traveler tried to content herself with rice and salsa (even the beans had lard), but grew frustrated, and asked for a vegetarian *sopa* (soup). While the broth may have derived solely from veggies, floating within the bowl was a solitary chicken foot.

Make restaurant reservations. Plan ahead if you're determined to snag a table at a sought-after restaurant. Some renowned eateries are booked weeks or months in advance. But you can get lucky at the last minute if you're flexible—and friendly. Most exclusive restaurants keep a few tables open for walk-ins and VIPs. Show up for dinner early or late, and politely inquire about any last-minute vacancies or cancellations. If you're calling a few days ahead of time, ask if you can be put on a waiting list. Occasionally, a restaurant may ask you to call the day before your scheduled meal to reconfirm: Don't forget or you could lose out.

Let the concierge know what you want in a restaurant. You get what you ask for. Make sure he or she understands whether you want to dine with other visitors or seek a place with plenty of locals. If you want to experiment with cuisine, make that clear, too.

WORD OF MOUTH. **"I think that tapas are the perfect food for picky eaters. There's loads to choose from—just pick and eat what you fancy and ignore what you don't like! And it's easy to try new things without having to order/eat a whole plateful." —hanl**

Try what other diners are eating. Kindly ask the diners at an adjacent table what they're eating or, lacking language skills, carefully point to the meals of others while politely nodding, so your food server can effectively interpret.

Dine with the locals. This might not be such a big surprise, but many destinations, even in big cities where there are lots of choices, have tourist traps where the food is mediocre (or worse) and the prices are unreasonably high. There's a reason New Yorkers don't usually eat in Times Square, for example. You'll almost always have a better meal—and at a price that's right—when you eat where the locals do. If you can't land a local newspaper or travel guide, ask the hotel staff where they'd go for a special meal, or seafood, or a cheap meal, or the like.

Eat at the bar. It's a more casual and relaxed way to enjoy a high-end or even moderately priced restaurant; you can chat with the bartender to learn more about the restaurant, the local dining scene, or other local topics, and also with your fellow diners, who may be interesting people or have good tips on what's going on in the area; and you can generally show up without reservations and get a seat fairly quickly. The only downside to bar dining is that smoking may be permitted. If that matters to you, find out the policy before you sit down.

To get good food service, be nice. "It's nice to be nice," and no one appreciates it more than a food server, who will easily distinguish you from the bossy, finicky, overly entitled diners filling up the restaurant. A simple "How are you?" or willingness to ask questions (not too many!) about a dish before it's served can help predispose your server to act friendly and eliminate disappointments with your food choice.

Don't suffer bad restaurant service in silence. If you feel you've gotten poor service, don't keep quiet and then slink out without leaving a tip. Talk with the server—politely—about the problem. Keep in mind that delays in service may not be the server's fault: Maybe the kitchen is backed up. However, if the issue isn't addressed to your satisfaction, speak with the manager. But be polite. If, in the end, you decide not to leave a tip, the server should know why.

Know what local reviewers say about a place. Unless you're traveling way off the beaten path, many restaurants in any given city are written up in guidebooks, newspapers, and magazines. Short of dining with a local who knows the ropes, these can be essential for finding a place to eat in a country where the language is unfamiliar and the cuisine mystifying.

WORD OF MOUTH. "Now a day's sites like Restaurants.com, Boorah.com, and Yelp.com and their reviews have become very popular. They are really useful and provide ideal dining experience." —emilyjhon

Speak up if something's wrong with your food. If something is incredibly, and inedibly, salty or burned or has meat in it and you're a vegetarian, politely let your server know. The server wants you to be happy, because you're the primary source of his or her income, and may offer another meal in its place or perhaps a free dessert as a gesture of good will.

ORDERING

12

Get a traveler's picture dictionary. Sold in many travel stores, these laminated books more resemble children's primers than tools for traveling adults. But before you make fun, consider it's a sound way to communicate without learning to read a tough language like, say, Tamil. (One such book is Dieter Graf Verlag's *Point It*, sold for about $10 at Flight 001 in New York; ⊕*www.flight001.com.*) You simply flip to one of the many pages dedicated to food items, politely get your food server's attention, and point.

WORD OF MOUTH. **"I'm allergic to mushrooms, and though I have never bothered in all my previous travels (feeling that I could always work it out), one time I took cards that I ordered over the Internet (www.selectwisely.com). The cards simply asked if the dish contained mushrooms, and said that I was allergic to mushrooms. I had one for each language." —shandy**

Ask for help deciding what to eat. Ask, "If I could only eat here once in my life, what should I order?" Food servers will usually have lots of great advice when you put it to them that way. (Although you could simply ask what's popular, you might not approve of the local clientele's selection.)

Sample the cuisine your destination is known for. Or, if you're a serious food lover and know what to expect, find out what chefs are locally famous. A terrific way to learn about a place is to eat there.

Beware of "American" food. Some places do a poor imitation of pretty basic American dishes. Don't blame them: Local ingredients and cooking styles don't often lend themselves to creating an exact replica of, say, a thick, juicy hamburger.

EATING LIKE A LOCAL

Don't eat with your left hand. In many countries this is offensive, as is using it to pass food. Always observe local manners and taboos. Is yours a destination where no implements or napkins are used, but a sink is nearby (southern India)? Where pointing or piercing food with chopsticks is downright rude (Japan)? Or perhaps you're going to Bangkok, where the fork is not raised to the mouth but rather held in the left hand and used to push food to the center, where it is scooped up with the spoon and eaten. Make it your business to know the eating customs before you go—or enlist someone to teach you when you arrive.

Know when to eat. Many restaurants close between lunch and dinner, either to prepare for the next shift or for traditional reasons, like observing a siesta. In addition to off hours, be aware that both breakfast and dinner might start earlier or later than you're used to at home. If you don't know the hours and customs of the place you're going, you may find yourself cranky and hungry while waiting for mealtime to roll around again. That said, if you eat early or late you may be able to take advantage of a prix-fixe deal not offered at peak hours. Most upscale restaurants offer great lunch deals with special menus at cut-rate prices designed to give customers a true taste of the place.

Know what to wear when dining out. As unfair as it seems, the way you look can influence how you're treated—and where you're seated in a restaurant. In major cities jeans or khakis and a button-down shirt will suffice at most inexpensive to mid-priced table-service restaurants. Moving up from there, many pricier restaurants require jackets, and some insist on ties. Elsewhere, in tropical destinations, casual dress is permitted at all but the most formal restaurants. When packing, it's generally a good idea to bring at least one "dress-up" outfit.

Watch for restaurants' hidden charges. If you're watching your budget, be sure to ask the price of daily specials recited by the waiter or captain. The charge for specials at some restaurants is noticeably out of line with the other prices on the menu. Beware of the $10 bottle of water; ask for tap water instead. And always review your bill. Note that some restaurants offer freebies: in a Mexican restaurant in most U.S. cities the first basket of chips and salsa often comes without charge. In upscale French restaurants, the chef may send out a complimentary *amuse bouche* (a small treat from the kitchen; literally a "mouth teaser") before or between courses. But in Portugal and Brazil the lavish dishes of cheese, olives, spreads, and bread put before you are not free.

Make lunch your big meal. In many countries, from Egypt to Costa Rica, lunch is the main meal of the day, when a larger array of entrée options is proffered and portions are big. Although some restaurants will cater to American customs, smaller places may not.

Don't enforce strict diet plans on vacation. How will you truly know that New Zealand is the land of "milk and honey" if you eat just celery sticks? Let yourself have a scoop of the nation's world-renowned Hokey Pokey ice cream and just plan to have a good walk home and a light dinner later.

12

Eat internationally. Many cities have an international district where you eat your way across the world without having to travel there. London is renowned for its Indian and Pakistani cuisine, for example, while San Francisco has a major concentration of Asian restaurants in Chinatown and throughout the city. Typically, these ethnic eating experiences are budget-friendly.

Know how to tip. Servers in some countries expect a tip from Westerners but not from locals. Others expect a bit of change left over from the bill. In China a tip of 3% of the bill is fine; in New York City food servers expect 20%. In Miami the tip might already be added to your bill. To keep up with the rules, consult your travel guide.

Hotel Stays

WORD OF MOUTH

"If we're traveling with our son, we look for large rooms, a pool, and a kitchenette. If it's just me and my husband, we want over-the-top gorgeous (if we can find it) and a really comfy bed."

—Devonmcj

"I faxed the hotel concierge with my restaurant requests and dates . . . and the concierge made all the arrangements. I got a fax back with all the details signed by the concierge. When I arrived at the hotel, I . . . thanked him for his help, and gave him an appropriate tip."

—A_Traveller

Updated by Alexis Kelly

According to industry analysts, the average traveler's largest single expense is lodging. But although many travelers spend hours seeking the best possible airfare, some spend comparatively little time researching their lodging options. To make things easier, we've broken down the process of selecting a hotel—and having a good stay—into a few simple steps. Three basic things to remember: shop around, ask questions, and document your complaints if the lodging you choose doesn't live up to its guarantees.

13

CHOOSING A HOTEL

Prioritize your lodging needs. Focus on hotels that will best meet your needs. Amenities, location, and price all come into play in making a determination, but do you care about a spa you won't use, a pool when it's the beach you're after, or that the clientele is all under 25? Do you want anonymity or the coziness of a small B&B? Luxury or rustic simplicity? A splurge or a super-saver? Look at photos online, ask around for recommendations, check user reviews at Fodors.com or call the hotel and ask them to explain what they have to offer and who or what age their regular customers are.

Know what facilities are included in the hotel price. Bathroom facilities in B&Bs and in hotels in France determine price. In France, state your preference for shower (*douche*) or tub (*baignoire*)—the latter always costs more. If you want a double bed, you should request one (*lit matrimoniale* in France); in many places twin beds are still common. If you're counting on air-conditioning or an in-room safe, ask whether there's a surcharge. Staying in a remote jungle lodge? A Japanese *ryokan*? It might be tough to know what to expect, and your assumptions may be way off. For exotic and unique properties, it's even more important to call the property or do a little research if you don't like surprises.

WORD OF MOUTH. **"If you're staying in a Portuguese hotel you will almost certainly have breakfast, including coffee, included in your room rate. (I can't think of a place in Portugal where it wasn't.)" —thursdaysd**

Ask whether there's a restaurant or room service. Many lodgings offer room service, but not necessarily 24 hours a day. Moderately priced business-oriented hotels often keep menus of local restaurants that will deliver to your room.

Expect to forego some basics at budget hotels. Most hotels have in-room phones, for example, but double-check this at inexpensive properties, especially if you are traveling outside the United States. The same goes for TVs and air-conditioning. Most hotels and motels have in-room TVs, often with cable, in the United States, but the terms change when outside North America. International chain hotels tend to be the most predictable in terms of what in-room amenities you can expect.

Find out about hotels' fitness amenities. If you care about specific features in a gym, speak up and ask what you can expect. It could be anything from a room with a single treadmill to a fully stocked gym with exercise classes. Don't forget to ask about the hours, too.

ON THE WAY TO YOUR HOTEL

Before you go, reconfirm the room rate. If you have a hotel reservation and you suspect business might be a little slow, call the front desk directly—not the 800 number—just before you arrive and ask what the best rate is for the evening. In many cases, if it's late and the hotel is not full, you will be quoted a better rate than the one you got when you made the reservation—hotel managers are fully aware that an empty room generates no revenue. If the rate is not better, simply show up with your reservation as planned. However, if you have guaranteed reservations—the kind that charge your card even if you don't show up—this trick won't fly.

Make sure you're listed in the hotel's computer. If you haven't booked the room yourself or with the hotel directly, there is room for error. Double-check that your reservation has been honored before you leave home, and if your hotel engages in the practice of double-booking, they'll know you intend to honor your reservation.

Find out when your room will be available. It might make more sense to head from the airport to a restaurant for lunch if your plane gets in at 11 AM and you can't check in until 2.

Call if you're going to arrive at your hotel late. If your reservation is for a certain hour, alert the hotel if you will be arriving later—even if it's only 15 minutes later. Hotel managers are under pressure to keep occupancy rates high, so unless they know for sure you're arriving, they may give your room to someone else.

Bring your hotel confirmation information. Show it to the staff person when checking in. This is particularly important if you've booked online or through a third party, or are traveling as part of a tour package.

Don't head for the wrong hotel. This may sound obvious, but in larger cities where chains have multiple properties you need to know whether you're heading to the Heavenly Hotels Downtown, the Heavenly Hotels Seaport, or the Seaside Heavenly Hotels Resort and Conference Center. Keep both the name and address handy, and ask about nearby landmarks when booking.

Let your hotel know if you're expecting phone calls. If you've left the kids with Grandma or are traveling for business and it's important that you can be reached at your hotel while you're en route, let the staff know ahead of time. Calls may not be waiting for you when you arrive otherwise. Similarly, late arrivals are often handled by night auditors who give you your key and leave the paperwork for the morning desk clerk; make sure he or she adds your name to the hotel's guest roster—particularly if you're expecting an early morning call.

AT THE HOTEL

Give up a copy of your passport to your hotel—not the original. The policy of leaving your passport with the desk is now somewhat moot—in-room safes mean travelers can store them there, and all a hotel really needs for their protection is to see your passport and copy down the passport number. It's best not to be separated from your identification—this has become even more important in our post-9/11 world. Bring along a few extra copies of your passport information page and hand over those instead.

Ask to leave your bags if your room isn't ready. You can start your vacation right away. Go grab something to eat, tour a museum, or head to the hotel pool or beach.

Request a late checkout, if there's no extra charge. As a courtesy, most hotels will grant you an extra hour or two to leave your room, especially if it isn't booked for the upcoming evening. But you must call the front desk in advance and request a late checkout. If not, you'll likely be billed

WORD OF MOUTH: BREWS TO GO

"I pack a little French press and my own coffee. Hot water is almost always available but American coffee is rare." —kilikavc

"I would go with a cup, immersion coil, and instant coffee packets (Starbucks or Medaglia D'oro are both pretty good)." —suze

"I decided that the kettle and a drip cone would be more versatile, and no cleaning up. [I can] boil eggs in the kettle. I can also do tea, instant noodles, and instant oatmeal. I think I will spend the next few trips to the grocery store to see what else can be reconstituted with boiling/hot water. It's a whole new world for my budget travel side." —spcfa

"Taster's Choice has individual packets of instant coffee that are very convenient. You don't have to take along a jar of instant coffee; with the individual packets/tubes you gain space as you use them." —bratsandbeer

"I have a hot stick which is fine. Works great, fast, no mess, and nothing to clean up. Takes less space in the suitcase also." —Jedmo68631

"Instead of using "instant," I buy single serving Folgers coffee bags. They look like tea bags, but are actually brewed coffee. I also bring along a few packs of hot cocoa. Sometimes I just want to sit back and relax before or after a long day with a cup of coffee or hot chocolate. If my apartment has a terrace, it makes all the difference in the world." —daveesl

for additional hours or an entire day. If late checkout isn't available and you don't want to deal with your bags, ask to leave your bags with the bellhop.

WORD OF MOUTH. "In hotels, place the tip on the pillow when you leave each morning, so there's no confusion about what its for. Sometimes there's a little envelope with the maid's name on it. For luggage handlers, deftly slip folded bill(s) to the guy (sort of like a handshake) when you receive your bags." —capxxx

Leave a fair tip. Give inn staffers and porters $1 per bag carried to your room, and leave about $2–$5 per night of your stay for maid service—more if extra service, like shoe shines, warrants it.

IN YOUR ROOM

Toss off that bedspread. Many hotels still use fancy patterned bedspreads that can't take the wear-and-tear of regular washing, so it may not have seen the inside of a washer for awhile. Consider casting the spread off the bed and into a closet—you never know who used the room before you. If you're concerned about sanitization, you also may want to wash out the water glasses in the bathroom with hot water, and use sanitizing wipes to disinfect the remote control and phone.

See if everything in your room is working. Upon arriving, check lights and lamps, TV and radio, sink, tub, shower, and anything else that matters. Report any problems immediately. Also, check out the fire emergency instructions. Know where to find the fire exits, and make sure your companions do, too.

Make sure your hotel room has everything you need. If you're going to need extra pillows or blankets or an ironing board, call housekeeping right away so the items will be there when you want to use them.

Go easy on the unpacking. If you will be staying in a hotel room for only one night, put anything you take out of your suitcase in one place or into a single drawer. That way you won't have to go looking through closets and under beds to make sure you didn't leave anything.

Use on-site safes smartly. Don't leave anything of value out in the room. Either lock things in the room safe or, for particularly valuable items, in the hotel safe. Be sure to itemize the objects you're asking the hotel to store in its safe and have a staff person sign the itemized list.

Sleep more soundly away from home. Raucous Las Vegas partying keeping you up at night in your hotel? Pack a small transistor radio and turn the dial to one of the channels that only beams "static"—white noise that sounds like an air-conditioner. Play this at sufficient volume and the noisy world outside your window will disappear. Or, just wear earplugs.

Let the hotel know if your neighbors are noisy. Some amount of noise is par for the course, but if it continues into the wee hours, let the hotel know and have them correct the problem. One way of convincing a hotel to take immediate action is to imply that there might be some destruction of property going on.

USING THE CONCIERGE

■ **Help your concierge help you.** When asking for help, focus on what you like. Avoid unhelpful statements such as "Where should I eat? I don't like fish, I don't like steak, and I don't like Chinese." You'll get better results by revealing your preferences, as in, "I love candlelit French bistros, but tonight I feel like something livelier, more casual, maybe Italian." Also, nothing drives a concierge crazier than a guest asking, "I'm in town for two weeks, and I've never been here before. What should I do?" Pick up a Fodor's guide, and do a little homework.

■ **Keep expectations realistic.** At a typical tourist-class hotel you can expect a concierge to give you the basics: to show you something on a map, make a standard restaurant reservation, or help you book a tour or airport transportation. In Asia concierges perform the vital service of writing out the name or address of your destination for you to give to a cab driver. It's not uncommon for restaurants to ply concierges with free food and drink in exchange for steering diners their way; European concierges often receive referral *fees*. Hotel chains usually have guidelines about what their concierges can accept. The best concierges, however, are above reproach.

■ **Leave time for your request to be fulfilled.** Don't expect to breeze by the desk with a laundry list of requests and get immediate attention. Concierges are busiest in the morning at checkout time, when business travelers need the most assistance, and in the late afternoon and early evening at check-in time, when guests want dinner reservations. The ideal time to chitchat is usually between noon and 4 PM and 8 PM and 10 PM. If you have a complicated request, leave your cell-phone number, or ask that a message be left in your room.

■ **Know how to tip.** For the best service, give half the money up front, then the other half once your request has been fulfilled. If the staff knows you're a good tipper, they'll work extra hard to ensure you get what you want, when you want it. Base the amount of your tip on the time spent arranging your request. For simple matters that require only one phone call, such as an airport shuttle, tip $2. For restaurant recommendations and reservations that require discussion and opinion, $5 to $20, the latter for harder-to-book tables. For itinerary planning, tip $20 to $100, depending on how complicated it is.

COMPLAINTS

Know how to handle hotels' overbooking. Hotel managers routinely deal with problems associated with "oversales," the industry term for booking more reservations than there are rooms. Even the best hotels engage in the practice, because a consistent percentage of all reservations are either canceled or result in no-shows. Often the hotel will have a nearby "sister" property or an arrangement with another chain or hotel to honor overbooked reservations. If this is the case, you can usually get an upgrade to a larger room or suite at the substitute property for no extra charge. If the room is the same or inferior to the one you have reserved, demand a rate reduction for your inconvenience and ask when a room at the hotel you originally chose will become available.

If there's a problem with your room, deal with someone in authority. Try to settle your dispute with the front-desk personnel, but if you're still not satisfied, ask to speak to the general manager. Keep in mind that it's the job of the front-desk staff to solve problems without involving the general manager. Use this knowledge to your advantage in disputes over small matters. If your problem is a big one, though, cut to the chase and demand an audience with a person in authority.

In a dispute with a hotel, pretend you're already in court. Write down the names of everyone you speak with, when you spoke with them, and what he or she said. If you have a camera, take photos relevant to your complaint. This information is handy for presenting to corporate public-relations personnel, who are very sensitive to these occurrences, and are often quick to compensate unhappy guests—sometimes quite generously—for their troubles.

Ask for an adjustment or complete refund. If hotel personnel are unable to deliver what you were promised, ask for an adjustment—a lower rate, for example, if you've gotten a lesser room than the one you were promised. If you received a confirmation notice and brought it with you, your claims will be all the more convincing.

Be specific, focused, and fair when resolving problems with hotels. Regardless of the problem, be very specific about how you would like to see the situation resolved, but be fair: If noisy neighbors kept you awake one night of your two-night stay, don't demand a refund for both nights.

EFFECTIVE COMPLAINING

Things don't always go right when you're traveling, and when you encounter a problem or service that isn't up to snuff, you should complain. But there are good and bad ways to do so.

■ Take a deep breath. This is always a good strategy, especially when you are aggravated about something. Just inhale, and exhale, and remember that you're on vacation. We know it's hard for Type A people to leave it all behind, but for your own peace of mind, it's worth a try.

■ Complain in person when it's serious. In a hotel, serious problems are usually better dealt with in person, at the front desk; if it's something quick, you can phone.

■ Complain early rather than late. Whenever you don't get what you paid for (the type of hotel room you booked or the airline seat you prereserved) or when it's something timely (the people next door are making too much noise), try to resolve the problem sooner rather than later. It's always going to be harder to deal with a problem or get something taken off your bill after the fact.

You have a better chance of resolving your dispute if your expectations seem reasonable. Also, hotel managers have been trained to let aggravated customers vent until they tire of arguing, so be sure to initiate a dialogue rather than droning on ad nauseam. Stay focused, and reiterate your specific demands if the conversation veers away from the problem at hand.

Get confirmation of the resolution in writing. Hotel managers have been known to say anything to put an end to a disagreeable situation. Once you and management have agreed on a solution, get confirmation of your agreement in writing.

Contest hotel charges. If you believe your complaint was not handled satisfactorily, get the names of the people involved, keep your receipts, and call your credit-card company when you get home. Major credit-card companies have departments that deal with contested charges, and most companies will not charge your card while the matter is under investigation.

Destination Tips

WORD OF MOUTH

"If a guide or driver will be with you for multiple days then it's ok to tip each at the end of your trip. Do check with them as to how long they'll be with you when you first meet them. The tour rep usually only sees you when you first arrive and then when you leave the city or country"
—Axel12DP

AFRICA AND THE MIDDLE EAST

EGYPT

Get the big picture. Before you visit any of the monuments at Giza, drive out to the viewing area beyond the third pyramid for a commanding view of the entire site—nine pyramids, one view, as the camel drivers will tell you.

Plan to eat late. Lunch is from 2 to 4, and dinner often starts at 9 or 10. In summer all this shifts by an hour, and during Ramadan it goes absolutely haywire.

Beware of people trying to sell you antiquities. Most of them are forgeries, sometimes very good ones, but at any rate it's illegal to trade in any sort of antiquities in Egypt. Even good forgeries could cause you problems at customs. As a rule, you cannot take anything more than 100 years old out of the country. This doesn't necessarily apply to items of European origin, but it can apply to carpets, paintings, and some books.

Know that tipping is a way of life in Egypt. Everyone who performs a service expects a *baksheesh*. People might even engage you in conversation or present you with a "free" gift and then ask for a little *something*. Amounts are small—£E1 is sufficient for restroom attendants, £E2 or £E3 for other small services. Restaurants generally add a 12% service charge to tabs, but, even then you're still expected to tip an extra 5% to 10% in cash (especially if using a credit card) for good service. In hotels, leave at least $1 per day for the hotel maid; porters expect at least $1 per bag. Don't tip cabbies for short in-town journeys, but if you engage a driver to take you to attractions with waiting time or you book a driver for a day, add 10% to the agreed fee.

WORD OF MOUTH. "Overall I really liked Cairo. I had heard that it can be scary, especially for American women traveling without a male, but I never felt threatened or in danger. It's a big city with a big-city vibe. Yes it's dirtier than many American cities, but anyone who has traveled to developing countries shouldn't be shocked by Cairo." —memejs

ISRAEL

Time visits to religious sites. Muslim sites are generally closed to tourists on Friday, the Muslim holy day. Avoid the Muslim Quarter of Jerusalem's Old City between noon and 2 PM on Friday, when the flow of worshippers in the streets can be uncomfortable or even rowdy. Some Christian sites close on Sunday; others open after morning worship. Many Jewish religious sites, and some museums and historical sites, close early on Friday; some remain closed through Saturday (the Jewish Sabbath).

Try the bus to get around. You can get almost anywhere in Israel by bus, and the central bus station is a fixture in most towns. Ask for the *tahana merkazit*. Egged handles all in-city bus routes, except those in Tel Aviv, where Dan operates. City fares are a flat rate per journey, not based on distance. For both local and intercity travel, bus drivers accept payment for tickets (payable only in shekels). They don't make change for a bill more than NIS 100; try to have smaller denominations. It's faster to buy tickets at the bus station.

14

Remember the Sabbath. The Jewish Sabbath extends from sundown Friday until dark on Saturday. Most shops and restaurants in Jewish neighborhoods will be closed, but Arab areas in Jerusalem's Old City, and in towns like Nazareth and Akko will be bustling. While Jerusalem quiets down by Friday afternoon, Tel Aviv remains lively. Public transportation is generally suspended during the Sabbath, from about two hours before sundown Friday to sundown Saturday. Sunday is the first day of the regular work and school week.

Make the most of shopping in the souk. Markets like Jerusalem's Old City souk are full of local color, with exotic spices, fresh-baked delicacies, embroidered dresses, tourist baubles, and more. Bargaining can be a fun part of any market experience—but there are some useful pointers. Never answer the question "How much do you want to pay?" When the seller names a price, come back with about half. If the seller balks, be prepared to walk out; if you're called back, they want to make a sale. Not every vendor will be in the mood for bargaining: don't even begin the process unless your intentions of buying are sincere. Women should resist invitations to inspect the merchandise at the back of the store in places like Jerusalem's Old City souk.

Save room for breakfast. If you're staying at a hotel, expect a substantial (even extravagant) buffet with breads and rolls, yogurts, hummus, cheeses, fresh vegetables and chopped salads, fruits, and even American-style foods such as pancakes and granola. This Israel breakfast is often included in the room price, but check. Some cafés serve the same spread. It's enough to hold you for hours.

Be flexible about tipping. There are no hard-and-fast rules for tipping in Israel. Taxi drivers don't expect tips, but a gratuity for good service is in order. If you've negotiated a price, assume the tip is been built in. If a restaurant bill doesn't include service, 15% is expected—round up if the service was good, down if it was dismal. Hotel bellboys should be tipped a lump sum of NIS 10–NIS 20, not per bag. Bus groups tip guides NIS 20–NIS 25 per person per day, and half that for the driver. Private guides get tipped NIS 80–NIS 100 a day from the whole party. Leave NIS 10 per day for your hotel's housekeeping staff, and the same for spa personnel.

WORD OF MOUTH. "The large bus companies and the trains do not run on Shabbat. However, the intercity sherut (communal) taxis and private taxis operate everywhere as usual. Private transportation is unrestricted (except for a few streets in ultra-Orthodox Jewish areas). Many local car-rental branches are closed on Saturday, like most businesses, and close earlier on Fridays. Check the hours carefully if you plan to pick up the car on a Friday." —mbgg

---

KENYA AND TANZANIA

Notify your credit-card company that you'll be traveling to East Africa. If you don't do this your transactions might be flagged as unusual and then denied. MasterCard, Visa, and American Express are accepted almost everywhere, but Diners Club is not. Discover is not recognized.

Reconfirm international flights. Call about flights to and from East Africa at least 72 hours before departure. Reconfirm your internal flights at least 48 hours before departure.

Bring your child"s own car seat. You may not be able to obtain one here.

On foot, look right before crossing the street. Kenyans drive on the left.

Fend off mosquitoes. Bites transmit malaria. In the evening cover your arms and legs and apply plenty of insect repellent. Burning mosquito coils at night also helps to ward off mosquitoes; coils can be purchased everywhere. Travel with mosquito netting in case this is not provided by a hotel.

Dress conservatively. East Africans, as a rule, are a reserved and religious people. Wearing revealing clothing is considered very disrespectful.

Stay calm. If you are unhappy with something, discuss your dissatisfaction calmly and clearly. East Africans don't respond well to displays of anger, which often make people less inclined to help resolve a problem.

14

Tip your porters and guides in Kenya. Tipping is not mandatory here, but porters do expect to be tipped, and 10% is customary in restaurants. Some hotels and lodges have a gratuity box for you to put a tip for all of the staff at the end of your stay. Tip your safari driver and guide approximately US$10–US$15 per day.

Carry small bills for tipping in Tanzania. For a two- or three-night stay at a lodge or hotel tip a couple of dollars for small services, US$2–US$5 per day for room steward and waiter. Your guide will expect a tip of US$15–US$20 per day per person; if he's gone out of his way for you, then you may wish to give him more. It's a good idea to carry small bills. U.S.dollars are acceptable almost everywhere, but if you're planning to go to more remote places, then shillings are preferred.

MOROCCO

Avoid visiting Morocco during Ramadan. During this month-long fast all cafés and nearly all restaurants are closed during the day, and the pace of work is reduced. Note that the Muslim calendar is lunar, and dates for Ramadan and other religious holidays shift back 11 days each year.

Learn Moroccan customs. People come first; the actions to be accomplished are secondary. Moroccans shake hands with each other every time they meet. Nothing can happen without politeness: if you have a problem and lose your temper, you give up hope of solving it. Using the left hand for any right-hand activities (like eating from a communal dish at a traditional meal) is generally thought of as rude, since the left is used for attending to personal hygiene.

SAFARI MUST-HAVES

"Binoculars. I [use] the Nikon Monarch 8 x 42. I also recommend purchasing a good-quality neoprene strap; it makes it more comfortable on your neck." —Elizabeth S

"Nights and mornings can be cooler than daytime temps in many places, so [be sure to pack] a fleece or heavier sweater/cardigan or crewneck. You may even need these on the planes." —sandi

"Have a good big hat, but one that's floppy and can be rolled up or packed." —TC

"A journal is a must." —LyndaS

"Pepto, sleeping pills, and a very small good-quality brush to get dust out of camera lens. My point and shoot lens would not open from the dust. Brushed it out and then took many more phots." —Elainee

"Bring about 50 American $1's for tips. It is very difficult to get them once you are there." —irecommend

Dress and behave conservatively in Morocco. Although this is a moderate Islamic society, it's best to adhere to modest dress in public. Shorts simply aren't acceptable for either sex anywhere, except at the beach. Public displays of affection aren't common between straight or same-sex couples. Furthermore, there's no "out" gay life in Morocco. Homosexual acts are strictly illegal, and travelers have been imprisoned as a consequence.

Go with a guide. In the often labyrinthine cities, guides make a lot of sense. In places like Fez you'll find you need a guide just to protect yourself from being approached by other guides. Official guides have a badge to prove that they're official, and they generally charge fixed fees of around 200 DH–250 DH for a half day and 300 DH–350 DH for a full day. To find an official guide, check with hotel staff or the tourist board. If you opt for an unofficial guide, fees will be negotiable; establish them in advance.

Bargain in Moroccan markets. You must negotiate when purchasing Moroccan specialties. There's no rule for the percentage by which you should aim to reduce the price, because some vendors start with a decent price and others start by inflating the price 10- or 20-fold. Any kind of intermediary, like a guide, will inflate the price.

Plan to tip in Morocco. Although it's not done as commonly as elsewhere in the world, you can never go wrong by tipping in Morocco. You should always give waiters in proper restaurants who provide good service 10% of the bill; tip those in cafés 4 DH or 8 DH per person in the dining party. In taxis round up to the nearest 5 DH (e.g., if the meter says 12 DH, pay 15 DH). Porters appreciate 8 DH or 16 DH per bag; chambermaids the same per day.

SOUTHERN AFRICA

Monitor your passport's empty pages and expiration date. American citizens need a valid passport with two blank facing visa pages to enter South Africa for visits of up to 90 days; this includes infants. If your passport will expire within six months of your return date, you need to renew your passport in advance, as South Africa won't let you enter with a soon-to-expire passport.

14

Set up international roaming cell-phone service before you leave home. This is your best, cheapest, and least complicated way of making and receiving phone calls here. In Botswana and Swaziland there are no access agreements to allow you to use U.S. long-distance services. Thus, you will not be able to make calls using your U.S. calling card from Botswana or Swaziland.

Be sure you can access your money. Program your credit cards for ATM use in South Africa before leaving home. (Most South African ATMs take five-digit PIN numbers.) In both Namibia and Zambia MasterCard and Visa are preferred by business owners over American Express, because of substantial charges levied by Amex to proprietors. Business owners in Zambia often prefer cash (or traveler's checks) rather than credit cards, and some smaller hotels levy a fee up to 10% to use credit. Foreign currency is the only acceptable method of payment in Zimbabwe. It's advisable to stick to U.S. dollars for all activity payments to both the Zimbabwean- and the Zambian-based operators (all activities are quoted in U.S. dollars).

On foot, look right before crossing the street. Southern Africans drive on the left.

Be car savvy. Keep your car doors locked at all times, and leave enough space between you and the vehicle in front so you can pull into another lane if necessary.

Avoid areas with land mines. Never, under any circumstances, drive off the road in Mozambique unless it is a detour that

ON SAFARI

■ **Budget extra for the extras.** If you have to get every shot and/or prescription that the CDC recommends, you're looking at anywhere from $1,000 to $2,000. Also budget money for visas, which usually cost $50. Not digital yet? Stock up on film before you head out; a roll costs about US$20 in a safari camp. And, don't forget to save some money for souvenirs.

■ **Don't forget tipping.** Plan to spend US$15 to US$25 a day (per traveler) on gratuities. In South Africa tips are on the higher end of this range and usually are paid in rand (the local currency); you may also use U.S. dollars for tips, however. Elsewhere in southern Africa, U.S. currency is preferred.

■ **Make sure your name is the same on all your documents.** Be on guard especially if you're honeymooning. If one document has your maiden name while the other has your married name, your trip could be over before you say Mr. and Mrs. Smith.

■ **Go with soft, light bags.** For most fly-in safaris the maximum weight for luggage is 26 kilos (57 pounds). Your bag should be a soft-sided duffel with a lock or something similar, so the pilot can easily fit it into the small cargo area. At most private lodges laundry is included. If your bag is over the weight limit, or if you weigh more than 220 pounds, you will be required to purchase an additional plane seat (usually about US$100).

■ **Define "all-inclusive."** Does your all-inclusive fee include park fees? Visas? Lunch?

■ **Protect yourself from malaria.** Travelers heading into malaria-endemic regions should consult a health-care professional at least one month before departure. Take great care to avoid being bitten by mosquitoes. Always sleep in a mosquito-proof room or tent, and if possible keep a fan going in your room. If you are pregnant or trying to conceive, avoid malaria areas if at all possible.

■ **What to pack.** Light, khaki, or neutral-color clothes help to deflect the harsh sun and, unlike dark colors, are less likely to attract mosquitoes. Do not wear camouflage gear. Do wear layers of clothing that you can strip off as the sun gets hotter and put back on as the sun goes down. Make sure you have something that can double as a raincoat.

■ **Check your existing health plan.** Make sure you're covered while abroad, and supplement it if necessary. Southern African nations have no (or limited) national health systems.

has obviously been used by lots of other vehicles. There may still be land mines in the least likely places.

Don't walk alone at night. Be cautious even by day. Avoid wearing flashy jewelry (even costume jewelry), and don't invite attention by wearing an expensive camera around your neck.

ASIA

CHINA

Keep packets of Kleenex and antibacterial hand wipes in your day pack. Paper isn't a feature of Chinese restrooms, and you often can't buy it in smaller towns. A small flashlight with extra batteries is also useful. The brands in Chinese pharmacies are limited, so take adequate stocks of your potions and lotions, feminine-hygiene products (tampons are especially hard to find), and birth control. All these things are easy to get in Hong Kong.

Do the immunization thing. No shots are required for entry into China, but it's a good idea to be immunized against typhoid and hepatitis A and B before you go, as well as to get routine tetanus-diphtheria and measles boosters. In winter, a flu vaccination is also smart, especially if you're infection-prone or are a senior citizen. In summer months malaria is a risk in tropical and rural areas, especially Hainan and Yunan provinces—consult your doctor four to six weeks before your trip, as preventative treatments vary. The risk of contracting malaria in cities is small.

Know the e-mail trick for finding accommodation. The current hotel glut in China means proprietors have extra incentive to offer you a deal. Although it's always worth a quick look at online accommodation sites, sometimes even dropping an e-mail directly to the hotel itself can get you similar, if not better, rates.

Hire a driver, not a car. In a nutshell, driving yourself around is not a possibility when vacationing in mainland China, as the only valid driver's licenses are Chinese ones. However, this restriction should be cause for relief, as city traffic is terrible, drivers are manic, and getting lost is practically inevitable for first-timers. Conditions in Hong Kong aren't much better, but you can drive there using a U.S. license.

Save face. "Face" is the all-important issue in China. A cross between pride and social status, it's all about appearances, yet its cultural roots run deep. Shame someone publicly, and you may lose their friendship for life; make them look good, and you'll go far. What makes people lose and gain face is complicated, but respect is the key issue. Don't get all upset if things go wrong, especially when reserving tickets and hotel rooms. Instead, be stern but friendly—raising your voice and threatening will get you nowhere. Keep facial expressions and hand gestures to a minimum; when pointing, use your whole hand, not a finger.

Steel yourself for shopping at a Chinese market. It's great fun for the savvy shopper. Do haggle—with histrionics at the seller's first asking price but with a polite, positive attitude throughout, and never with finger pointing (use your whole hand instead). That said, be prepared to be grabbed, pushed, followed, stared at, and even have people whispering offers in your ear. Personal space and privacy aren't thought of in the same way as in the West, so the invasion of them is common. Also, many Chinese love to touch foreign children, so make sure any younger traveling companions are aware of and prepared for this.

Eat like a local. The standard eating procedure is to hold the bowl close to your mouth and shovel in the contents without any qualms. Noisily slurping up soup and noodles is also the norm, as is belching when you're done. Covering the tablecloth in crumbs, drips and even spat-out bones is a sign you've enjoyed your meal. It's considered bad manners to point or play with your chopsticks, or to place them on top of your rice bowl when you're finished eating (place the chopsticks horizontally on the table or plate). Avoid, too, leaving your chopsticks standing up in a bowl of rice—they look like the two incense sticks burnt at funerals.

Share and share alike. Instead of ordering individual main dishes, it's usual for those around a table—whether 2 or 12 people—to get several. Four people eating together, for example, might order a whole or half chicken, another type of meat, a fish dish, a vegetable, and fried noodles—all of which would be placed on the table's lazy Susan so everyone can reach. Portions and prices may be altered according to the number of diners.

Mind your manners. The Chinese aren't very touchy feely; opt for greeting with handshakes over European-style cheek kissing. Also, limit public displays of affection to hand holding. Always use a person's title and surname until invited to do otherwise. Respect silences in conversation; don't hurry things or interrupt.

Know when not to tip. It's officially forbidden by the government, and locals simply don't do it. In general, follow their lead without qualms. Nevertheless, the practice is beginning to catch on, especially among tour guides, who often expect Y10 a day. Official CTS representatives aren't allowed to accept tips, but you can give them candy, T-shirts, and other small gifts. You don't need to tip in restaurants or in taxis. In Hong Kong, hotels and major restaurants usually add a 10% service charge; in almost all cases, this money does not go to the waiters and waitresses. Add on up to 10% more for good service. Tipping restroom attendants is common, but it is generally not the custom to leave an additional tip in taxis and hair salons.

Pass on the antiques. In China it's against the law to take anything more than 120 years old out of the country.

WORD OF MOUTH. "The taxis have meters in Suzhou, Beijing, Chengdu, and Shanghai. We never had to bargain for taxi fare anywhere. It was always cheap and fair. Don't forget, you do not need to tip, but you do pay for tolls. Also, what you read about the taxi drivers NOT speaking English is correct. Most do not even understand proper names like Ramada or even the word airport." —luv2globetrot

HONG KONG

Check in with the tourist board to find great deals on activities. Offerings include feng shui tours, tai chi and tea appreciation classes, and even free rides on the fully restored fishing junk the *Duk Ling* (bring your passport to prove you're from out of town).

Use the MTR. Not many cities have a metro system as efficient, reliable, spotless, and user-friendly as Hong Kong's Mass Transit Railway. All signs and maps are in Cantonese and English, and the six train lines take you all across Hong Kong Island and the Kowloon Peninsula.

Get your bearings. If you're on Hong Kong Island and feeling a little disoriented, remember that Victoria Harbour is always north; in Kowloon it's always south. You can use the Island's mountains as a guide, too; the Central district backs onto the slopes of Victoria Peak, so the districts south of it—the Midlevels and the Peak—look down on it.

Know that you can go antiquing. Although mainland law forbids that any item more than 120 years old leave China, Hong Kong isn't held to this rule. It's perfectly legal to ship your antique treasures home.

Visit a tailor. No trip to Hong Kong would be complete without doing so. In often humble, fabric-cluttered settings, customers on record include such notables as David Bowie, Kate Moss, Jude Law, and Queen Elizabeth II.

Leave enough time to get the suit you want. A fine suit requires six or more days to create. That said, be wary but not dismissive of "24-hour tailors." Hong Kong's most famous craftsmen have turned out suits in a day.

Eat dim sum. The city is famous for its near-endless varieties.

Stear clear of shark. Hong Kong accounts for 50% of the world market for shark. The expensive shark's-fin soup, considered by locals to be an aphrodisiac, is made with the great beast's pectal, dorsal, and lower tail fins. Not only are there environmental and moral issues involved, but the soup has very little flavor, making it one of the biggest wastes of money in the culinary universe.

WORD OF MOUTH. "In general in Hong Kong, a well-made men's suit or women's suit made with quality fabric will cost the same, or perhaps more, than a good quality off-the-rack suit in the US (excluding designer brands in the US which will most likely cost more)." —Cicerone

SHANGHAI

Dress nicely to fit in. Forget Paris, New York, and Milan—the new center of the fashion universe is Shanghai. People in the rest of China dress for comfort, but the Shanghainese dress to kill. This is a city where suits are still de rigueur for meetings and business functions. Slop around in flip-flops and worn denims and you will feel like there's a neon "tourist" sign over your head. Pack your nicer pairs of jeans or capri pants for sightseeing—there are plenty of fake handbags around with which to dress them up come dinner.

Research hotels carefully before booking. The choice of accommodation is wide, and takes in most tastes and budgets. However, that's not to say choosing a hotel is always easy: The Chinese star system is a little unpredictable, and Web sites are often misleading for all but the biggest names. For lesser establishments, try to get recent personal recommendations: the forums on Fodors.com are a great place to start.

INDIA

Respect religious monuments. Remove your shoes before entering a shrine, even if it appears to be in ruins. Be aware that some temples and mosques are off-limits to travelers who don't practice the faith, or to any women. Women visiting sacred places should dress modestly—no shorts or tank tops—and cover their heads before entering a Sikh temple or a mosque. Cameras and video cameras are sometimes prohibited inside houses of worship.

14

Use prepaid taxi and rickshaw counters at airports and railway stations in major cities. You tell the clerk your destination and pay in advance. Don't get waylaid by aggressive drivers who try to persuade you to come to them instead of going to the counter: They'll without doubt charge you more than the published rate at the counter.

Tip correctly. It's true that much of India runs on tips, but the best advice we can give is to trust your instincts and reward good service accordingly wherever you are. Always tip in cash. You should leave up to 10% on any restaurant bill, 15% for exceptional service. Taxi drivers don't expect tips unless they go to a great deal of trouble to reach your destination; in such a case Rs. 10–Rs. 15 is fair. If you hire a car and driver, tip the driver about Rs. 50–Rs. 100 per day, depending on the distance traveled, and about Rs. 25 for each lunch or dinner; also give him a larger amount at the end of the journey if you have been using him for many days. Tip local guides 10% of the price of the tour.

WORD OF MOUTH. "No matter how much you have traveled you have never seen anything like India! It is a joy, interesting, disgusting, aromatic, disgusting, spiritual, dirty, rewarding, enlightening, disgusting, and simply the most interesting experience of your lives." —rhkkmk

JAPAN

Do not try to open the taxi door. Japanese taxis have automatic door-opening systems.

Direct taxi drivers by naming nearby landmarks. Do not assume the taxi driver will be able to find your destination with just a written address. Better yet: Carry a map and point to where you want to go.

Be sure of your bus route and destination. The bus driver, particularly on routes outside Tōkyō, probably won't speak English.

Use care crossing the street. In Japan driving is on the left. Look right when crossing.

Don't flaunt your tattoos. These personal expressions are strictly forbidden in many hot springs and other places because of the association between tattoos and the *yakuza* (Japanese mafia). Some places even post signs reading PEOPLE WITH TATTOOS ARE NOT ALLOWED.

Know your chopsticks. Life will be easier for you in Japan if you've had some experience with chopsticks. The secret is to learn to move only the chopstick on top rather than both at once. Don't point, lick, or gesture with chopsticks. Also, never take food from a common serving plate with the ends of the chopsticks you've had in your mouth. Never use your chopsticks to take food from someone else's chopsticks, as this denotes a funerary custom.

Get a Japan Rail Pass. This pass offers unlimited travel on Japan Railways (JR) trains. A one-week pass is less expensive than a regular round-trip ticket from Tōkyō to Kyōto on the Shinkansen. Note that you must obtain a rail-pass voucher prior to departure for Japan, and the pass must be used within three months of purchase. The pass is available only to people with tourist visas, as opposed to business, student, and diplomatic visas.

Be prompt for both social and business occasions. Tardiness is a major faux pas. Japanese addresses tend to be complicated, and traffic is often heavy, so allow for adequate travel time.

Greet with a bow. Japanese of all ages and backgrounds bow in greeting each other (even on the telephone!), and foreign visitors who at least bob the head will get a smile of recognition. However, Japanese know all about handshaking, and the visitor's head may crash with an out-stretched hand. In business, exchanging name cards is essential.

Get a handle on what to expect in the bathroom. The most hygienic restrooms are in hotels and department stores, and are usually marked with international symbols. You may encounter Japanese-style toilets, with bowls recessed into the floor, over which you squat facing the top. If squatting is not an option, the last cubical in the row may be a Western-style toilet. In many homes and Japanese-style public places there will be a pair of slippers at the entrance to the restroom. Change into these before entering the room, and change back when you exit. Many public toilets don't have toilet paper, though there are dispensers where packets can be purchased for ¥50 (45¢) or so.

Stick to last names and use "san" after the name. In business situations, most Japanese aren't accustomed to using first names. Even coworkers of 20 years' standing use surnames. Unless you are sure that the Japanese person is extremely comfortable with Western customs, it is best to use last names only, followed by the honorific "san."

14

Pack your best socks and stockings. Japanese don't wear shoes in homes, temples, or traditional inns. Having shoes you can quickly slip in and out of is a decided advantage. Take wool socks (checking first for holes!) to help you through those shoeless occasions during the winter.

Don't pour your own drink. Similarly, if a glass at your table is empty, show your attentiveness by filling it for your companion.

Take instant coffee. All lodgings provide a thermos of hot water and bags of green tea in every room, but for coffee you'll either have to call room service (which can be expensive) or buy very sweet coffee in a can from a vending machine.

WORD OF MOUTH. "I visited Japan in January of 2010 for one week, and had an amazing time. Although it was a bit chilly, there were very few tourists regardless of where I went. The only downside to visiting during the winter season was probably the lack of cherry blossoms, which I had always been so drawn to. So if you're hoping to avoid the tourist season, I would definitely recommend visiting during winter." —Litecast

Know that tipping is not common in Japan. It's not necessary to tip taxi drivers, or at hair salons, barbershops, bars, or nightclubs. Porters charge fees of ¥250–¥300 per bag at railroad stations and ¥200 per piece at airports. It's not customary to tip employees of hotels, even porters, unless a special service has been rendered. In such cases, a gratuity of ¥2,000–¥3,000 should be placed in an envelope and handed to the staff member discreetly. Note that even in these instances, the employee may still refuse your tip.

NEPAL AND TIBET

Know the health risks. Check with the Centers for Disease Control and your physician about current risks and recommended vaccinations before you go. Immunizations for hepatitis A, meningitis, and typhoid fever are advised.

Don't plan on traveling independently in Tibet. In addition to a visa for the People's Republic of China, you will also need to get a Tibet Tourism Bureau travel permit, which is arranged by the travel agent who books your tour or transportation to Lhasa. Travel by train or plane without a permit is next to impossible—on Internet forums you may hear of the odd person who claims to manage it, but it's more than likely that you will be refused boarding with no refund. At this writing, no independent travel to Tibet was permitted; only individuals booked on tours to Tibet could travel there. These restrictions change depending on the political situation in Tibet, so it is best to contact travel agents, tour groups, or hotels in the region for information on current policies.

Reconfirm all flights. This goes for both domestic and international flights out of Kathmandu. Do it at least 24 hours in advance, particularly because weather often causes delays and cancellations of domestic flights.

Never touch anything with your feet. It's considered rude.

Know the etiquette for visiting religious buildings. You must always ask permission before entering a Hindu temple. You should not bring leather in with you. If you visit a stupa, the traditional way to see it is to walk clockwise.

Dress modestly. Dress in Nepal and Tibet is informal but conservative. Shorts, short skirts, and revealing tops put women at risk of encountering unflattering remarks and, increasingly, unwanted touching.

Be careful what you eat and drink. Leafy vegetables are known to carry parasites, so avoid those of dubious origin or those likely to have been washed in tap water. Also, try to eat only fruit that has a skin you can peel. Avoid drinking tap water as well as beverages with ice, which often is made of local water. Most good restaurants either make their own ice using boiled water or buy ice in bulk from huge freezer warehouses, where purified water is used.

WORD OF MOUTH. "Since the railroad and the railcars (on the Llasa Express) are all new, and since the speed was limited on the permafrost at 100km/h (62MPH), the ride was very smooth, and I had no problem getting to sleep at all." —rkkwan

SOUTHEAST ASIA

Don't touch food or people with your left hand. It is considered unclean, as the left hand is used for washing oneself—with soap and water—after using the toilet. Never offer anything, even money to a vendor, with your left hand.

Use common sense when eating from street vendors. If the vendor is getting a lot of business, that's a good indication of the quality of his product.

14

Watch public displays of affection. In Muslim countries it's often considered improper for a male to kiss a female acquaintance on the cheek or even offer his hand to most women until she has offered hers first. But such modesty isn't limited to Muslim countries: Cambodians find public affection so egregious that even newlyweds are forbidden to kiss at their wedding ceremony. Note that in some countries same-sex affection is common, but strictly social. The rights of gays and lesbians aren't respected or even protected in many areas.

Avoid inadvertent offense. Don't point your feet at anyone; keep them on the floor, and take care not to show the soles of your feet, particularly when seated, as in places like Thailand and Bali it's considered rude. In Bali it's also impolite to point with your index finger. Gesture with your whole hand instead. Never touch a person's head, even a child's (the head is considered sacred), and, if you are a woman, you should avoid touching a monk. Also, in many places, displays of anger—which include crossing your arms and putting your hands on hips as well as raised voices and confrontations—are considered very bad form.

Brush up on temple etiquette. In Balinese Hindu temples you must wear a sash, which you can usually rent on-site for a few thousand rupiah. In other places, temples have wraps you can borrow; but you're better off having your own wrap or scarf. It's considered improper to wear shorts and other above-the-knee clothing in temples, so avoid them. Women should wear a shirt that covers the shoulders. Short sleeves are OK, but tank tops are not. Also, be sure to remove your shoes before entering. You'll see a pile of shoes at the entrance—that's your cue to take yours off. Oh, yes, and don't point your toes at any image of the Buddha, as it's considered sacrilegious.

Learn how to tip in Southeast Asian countries. Tipping is not a local custom, but it is expected of foreigners, especially at larger hotels and restaurants and for taxi rides. If you feel the service has been less than stellar, you are under no obligation to leave a tip, especially with crabby cabbies.

WORD OF MOUTH. "Bali's attractions are not necessarily the beaches but the Balinese Hindu culture, and Ubud is really the best place to experience it. There are nightly dance and gamelan performances in small open-air venues, many temples and beautiful scenery, and Ubud life is much more the traditional culture that people here live every day." —kuluk

BALI

Get familiar with the Indonesian toilet. There are several models: the long porcelain bowl in the floor, which flushes; the usual Western throne; its seatless cousin, often used in mid-price hotels, which is flushed with a dipper of water; and the hole in the ground. Instructions for floor toilets: squat and go—but if you want toilet paper, you'll have to bring it. (Instead of paper, Indonesians use water and soap to wash their nether regions after using the bathroom.) The floor toilet requires balance, but most people actually find it easy with practice. Most tourist hotels and restaurants have Western-style toilets. Note that the sink is often outside the room with the toilet, and there is sometimes a nominal charge (rupiah 100) for restroom use in such public places as bus terminals. If you need to find a bathroom, ask for the WC (way-say).

Agree to a fare before you get into a taxi or *becak* (BAY-check, similar to a tuk-tuk). If not, the fee will likely be exorbitant. Clarify with the driver that the fare you agree to is the *whole* fare. Don't leave room for mysterious taxes and additional charges to appear.

Don't open a gift in front of the giver. It's customary to wait and open it later in private. The practice is supposed to indicate that the receiver is gracious, not greedy.

Expect touching as part of conversation. The Balinese are extremely polite. Shaking hands has become a common practice, and Indonesians are very tactile, so touching happens often. Smiling is the national pastime, so do it frequently, and you'll have a much easier time transcending language barriers.

Avoid highway scams. In northern Bali, for example, a car will pull up, its occupants waving their arms, implying that something is wrong with your car. Ignore them. This is likely to be a scam in which they will have you pull over, "fix" a problem that doesn't exist, and then charge you for it. Pay attention to similar warnings that come from car-rental operations.

Don't fall prey to a "tour guide" in Bali. Some attach themselves to you and then proceed to drag you to all the stores of their friends and relatives (in the hope that you will buy something and make a commission for them in the process).

14

Learn the ins and outs of tipping in Bali. The more expensive tourist restaurants include a service charge; if service isn't included, tip 10%. In addition to built-in hotel service charges, be prepared to tip about $1 or $2 per bag you may also want to tip room service personnel if you request a special service. Taxi drivers aren't tipped on Bali or Lombok, although they always appreciate it if you leave them small change. Private guides expect a gratuity, perhaps $3–$6 per day.

CAMBODIA

Don't give money to panhandlers. Beggars will approach you in Cambodia. Many NGO workers who work with the homeless advise against giving handouts on the street. Instead, you should acknowledge the people who greet you, politely decline, and make a donation to an organization that operates larger-scale programs to aid beggars and street kids.

Time your trip wisely. It's important to book in advance if you plan on visiting during mid-April's New Year celebrations or for the Water Festival in Phnom Penh in November. Strangely, the New Year is one of the best times to see the capital—at least in terms of lower rates and crowds— because the majority of Phnom Penh residents come from somewhere else and they all go home for the holidays.

Stay on the beaten path. Land mines laid during the civil war have been removed from most major tourist destinations. Unexploded ordnance is a concern, however, around off-the-beaten-track temples, where you should only travel with a knowledgeable guide. As a general rule, never walk in uncharted territory in Cambodia, unless you know it's safe.

Sample the local seasoning. Down south, Kampot Province grows world-renowned pepper. If you're coming from a northern climate, try a seafood dish with whole green peppercorns on the stalk. You won't find them (not fresh, anyway) in your home country.

Get out into the countryside around Siem Reap. This is the best way to get a feel for the way Cambodian farmers and fisherman live. Take a day to tour some of the outlying temples, some of which are still covered by jungle growth; others are incorporated into village life. Most guesthouses can arrange such a trip.

WORD OF MOUTH. "The big draws—Angkor Wat, the Bayon—rightfully deserve their reputations and are somewhat overwhelming on the first go. They can also be literally overrun by our fellow travelers. My approach was to try to get an overview, an orientation as it were, then to return a day or so later to absorb the details." —marmot

Tip even though it's not the local custom. In Cambodia, the locals don't often tip for services, but as a visitor your tips are welcomed. If service for a meal isn't already on the bill, tip up to 10%; tour guides can be tipped between $10 and $20 per day depending on the level of service.

LAOS
Know how to greet people. Laotians traditionally greet others by pressing their palms together in a sort of prayer gesture known as a *nop*; it is also acceptable for men to shake hands. If you attempt a nop, remember that it's basically reserved for social greetings; don't greet a hotel or restaurant employee this way. The general greeting is "sabai di" ("good health"), invariably said with a smile.

Bring your appetite with you. For such a sleepy somewhat off-the-beaten-path country, Laos has some excellent eating options. Choices in Luang Prabang as well as Vientiane are endless, from high-end French restaurants and Indian curry joints to pizzarias and Japanese sushi houses, not to mention fantastic bakeries and coffee shops. In smaller spots, you may have to make do with sticky rice and grilled meats/fish, but most towns do have at least one or two "fancier" places with decent menus. Lao food is similar to Thai, but not quite as spicy or varied.

Play it safe. Laos is fairly free of crime in tourist areas. Pickpocketing is rare, but you should still be careful in crowded areas. Never leave luggage unattended.

WORD OF MOUTH. **"I think Luang Prabang is the first place I've been on this trip that I can say I truly LOVED. It just seemed so unique—while focused on tourism, it didn't have any of that plastic or phony tourist glitz going. And the people everywhere were charming. Even the tuk tuk drivers would simply say gently 'tuk-tuk?' or 'waterfall?' and if you said no, they just let you go." —NeoPatrick**

14

Know that tips aren't customary in Laos. However, tipping 10% on a meal (as long as service isn't already included) is a nice gesture, as are small tips for services you'd customarily provide a bit extra for at home.

SINGAPORE
Visit a food hawker center. These government-regulated food courts are clean and safe, and are a good way to eat what the locals do at about the same prices. Prices vary depending upon the center, and some try to fleece tourists, so ask at your hotel or check your guidebook for specific recommendations.

Stick to public transportation. Taxis can't access the reserved bus lanes, which means that buses whiz by those stuck in traffic. It's usually unnecessary to rent a car—and there are confusing driving restrictions to know and extra licenses to acquire if you do. Plus,, driving is on the left in both Malaysia and Singapore.

Know who to tip—and who not to. Tipping's prohibited at the airport and discouraged in hotels (except for bellboys, who generally receive S$1 per bag) or restaurants that levy a 10% service charge. Unlike in other countries, though, waitstaff don't receive a percentage of this service charge, except in the more progressive establishments. Taxi drivers don't receive tips from Singaporeans, who become upset when they see tourists tip.

THAILAND
Choose your dishes wisely. Ask for your dishes *mai phet* ("not spicy"). Thai food can get really spicy—know what you're in for. (Phet means spicy.) Skip the *nam pla* if you're on a low-sodium diet. This fish sauce is used instead of salt, and is added just as commonly.

Don't assume that Thais eat with chopsticks. Unless they're eating Chinese dishes, Thais use a fork and a spoon.

Carry toilet paper or a small package of tissues. It's rarely provided in older buildings or in rural areas, where you still may find squat toilets. Often a bucket is placed under a tap next to the toilet; you are expected to fill the bucket with water and flush out the toilet manually. Note that Western-style facilities are usually available in the main tourist areas and are the norm in hotels.

Leave a tip if the service was good. In Thailand tips are generally given for good service, except when a price has been negotiated in advance. If you hire a private driver for an excursion, do tip him. With metered taxis in Bangkok, however, the custom is to round the fare up to the nearest B5. Hotel porters expect at least a B20 tip, and hotel staff who have given good personal service are usually tipped. A 10% tip is appreciated at a restaurant when no service charge has been added to the bill.

WORD OF MOUTH. "Casual is the rule in Bangkok, whether at a 'nicer' restaurant or something with more 'local' flavor . . . long pants for the guys, with a polo or casual button shirt. For women, pants and skirts or lightweight dresses are fine. Lightweight fabrics work best. Cotton, linen, gauze. these are my favorites. Again, maybe a sweater or pashmina-style wrap as restaurants tend to set the AC waaaaaay down, so I'm sometimes chilled a bit." —simpsonc510

VIETNAM

Plan around the Tet Festival. If you're planning to travel during late January or early February, be sure to take the Tet Festival into account. Hotels are often fully booked far in advance, and many services are closed down for extended periods.

Know how to tip. Most government-run hotels and tourist restaurants add a 5% service charge to the bills (though the staff may not receive any of it). Tip anywhere from 5% to 10% when eating out. Be sure to give at least 10% to hired drivers and guides—it's expected and greatly appreciated.

Beware of traffic. Crossing the street in Vietnam is a dangerous game, and though traffic lights are all over Hanoi and Ho Chi Minh City, you shouldn't put too much faith in them; red lights are often ignored, especially at night and especially in Hanoi. One-way streets are also dangerous—there is almost always a trickle of traffic flowing the wrong way. And although the Vietnamese technically drive on the right side of the road, the concept of lanes has yet to catch on.

BERMUDA, BAHAMAS, AND CARIBBEAN

BERMUDA

Err on the formal side when it comes to dress. It is an offense in Bermuda to appear in public without a shirt, even for joggers. Also, leave your cutoffs, short shorts, and halter tops at home. This rule may seem arcane, but most Bermudians appreciate the decorum. This also holds true for the beach—thong bathing suits and topless sunbathing aren't acceptable.

Don't plan on renting a car. In fact, you *can't* rent a car in Bermuda. The island has strict laws governing against overcrowded roads, so even Bermudians are only allowed one car per household. A popular (albeit somewhat dangerous) alternative is to rent mopeds or scooters, which are better for negotiating the island's narrow roads.

Use American money. The Bermudian dollar is on par with the U.S. dollar, and the two currencies are used interchangeably. (Other non-Bermudian currency must be converted.) Know that though you can use American money anywhere, change is often given in Bermudian currency. Avoid accumulating large amounts of local money, which is difficult to exchange for U.S. dollars in Bermuda and expensive to exchange in the United States.

Check Horseshoe Bay Beach's notice board for jellyfish updates before you go swimming. The Portuguese man-of-war variety looks like an innocuous blue plastic bag, but its sting is extremely painful and poisonous.

Consider visiting a less touristy area. The northern end of Court Street in the City of Hamilton is off the typical tourist trail, so you can find some great local eateries and a taste of day-to-day Bermuda life. Be warned, this area is not advisable after dark.

Always be cautious if you're tooling around on a scooter. The island's notoriously narrow, twisting roads have a particularly high accident rate, and drinking-and-driving is a problem. Don't be scared, just be aware.

Tip in Bermuda. Tipping in Bermuda is fairly similar to tipping in the United States. A service charge of 10% (or an equivalent per-diem amount), which covers everything from baggage handling to maid service, is added to your hotel bill, though people often still tip a few extra dollars. Most restaurants tack on a 17% service charge; if not, a 17% tip is customary (more for exceptional service).

BAHAMAS

Stay safe in Nassau. Be mindful of your surroundings, especially near the cruise-ship dock and in areas less visited by tourists. Police presence has increased on the streets of downtown Nassau for added security.

Be a choosy shore snorkeler. Remember that the better the sandy beach, the less likely you are to find colorful coral and fish.

Don't try to haggle at upscale Nassau shops. This includes those at the resorts; prices are set and not subject to being talked down.

Go easy at first on new foods. Mangoes, conch, and rum punch top the list. The major health risk is traveler's diarrhea, caused by ingesting fruits, shellfish, and drinks to which your body is unaccustomed.

Don't forget to drive on the left. This can be confusing, because most cars are American with the steering wheel on the left. Similarly, pedestrians must look right, left, right when crossing the street.

Bring lots of small bills. This pertains to taxi fares and for shopping at places like the Straw Market, as drivers and vendors either won't have change for big bills or will claim not to in the hope of getting a bigger tip or a higher price for that T-shirt.

Be aware of the spring-break factor. Between the end of February and mid-April you'll find a lot of vacationing college students on spring break, which includes beach parties, sports events, and entertainment. Plan accordingly.

Tip right. In the Bahamas, the usual tip for service from a taxi driver or waiter is 15%, and $1–$2 a bag for porters.

Many hotels and restaurants automatically add a 15% gratuity to your bill.

WORD OF MOUTH. "FYI—most of the Bahamas Islands are fairly far north in the Atlantic and can be 'cool' in February, in some cases it could be too cool for swimming." —RoamsAround

CARIBBEAN

Reconfirm your flights on interisland carriers. You may be requested (actually, told) to take another flight or departure time that's more convenient for the airline, or your plane may make unscheduled stops.

14

Ask about island-hopping passes. They're cost-wise if you're flying to more than one island. Air Jamaica, American Airlines, American Eagle, and LIAT are among the airlines that offer them.

Save up to 50% at resorts off-season. From April 15 through December 15 you can save a bundle. That said, be mindful of hurricane season. It's roughly from June through November, with greatest risk for a storm from August through October. Delays and flight cancellations are common during this time.

Know which side of the island you want. Decide whether you want a hotel on the leeward side of an island (with calm water, good for snorkeling and swimming) or the windward (with waves, good for surfing, not good for swimming).

Take in (or leave out) the view. At less expensive properties an ocean-view room may mean a difference in price of only $10–$20 per room; at luxury resorts on pricey islands, however, it could amount to as much as $100 per room. If you're the active type who really uses a room only to sleep, then you can save a bundle by choosing a garden-, mountain-, or town-view room. Smaller hotels and guesthouses or those that are a short walk from the beach offer very pleasant accommodations that are priced considerably lower than their larger, beachfront neighbors.

Don't overlook local firms when renting a car. Their cars are mechanically sound, and prices are competitive. It's not crucial to reserve a rental car prior to your arrival.

Mind those driving permits. Several Caribbean islands require a temporary local driving permit for car rental. Anguilla, Antigua, Barbados, the BVI, Cayman Islands, Dominica,

Grenada, St. Kitts, St. Lucia and St. Vincent, and the Grena-
dines require you to present your valid driver's license and
pay a small fee to obtain a local driving permit. An International Driving Permit (available from AAA) is sufficient
on St. Lucia and St. Vincent.

Use a good repellent to ward off tiny no-see-ums. Sand flies
often appear after a rain, near swampy ground, and around
sunset; mosquitoes also can be annoying.

PUERTO RICO

Spend a day in Old San Juan. Many people find themselves
with a single day, or less, to explore San Juan (it's one of
the Caribbean's largest home bases for cruise ships). If
you've only got one day, head straight for Old San Juan.
The incredible scenery, history, shopping, and dining here
make this compact, walkable area the best place for single-
day exploration.

**Leave your rental car behind for two destinations in Puerto
Rico.** Old San Juan: This is a walking city, with narrow,
one-way streets, narrower alleys, little parking, and sights
and shops packed together in an area hardly larger than
one square mile. Vieques or Culebra: The cargo ferry runs
at an erratic schedule, and may bump your vehicle at the
last minute if there is no room. Besides, you need a 4x4 to
navigate the island roads.

Reserve your car from home in peak seasons. This isn't only
because of possible discounts, but also to ensure that you
get a car and that it's a reliable one. Also, always opt for
air-conditioning; you'll be glad you did when it's high noon
and you're in a San Juan traffic jam.

Wear a shirt and shoes. It's considered disrespectful to enter
a store or a restaurant in a bathing suit or other inappropriate attire, even though you may be spending a great deal
of time on the beach.

Tip appropriately. Some general guidelines for tipping for
good service on Puerto Rico are: restaurant waitstaff, 15%
to 20% (if a service charge isn't included); hotel porters, $1
per bag; maids, $1 to $2 per day; taxi drivers, 15% to 18%.
Some hotels automatically add a 5% to 12% service charge
to your bill. Check ahead to confirm whether this charge is
built into the room rate or will be tacked on at checkout.

U.S. AND BRITISH VIRGIN ISLANDS

BVI

Pick your island carefully. Tortola gives you a wide choice of restaurants, shops, and resorts. Virgin Gorda has fewer off-resort places to eat or shop, but its resorts are often better than those on the other islands, and its beaches are exquisite. Diving and snorkeling don't get any easier than around remote Anegada, where vibrant reefs are often just feet from the shore. Jost Van Dyke has classic Caribbean beach bars and basic accommodations.

Head elsewhere for wild nightlife. The BVI are mostly quiet and casual, so don't expect to party until dawn, and definitely leave the tux at home. Luxury here means getting away from it all rather than getting the trendiest state-of-the-art amenities.

14

Know that tipping in the BVI is straightforward. Hotel porters get $1 per bag. Sometimes a 10% service charge is added to restaurant bills; if so, it's customary to leave another 5%. Otherwise, tip 15%. Cabbies normally aren't tipped, as they usually own their cabs, though you could round up the fare to the nearest whole number; if service was above and beyond, tip 10%–15%.

USVI

Pick your island carefully. St. Thomas is the most developed, great if you want to shop, see historic sights, play golf, or dine out a lot. The more luxurious resorts are on the island's eastern end. St. John is mostly national park, and as the least developed of the three islands is good if you want a small-island feel and easy access to great hiking. That said, most of the villas aren't right on the beach. St. Croix has everything from simple inns to luxury resorts, including some places that specialize in diving on the north coast. That said, none of its beaches rivals those on St. Thomas or St. John.

Avoid Charlotte Amalie when the ships pull in. St. Thomas's hub is the Caribbean's busiest cruise-ship port. On a busy port day in high season as many as eight ships may anchor in the harbor. Plan accordingly.

Plan to tip on the USVI as you would on the U.S. mainland. Many hotels add 10%–15% service charge to your bill, but it's not always a sure thing that all the money reaches the staff. If you want to err on the side of generosity, tip porters $1 per bag and chambermaids $1 or $2. Bartenders and waitresses get 10%–15%, but always check your tab first to see whether or not service is included. Tip cabbies 15%.

CANADA

Don't skip the tip—it's not included in your bill. In general, tip 15% to 20% of the total bill. This goes for waiters and waitresses, barbers and hairdressers, and taxi drivers. Porters and doormen should get about C$2 a bag. For maid service, leave at least C$2 per person a day (C$3 to C$5 in luxury hotels).

Know about the dough. The units of currency in Canada are the Canadian dollar (C$) and the cent, in almost the same denominations as U.S. currency ($5, $10, $20, 1¢, 5¢, 10¢, 25¢, etc.). The $1 and $2 bills have been replaced by $1 and $2 coins, known as "loonies"—because of the loon that appears on the coin—and "toonies," respectively.

Ship if the option's offered. Many shops ship purchases home for you; when they do, you may avoid having to pay the steep provincial taxes. By courier, a package takes only a few days, but via regular Canada Post mail packages often take a week—or longer—to reach the United States. Be sure to address everything properly and wrap it securely.

Remember that going to Canada from the United States means crossing an international border. All travelers now need a passport or other accepted secure documents to enter or reenter the United States. Naturalized U.S. residents should carry their naturalization certificate. Permanent residents who aren't citizens should carry their Permanent Resident Card, more commonly known as a green card. U.S. residents entering Canada from a third country must have a valid passport, naturalization certificate, or green card.

Carry insect repellent in the woods in summer. This is particularly true in northern Canada, and in June, which is blackfly season.

MONTRÉAL AND QUÉBEC

Learn a few French phrases. They'll be appreciated in the province of Québec or in French-Canadian communities elsewhere. And bring along a French-English dictionary.

Be hotel savvy. Canada doesn't have a national rating system for hotels, but Québec's tourism ministry rates the province's hotels and bed-and-breakfasts; the stars are more a reflection of the number of facilities than of the hotel's performance. Hotels are rated zero to three stars (B&Bs, zero to four suns), with zero stars or suns representing minimal comfort and few services and three stars or four suns being the very best.

Try some poutine. Poutine is everywhere. But it's no longer just hot french fries topped with cheese curds and a ladle-ful of thick brown gravy, as dozens of high- and lowbrow variations have sprung up. You might want to try poutine Michigan, for example, which replaces the gravy with spaghetti sauce, or poutine poulet, which adds chunks of barbecued chicken to the mix.

Enjoy hockey night. What soccer is to Brazilians and base-ball is to Americans, hockey is to the Québecois. It's not a game, it's a religion, and its winter-long rites are celebrated in hundreds of arenas across the province.

Be sure to explore Montréal's Underground City. Note that the network of tunnels, shops, and subway lines beneath the city's surface is so large that you'll want to use the Métro to save time and energy. Remember: It's easy to get lost. There are no landmarks, and routes are seldom direct, so keep your eyes on the signs (a Métro map helps). And if you start to feel panicky, come up for air.

Allot ample time for an Ile d'Orleans crossing. It may not look far when you have a map in hand, but it will take longer than you think to cross this island on one of the three roads—especially in winter—so plan accordingly.

Learn to say "eh." Canada's "eh" is like France's "*zut, alors,*" except that in Canada people actually say "eh," and say it all the time. Master this verbal tic and you'll fit in, even here in French-speaking Québec.

Check whether your bill includes gratuity. Tips and service charges aren't usually added to a bill in Canada. In gen-eral, tip 15% of the total bill. This goes for waiters and waitresses, barbers and hairdressers, and taxi drivers. Por-ters and doormen should get about C$2 a bag. For maid service, leave at least C$2 per person a day (C$3 to C$5 in luxury hotels).

TORONTO

Save on weekends and holidays using one C$10 TTC day pass. You can share with up to two adults and four children. Most downtown attractions are accessible by subway or streetcar. The single fare for subways, buses, and street-cars is C$3. An all-day unlimited-use pass is C$10. There are three subway lines, with 65 stations along the way: the Bloor–Danforth line, which crosses Toronto about 5 km (3 mi) north of the lakefront, from east to west; the Yonge–University line, which loops north and south like a giant "U," with the bottom of the "U" at Union Station; and the Sheppard line, which covers the northeastern section of the city.

Go underground to get around downtown in inclement weather. PATH, Toronto's underground city is an 11-km-long (7-mi-long) subterranean walkway lined with eateries, shops, banks, and medical offices. You can walk from beneath Union Station to the Fairmont Royal York hotel, the Toronto-Dominion Centre, First Canadian Place, the Sheraton Centre, the Bay, Eaton Centre, and City Hall without ever seeing the light of day, encountering everything from art exhibitions to buskers and walkways, fountains, and trees.

See what festivals are scheduled during your visit. Festivals keep Toronto lively even when cold winds blow in off Lake Ontario in winter. Themes range from art to food, Caribbean culture to gay pride. **Toronto Tourism** (☎416/203–2500 or 800/499–2514 ⊕ www.seetorontonow.com) maintains an online calendar of nearly every event in the city.

VANCOUVER AND VICTORIA

Be ready for changing weather in Vancouver and Victoria. Layering is the best solution, and unless "swank" is on your to-do list, ditch the tie, because West Coast casual means smart cotton dress pants or jeans and T-shirts. Ward off cool summer breezes with a light jacket or pashmina; bring Gore-Tex for warmth in winter and, year-round, it's never a bad idea to stash something waterproof. Vancouver and Victoria are walking cities, so pack comfortable shoes, and if you forget an umbrella, they're a dime a dozen at every corner store.

Get yourself to a noodle bar, sushi shop, or curry house. You'll find more authentic Chinese food in Vancouver's

Chinatown than almost anywhere in the world other than China–better than New York or Toronto—so come with an appetite.

CENTRAL AMERICA

Keep poor road conditions in mind. Given Central America's often difficult driving conditions, distances that appear short on a map can represent hours of driving on dirt roads pocked with craters. Always make sure that you have a spare tire and a jack before setting off.

Respect local etiquette. Revealing clothing is frowned upon, especially in more rural areas. Be quiet when visiting a house of worship, and don't photograph people praying. When on a bus, give up your seat to an elderly person or a woman carrying a child. Strangers still rely on a handshake for first introductions—although a hearty *abrazo* (hug) will sometimes replace the handshake on your second meeting. Other customs are more nuanced and vary from country to country, so you should observe locals and follow their lead.

14

Say "hello" appropriately. Greetings in Central Americas tend to be formal, especially among older people. The use of the formal "you" form, *usted*, is much more common than in other Spanish-speaking areas.

Don't count on using plastic. Carry enough cash or traveler's checks outside cities. Major credit cards are accepted at most of the larger hotels and more expensive restaurants throughout Central America. As the phone system improves, many smaller hotels, restaurants, and other facilities are accepting credit cards. Still, it's not common. Some hotels, restaurants, tour companies, and other businesses will give you a 5%–15% discount if you pay in cash.

Avoid people who offer to exchange money. They are notorious for shortchanging tourists unfamiliar with the local currency.

Be prepared for power surges. They're fairly common in Central America, so consider carrying a surge stabilizer if you'll be traveling with an expensive electrical device such as a laptop.

Bring a flashlight. Streetlights are rare, which means that when the sun goes down, it's dark. At jungle lodges and many resorts, power is often from generators. At a certain time of night, they are usually shut off and illumination is provided via lanterns and torches. During the rainy season, in El Salvador and possibly elsewhere, the electricity can go out for hours at time.

BELIZE

Know when to go. The rainy season lasts from around June through November; the tourist season (mid-November through April) coincides with the dry season, which runs from December through May. The busiest time is Christmas, followed by Easter and Thanksgiving.

Don't bother brushing up on your Spanish. The primary language spoken in Belize is English.

Pack for the regions you're visiting. For example, if you want to visit both the Cayo (cool nights) and the Cayes (hot, hot, hot), your wardrobe might include a warm polar-fleece jacket and some lightweight T-shirts and shorts.

Save by using the municipal Belize City airport for flights within Belize. Costs are as much as 45% lower on domestic flights, compared to similar flights to or from Philip Goldson International Airport, north of the city in Ladyville.

WORD OF MOUTH. "I think that while in Belize you should experience both sides of the 'Belizean Coin,' so to speak. The best way to do so is by visiting both the inland and island. There are many resorts which partner with each other to offer Rainforest and Reef Itineraries, which can be customized to your liking in order to enhance your experience." —Josue_CyoBze

Tip like a Belizean. Belize restaurants rarely add a service charge, so in better restaurants, tip 10%–15% of the total bill. At inexpensive places, leave small change or tip 10%. Many hotels and resorts add a service charge, usually 10%, to bills, so at these places additional tipping isn't necessary. In general, Belizeans tend not to look for tips, though with increasing tourism this is changing. It's not customary to tip taxi drivers.

COSTA RICA

Get to the capital and then get out. San José is not representative of what Costa Rica has to offer. Don't plan to stay long; use the city just as a transportation hub and for any last-minute necessities—although there are a few good international restaurants, if you do have a night to kill.

Reserve rental cars several months in advance. This is a must if you plan to rent any kind of vehicle between December 15 and January 3, or during Holy Week around Easter, in April.

Pack light. A luggage weight limit of 11.3 kilograms or 25 pounds is almost always enforced on the tiny domestic planes.

Hire a professional, bilingual nature guide. To get the most out of your trip, hire someone who can turn what looks like a mass of green foliage to the untrained eye into a widely diversified trove of plants and creatures great and small—one of the highlights of a trip here. For the full effect, bring or borrow binoculars.

14

Tip only for good service. Costa Rica doesn't have a tipping culture, but positive reinforcement goes a long way. Taxi drivers aren't tipped, but leave an extra 200 colones–300 colones if they've helped you navigate a complicated set of directions. Chambermaids get 1,000 colones to 1,500 colones per day; for great service, try to leave up to 10% of your room bill. Concierges are usually not tipped. Room-service waiters should be tipped about 500 colones, as should bellhops (more in the most expensive hotels). Restaurant bills include a 13% tax and 10% service charge—if the menu doesn't indicate whether service is included, ask. An additional gratuity is not expected, especially in cheap restaurants. Leave a tip of about 200 colones per drink for bartenders. Give $10 (or 5,000 colones) per day per person to guides, and about 10% of the rental to a hired driver of a small car. Give less to guides or drivers on bigger tours.

EL SALVADOR

Try *pupusa*. No food is more typically Salvadoran: it's a fried tortilla filled with beans, cheese, and/or *chicharrón* (pork skin). A pupusa called a *revuelta* has all three fillings mixed together. Delicious *pupusas de arroz* are made with rice flour and are not quite as thick; rather, they have a certain lightness, though they are still quite filling. *Loroco*, a sprouty green local vegetable, is also a popular and interesting filling. All are found in *pupuserías*, where they're served with spicy tomato sauce and a vinegary pickled cabbage and carrot concoction called *curtido*.

Be tip savvy. As in many Central American countries, a 10% to 15% tip is already built into the bill. Leave a little extra if your experience was really fantastic. Tour guides should receive the equivalent of US$1 to US$5 per day.

GUATEMALA

Get vaccinated. Malaria is prevalent in areas below 1,500 meters (4,900 feet)—both Antigua and Lake Atitlán are too high to be at risk. Another mosquito-borne disease, dengue, is also a threat, particularly on the Pacific coast. The best way to prevent both is to avoid being bitten: Cover up your arms and legs and use ample repellent, preferably one containing DEET. The CDC recommends chloroquine as a preventative antimalarial for adults and infants in Guatemala. To be effective, the weekly doses must start a week before you travel and continue four weeks after your return. There is no preventive medication for dengue.

Be smart about food safety. Drink only bottled water, called *agua purificada* or *agua mineral*. It is available even at the smallest stores, and is much cheaper than in North America. Use bottled water even when brushing your teeth. Ask for your drinks *sin hielo,* meaning "without ice." Skip uncooked foods, fruits with the skin on, and unpasteurized milk and milk products. Words to remember: "Boil it, cook it, peel it, or forget it."

Don't ride public buses in Guatemala City. Guatemala's network of red public buses logs dozens of thefts (and a few armed robberies) each day. Your chances as an outsider of escaping unscathed are slim, so we advise against using the system. Taxis are plentiful and reasonably priced; take them instead. The exception to the "no bus" rule is the TransMetro, a system of green public buses that travel on special lanes and stop at fixed stations with ample security.

Don't engage Antigua street vendors. Antigua's streets are full of women and children peddling their wares, but only converse with them if you're serious about buying. The vendors get aggressive, and will follow you around in the hope that you'll break down and buy something. If you're not interested, don't make eye contact and keep walking.

Don't hike alone. The lonely slopes of the volcanoes near Antigua and Lake Atitlán have been frequented by muggers, so go with a group of people, a reputable guide, or a member of the Tourist Police, and carry only minimal valuables.

Limit your interactions with children. The increase in adoption of Guatemalan children has provoked the fear by many here, particularly in rural villagers, that children will be abducted by foreigners. Limit your interaction with children you do not know, and never take photos of children without asking permission from their parents first.

Book early if your trip coincides with Easter. The busiest time of the year is around Holy Week, from Palm Sunday to Easter Sunday. Hotels in Antigua, Panajachel, and Chichicastenango fill up months ahead of time.

Spend the night at Tikal. The best way to experience the incomparable Maya ruins is to get up just before the birds do, from a hotel within the park, and head toward the deserted plaza with a guide. From the top of one of the scalable pyramids the well-trained guards can show you an enormous array of wildlife that disappears from the park during the day. It is unbelievably breathtaking.

Visit a market. Each major town has one—each seemingly better than the last. Some reach their pinnacle on Sunday, like the one in Chichicastenango, which is a favorite with locals and international visitors alike. Colorful handicrafts, leather goods, handwoven fabrics, and carved masks of mythological animals are just some of the gorgeous wares.

Travel in private shuttles. Private minivans hold up to eight passengers, are faster and more comfortable than public buses (former school buses), and maintain a fairly reliable schedule. All that said, they cost more than the alternatives and usually require reservations. Shuttles can be arranged at the airport, at travel agencies, and at most hotels.

Tip for good service. In Guatemala tipping is a question of rewarding good service rather than an obligation. Restaurant bills don't include gratuities; adding 10% is customary. Bellhops and maids expect tips only in the most expensive hotels. You should also give a small tip to tour guides, or to guards who show you around ruins. Rounding up taxi fares is a way of showing your appreciation to the driver, but it's not expected.

HONDURAS

Hire a reliable guide for any of the archaeological sites you visit. You can enjoy the majesty of Copán without much help, but to truly appreciate the rich symbolic meaning of everything you see around you, you'll need an interpreter. Local experts are good, but snag someone with real academic archaeological experience if you can.

Never use the wandering money changers. You'll see them around the plazas in most big cities. Use a bank instead.

Be aware of what you do with used toilet paper. Flushing it is usually discouraged. Even if there's no sign saying what to do, a basket next to the toilet will indicate that you should toss your paper there. Don't worry—these are emptied often.

WORD OF MOUTH. "I just spent several days in Tegus and quite enjoyed them. We hired our hotel driver to take us to Valle de Ángeles and Santa Lucía, which is a really pleasant trip. We also visited the art gallery and the new museum. The central square is an interesting place to hang out and people-watch. We also saw a performance of a Garifuna dance troupe." —Heather49

Check to see if the tip is already included in your bill. In Honduras, if you see the word *servicio* when you get your bill, the tip has been included in the main charge. Other places suggest a *propina voluntaria*, a voluntary tip. The bill may specify what the amount should be, or it may not. Still other places do nothing at all. In any case, 10% to 15% of the bill is a good amount to tip your waiter or waitress. A tip of about L20 per day is an acceptable tip for housekeeping staff, though the *servicio* may be included in your final bill at checkout. If in doubt, ask.

Tip in lempiras. A tip in dollars requires the recipient to stand in line at the bank—and they're usually long lines—to change your tip into local currency.

NICARAGUA

Tip appropriately. A tip is only expected at pricier restaurants, where it's often included (look for *servicio* on the check). Most servers receive only minimal compensation, so even a córdoba or two is a nice gesture at cheaper restaurants. Taxi drivers aren't tipped. Generally, any stranger who offers to do you a favor (like watch your parked car) expects a tip.

Refer to the locals the way the locals do. The term *Nica*, a shortened form of *Nicaragüense*, serves invariably as both noun or adjective no matter what gender is being referred to (in Spanish, masculine words tend to end in *o* and feminine ones in *a*).

Learn about Nicaraguan politics from Nicaraguans. Many people here love a spirited discussion about the direction the country should take. If your Spanish is up to the task, don't be afraid to listen in—though within the confines of the local cantina, take what you hear with a grain of salt. Do let your acquaintances take the lead in the discussion; you'll be amply rewarded with some amazing insights.

PANAMA

Stay healthy in Panama. If you're traveling anywhere outside the Canal Zone, you'll need a yellow fever shot. Dengue fever and malaria are prevalent throughout the country, but are particularly an issue in Bocas del Toro, Darién, and San Blas. Cover up, and use mosquito repellent and netting. Talk to your doctor about taking antimalarial drugs (there's no preventive medicine for dengue).

Choose your Panama Canal cruise with care. Many cruise itineraries include a crossing, but you miss out on the country itself, because ships don't actually call at a port in Panama. Companies in Panama City offer full (whole-day) or partial (half-day) transits, both guided, of the canal. Note, though, that partial transits only run a few days each month, and coast-to-coast transits run only once or twice a month.

Don't worry about currency exchange in Panama if you have U.S. dollars. The dollar is the de facto currency; the Panamanians refer to it as the *balboa,* named for explorer Vasco Nuñez de Balboa who "discovered" the Pacific Ocean and claimed it for Spain. You'll see prices written as B1 or $1, and although the country does mint its own coins (of the same size and value as their U.S. counterparts), both types of currency circulate freely.

Plan to tip in Panama. As taxis aren't metered and you should sort out the fare ahead of time, any intended tip should be part of that fare. Hotels generally tack a service charge on to your bill. Regardless, you should tip porters $1 per bag and chambermaids $1 per night. If there's no service charge on your restaurant tab, a 10% to 15% tip for decent service is appropriate.

EUROPE

Before booking travel between cities in Europe, compare modes of transport. Many cities are so close together that flying hardly makes sense. For instance, it may take just half an hour to fly between London and Paris, but you must factor in time spent getting to and from the airports, plus check-in time. A three-hour train ride from city center to city center might be a better alternative.

Buy Eurail Passes before leaving for Europe. You can buy passes in many major European train stations, but prices are typically 20% higher than if you buy in advance online, and not all types of passes are available.

Note that Eurail Passes aren't honored in Britain. They are effective in the following 25 countries: Austria, Belgium, Bulgaria, Croatia, the Czech Republic, Denmark, Finland, France, Germany, Greece, Hungary, Italy, Luxembourg, Montenegro, the Netherlands, Norway, Poland, Portugal, Republic of Ireland, Romania, Serbia, Slovenia, Spain, Sweden, and Switzerland.

Reserve a car before you leave home. This is the way to get the best car-rental rates.

Be euro-wise. The euro is the accepted currency throughout most of Europe, with the following exceptions: the Czech Republic, Denmark, Great Britain, Norway, Sweden, and Switzerland. Euro coins and notes are broken down into denominations similar to U.S. dollars, and are easy for North Americans to understand and use. In recent years the value of the euro has fluctuated between $1.25 and $1.65.

Bring a little starter money. It's a good idea to pick up a small amount of your destination's currency before you leave home. Many banks have limited supplies of foreign bills on hand, so you may have to order money a week or so in advance.

Once you're in Europe, use the ATMs. True, your own bank will probably charge a fee for using ATMs abroad, as well as the foreign bank you use. Nevertheless, you'll usually get a better rate of exchange at an ATM than you will at a currency-exchange office or even when changing money in a bank. And extracting funds as you need them is a safer option than carrying around a large amount of cash. Make sure before leaving home that your credit and debit cards have been programmed for ATM use abroad—ATMs in Europe usually require PINs of four digits.

AUSTRIA

If you're headed to western Austria, consider flying to Munich. The western sector of Austria—including Tirol and Vorarlberg—is actually closer to southern Germany's hub city than to Vienna, and Munich is very close to Salzburg or Innsbruck via train.

Be sure to get an Autobahnvignette sticker (sometimes called a Pickerl) if traveling the autobahns. Your car will need one of these stickers (which show a highway icon and Austrian eagle, or with a calendar marked with an "M" or a "W"). It's available at gas stations.

14

Greetings are an important part of day-to-day interaction. Remember it's customary to say *Grüss Gott* or *Guten Tag,* "good day," to the shopkeeper as if he or she were an old friend—and a hearty *Auf Wiedersehen,* good-bye, on leaving.

Watch out for that sneaky "bread and butter" charge. Most Viennese restaurants charge a small fee for each roll that is eaten. Increasingly, however, eateries are using a per-person cover charge, which includes all the bread you want, usually with an herb spread and butter.

Tip judiciously in Austria. Although virtually all hotels and restaurants include service charges in their rates, tipping is still customary, but at a level lower than in the United States. In small country inns, such tips are not expected but are appreciated. Tip the hotel concierge only for special services or in response to special requests; maids normally get no tip unless your stay is a week or more or service has been special. Big tips are not usual in Austrian restaurants, since 10% has already been included in the prices.

BELGIUM

Be sure to leave a small tip. Tipping 15% to 20% of the cost of a meal is not common practice in Belgium or in the Netherlands. Instead, it is customary to round off the total to a convenient figure, to reward good service. If paying with a credit card, pay the exact amount of the bill with your card, and leave a few euros in cash on the table for the waiting staff.

Plan ahead for beer. Almost as requisite as riding a bicycle in Brussels or hiking the high moors of Wallonia on your Belgian adventure is sampling the local brews, the making of which is a tradition that dates back centuries. Westvleteren Trappist comes highly recommended. Some breweries offer tours only by appointment; call ahead—it's worth it.

Be ready for linguistic overload. Belgium has three official languages—Flemish, French, and German—and many citizens have strong allegiances to their region's particular linguistic flavor (except Brussels, which is bilingual in Flemish and French). When in doubt, use English, which is widely understood and a less contentious choice; assuming incorrectly can be nearly as taboo here as bringing up politics.

Eat french fries. These are a Belgian invention. Stands (*friterie* in French or *frituur* in Flemish) serve them in large cones, with a selection of condiments that go far beyond banal ketchup. Another favorite snack is the famous Belgian waffle (*gaufres* in French, *waffels* in Flemish), which you can buy at stands and in some city bakeries. Waffles are considered an afternoon snack here, though.

EASTERN EUROPE

Never photograph Gypsies without asking. It's best to ask for permission and agree on payment. Photographing anything or anyone military, assuming you'd want to, is usually prohibited. Otherwise, although most other people are pleased to be photographed, it's respectful to ask first.

Buy fresh fruits and vegetables at street markets. Regular grocery stores often don't sell them.

Pack vitamins and protein bars if you don't eat much meat. Vegetarians and those on special diets may have a problem with the heavy local cuisine, which is based largely on pork and beef.

Beware of unpasteurized milk products. In Romania, unrefrigerated milk sold in outdoor markets or in villages may not be pasteurized and can make Westerners sick. In Bulgaria, mayonnaise-based fillings are very common in *sandvitchee*—the ubiquitous toasted sandwiches sold at many street kiosks; avoid them.

Bring necessities. Some items that you take for granted at home are occasionally unavailable or of questionable quality in Eastern and Central Europe, though the situation has been steadily improving. Toiletries and personal-hygiene products have become relatively easy to find, but it's always a good idea to bring necessities when traveling in rural areas.

Beware of pickpockets in crowded areas, especially on public transportation, at railway stations, and in big hotels. Crime rates are still relatively low in Eastern and Central Europe, but you should always keep your valuables with you; in open bars and restaurants, purses hung on or placed next to chairs are easy targets. Men: Make sure your wallet is safe in a buttoned pocket. Women: Watch your handbag.

Avoid getting ripped off as a tourist. In the Czech Republic and Slovakia ask taxi drivers what the approximate fare will be before getting in. Asking for a receipt (*paragon* in the Czech Republic and *potvrdenka* in Slovakia) might also discourage a driver from charging you an enormous fare—or it could be used when complaining about a fare to a taxi dispatcher. Carefully look over restaurant bills, be extremely wary of handing your passport to anyone who accosts you with a demand for ID, and never exchange money on the street.

BUDAPEST
Don't plan to shop on Sunday or see museums on Monday. Many shops close Saturday afternoon and all day Sunday; museums tend to close on Monday. Depending on your timing, it may be prudent to reshuffle these daily itineraries.

Take a tour to see Parliament. It's the only way travelers are allowed in; English-language tours run daily at 10, noon, and 2. To avoid long lines, it is advisable to reserve a place in advance.

Consider skipping the conventional boat tour along the Danube. Do-it-yourselfers can paddle around Budapest by canoe or kayak. In summer you'll find rental facilities on Margaret Island.

Take the shortcut to Castle Hill. If you're not staying on Castle Hill, getting up it may seem daunting. Spare your tired legs by taking the funicular between the Chain Bridge and the Castle Hill district.

Know that City Park is fun in winter, too. Its rowing pond doubles as a skating rink in winter and its outdoor thermal pools remain open year-round.

WORD OF MOUTH. "Most of the spas have two types of water pools: Pools for bathing/soaking (sitting and relaxing in hot water) and pools for swimming (doing laps and rounds) . . . I observed that caps were required in the communal swimming pools (men and women) but not in the separated bathing/soaking pools on the men's side." —Mathieu

Be tipping-savvy in Budapest. Taxi drivers expect 10% to 15% tips; porters should get 200 HUF to 400 HUF. Dressing room attendants at the thermal baths receive 50 HUF to 100 HUF for opening and closing your locker. Gratuities are not included automatically on bills at most restaurants, so you should add a 10% to 15% tip to the bill. It's not customary to leave the tip on the table.

CROATIA AND SLOVENIA

When to go: Factor in the birds. Slovenia can get hot in summer, so you may want to save this region for spring, late summer, or early fall. Indeed, given that hundreds of thousands of birds gather at the Kopački Rit Nature Park in April, May, and early June and again around September and into October, a visit during such a time would be optimal.

Raise a glass of rakija. Get two Croatians together, and somebody's bound to introduce this distilled herbal or fruit spirit that makes up an important part of Croatian culture. All across the country business deals are sealed, friendships are cemented, and journeys are begun to the clink of a few shot glasses of the fiery schnapps.

For budget eats, try the burek. This local take on the sandwich is a local delicacy. Although Zagreb is not exactly overflowing with budget sandwich shops, traditional bakeries have long fulfilled that role for locals. At such places, which are on practically every street corner, you can pick up a burek for as little as 10 Kn a piece.

Bring the kids—and some extra patience. Travel in Slovenia and Croatia is generally safe for families—you'll find playgrounds in nearly every city—but there isn't a lot of special attention paid to the needs of children otherwise. It's hit or miss as to whether you'll find a high chair in a restaurant, and very few have child-specific menus.

Know how to tip. When eating out in Croatia, if you've enjoyed your meal and are satisfied with your service, it's customary to leave a 10% to 15% tip. It's not typical to tip in cafes or bars. Maids and taxi drivers are not usually tipped either. Tour guides do receive a tip, especially if they're particularly good. For porters on trains and bell-hops at hotels, a 5–10 Kn per bag tip will be appreciated.

POLAND

Hang up or check your coat when at restaurants. Slinging your coat over the back of your chair is frowned upon. In nicer restaurants there will likely be a coat check; more casual restaurants usually have hooks next to the tables. Only put your coat on the back of your chair if there are no alternatives.

Dress and behave modestly when entering churches. Shorts, skirts noticeably above your knees, and any sleeveless tops are considered disrespectful. Keep your voice down and be sure to check for signs limiting photography before pulling out your camera. Catholicism in Poland may not be mono-lithic or orthodox, but its traditions infuse every aspect of Polish life. Even nonbelivers observe some of its traditions.

14

Avoid casual body contact. Polish people are not very physi-cally demonstrative, so avoid making lots of hand gestures, tapping people on their arms or shoulders, or other such contact. Handshakes are the most common greeting. On the other hand, direct eye contact *is* standard, especially when making a toast.

Try a Polish home remedy if you've had a bit too much vodka. If you're feeling the bite of the Polish national drink, revive with a bowl of red *barszcz* (borscht). A pale sour rye soup is also a popular hangover cure, but that's more of an acquired taste.

Know that tipping is a tricky in Poland. First, not tipping here really does indicate displeasure. Service charges may or may not be added in restaurants. If not, 10%–15% of the bill is fine. Here's the catch, though: You should only thank your waiter or waitress after he or she returns with your change, not before—unless you aren't expecting to get any change back. This also applies when dealing with cabbies, who should be tipped about 10%. Hotel porters get the equivalent of $1 or $2 per bag; chambermaids the same amount per night. Tour guides get about $10 per day.

FRANCE

If you can handle French, reserve train tickets in advance at voyages-sncf.com. To book in English and get the same full range of fares, go to tgv-europe.com. To keep the site in English and avoid being bumped to the Rail Europe site (which doesn't offer discount fares), just choose Great Britain as country of residence.

Know when to tip and how to get your check. In restaurants you must ask for the check (it's considered rude to bring it unbidden) except in cafés, where a register slip often comes with your order. Gratuities (*servis*) are included in the bill, but leave some small change on the table: a few cents for drinks, €1 for lunch, or €3 for dinner. You can leave more at a top restaurant, but note that more than 10% is considered extremely generous.

Make an effort to speak French. A simple, friendly *bonjour* (hello) will do, as will asking whether the person you are greeting speaks English. Be patient, and speak English slowly.

Call ahead. When planning to visit museums, restaurants, and hotels, phone in advance to make sure they will be open. With 11 national *jours feriés* (holidays) and five weeks of paid vacation, the French have their share of repose. In May there's a holiday nearly every week, so be prepared for stores, banks, and museums to be shut for days at a time.

Rent a car if you're traveling in a group. Though renting a car in France is expensive—about twice as much as in the United States, as is gas—it can pay off if you're traveling with two or more people.

Board trains early for good seats. A half hour before departure is optimal. Before boarding, you must punch your ticket (but not Eurail Pass) in one of the orange machines at the entrance to the platforms, or else the ticket collector will fine you €15.

Know the distinction between private and public beaches. All along the coast, private waterfront is roped off and advertised by color-coordinated awnings, parasols, and mattresses. For a fee, you can access some of these private beaches—which often have full restaurant and bar service—and rent mattresses, umbrellas, and lounge chairs by the day or half day. But interspersed between these commercial beaches is plenty of public space, with open access and (usually) the necessary comforts of toilets and cold-rinse "showers."

Forget your dieting plans. When was the last time you were in a country with more than 500 types of cheese? It would be a shame to come all this way only to deny yourself participation in the French culinary delights. Help yourself to big slabs of cheese and bread, and wash it all down with a good red wine.

PARIS

Eat at the counter. In many cafés and bars in Paris it's less expensive to eat or drink standing up at the counter than it is to sit at a table.

Opt for the fixed-price menu. If there is one, the fixed-price menu for lunch or dinner is definitely going to be less expensive than ordering à la carte. If it's not offered, feel free to ask for one. Note that on some fixed-price menus certain options come with a supplemental charge.

14

Get a Carte Orange for the métro. If you're going to be in Paris for a week, a Carte Orange will save you money with unlimited access, rather than paying per ride.

Learn how to read Parisian addresses. A site's location in one of the city's 20 arrondissements is noted by its mailing code or, simply, the last one or two digits of that code (for example, Paris 75010 or 10e, both of which indicate that the address is in the 10th arrondissement; Paris 75005 or 5e indicates that the address is in the 5th arrondissement).

PROVENCE

Take a bus to save money. Surely the biggest bargain in the south of France is the €1 bus ticket, valid anywhere between Cannes and Menton. The most scenic line is No. 100, running from Nice to Menton along the Moyenne Corniche. It runs every 15 minutes, but can get unpleasantly packed in high season. Buses connect Nice to Èze Village (20 minutes), St-Paul, and Vence (about an hour); be sure to check the schedule, because they are not frequent.

Reserve hotels in advance. Book way ahead if you're heading to art towns or *villages perchés* (hilltop villages). Many of these (St-Rémy in particular) have a tiny number of hotels and are always sold out in summer.

Bring your windbreaker if traveling in late autumn or early spring. Provence's infamous mistral is a bitterly cold and dry north wind that can drop the temperature in minutes, often triggering "mistral nerves" in locals.

GERMANY

Tip waiters directly. Instead of leaving the tip on the table, add it to the total amount when you pay. For example, if the bill is €2.70, tell the waitress "€3 please" when she comes to collect the money. When you get the check for something small, like a cup of coffee, round up to the next even euro. For larger amounts, tip 10%. German waitstaff are more than happy to split the check so that everyone can pay individually.

Always address acquaintances formally. Germans are more formal in addressing each other than Americans. Always address acquaintances as *Herr* (Mr.) or *Frau* (Mrs.) plus their last name; do not call them by their first name unless invited to do so. The German language has an informal and formal pronoun for "you": formal is *Sie*, and informal is *du*. Even if adults are on a first-name basis with one another, they may still keep to the *Sie* form. When addressing someone, always use the formal *Sie* until you are begged by them to switch to the informal *du*.

Don't be surprised by public nudity. Germans are less formal when it comes to nudity: a sign that reads FREIKÖRPER KULTUR or FKK indicates a park or beach that allows nude sunbathing. It's also normal to see children running around without clothes on in parks, at swimming pools, or at the beach.

Eat on a budget. *Imbiss* (snack) stands can be found in almost every busy shopping street, in parking lots, train stations, and near markets. They serve *Würste* (sausages), grilled, roasted, or boiled, and rolls filled with cheese, cold meat, or fish. Many stands sell Turkish-style wraps called *Döner Kebap*. Prices range from €1.50 to €2.50 per portion.

Under no circumstances use profanity or pejoratives. Germans take these very seriously, and a slip of the tongue can result in expensive criminal and civil penalties. Calling a police officer a "Nazi" or using vulgar finger gestures can cost you up €10,000 and two years in jail.

BERLIN

Buy a Berlin WelcomeCard. Buy Berlin discount cards to save on public transport. Sold by EurAid, Berliner Verkehrsbetriebe offices, the tourist office, and some hotels, the Berlin WelcomeCard entitles one adult and three children under age 14 to either two or three days of unlimited travel in the ABC fare zones for €18.90 or €25.90, respectively, and includes admission and tour discounts. The CityTourCard, good for two or three days of unlimited travel in the AB fare zones, costs €15.90 and €21.90, respectively, and includes 50 discounts, and up to three children under age 6 can accompany an adult. Tickets are available from vending machines at U-bahn and S-bahn stations.

Be willing to ride buses. Berlin is a spread-out city and distances between subway stations can be greater than they appear on a map. Consider taking the bus if your destination isn't near a subway—they move fairly quickly through the city and are well marked.

Validate your transportation card. It must be done the first time you use public transportation, whatever type of card you purchase.

14

Take a free tour. On both sides of the Brandenburg Gate walking-tour operators offer free tours of the Pariser Platz and the surrounding area in various languages. Although most of these are fairly entertaining and really free, be aware that some will end with a sales pitch for paid tours and request tips.

Consider a Berlin State Museums ticket package. For three days, you have access to more than 70 museums for €15.

GREAT BRITAIN

Save with sightseeing passes or memberships. These shave the high price of visiting castles, gardens, and historic houses. Some, including the Great British Heritage Pass and the English Heritage's Overseas Visitor Pass, are for specific lengths of time, from four days to a month. The National Trust's pass must be purchased before your trip. If you'll be spending time in Scotland, look into the Historic Scotland's Scottish Explorer Ticket or the National Trust for Scotland's Discovery Ticket. The VisitBritain Web site (⊕*www.visitbritain.us*) has information about these and other discounts; match what the pass or membership offers against your itinerary to see whether you'll save money.

Take a trip to the pub. Pubs aren't exactly bars; in Britain they're also gathering places, conversation zones, and even restaurants (some fancy ones are known as gastro pubs). Pubs are, generally speaking, where people go to meet their friends and catch up on one another's lives. You can order beer, soft drinks, or tea, and then proceed to mix with the regulars as you wish. Some pubs have restricted hours for children; check with the bartender. Pubs are now no-smoking, and relaxed licensing laws mean that they can stay open after the traditional 11 PM closing.

Drive on the left in Britain. This takes a bit of getting used to, and it's much easier if you're driving a British car in which the steering and mirrors are designed for U.K. conditions. Note that off main streets roads can be very narrow and winding. Pick up a copy of the official Highway Code (£2.50) at a service station, newsstand, or bookstore, or check it out online by going to ⊕ *www.direct.gov.uk* and putting "Highway Code" in the search bar. Besides driving rules and illustrations of signs and road markings, this booklet contains information for motorcyclists, cyclists, and pedestrians.

Always check whether tipping is necessary. Tipping is done in Britain just as in the United States, but at a lower level than you would back home. Tipping more can look like you're showing off. Do not tip theater ushers or bar staff in pubs—although you can offer to buy the latter a drink. There's no need to tip at clubs unless you're being served at your table. Many upscale or international restaurants and large hotels will add a 10%–15% service charge to your bill, so check before you hand out extra money. Bellhops get £1 to £3 per bag; hotel maids £2 to £3 a day. Taxi drivers expect 10% to 15%, but always round up to the next pound.

Expect to get your own drinks at pubs. Most pubs don't have any waitstaff, and you're expected to go to the bar and order a beverage and your meal—this can be particularly disconcerting when you are seated in a "restaurant" upstairs but are still expected to go downstairs and get your own drinks and food.

LONDON

Take advantage of free museums and the city's parks. Many of London's best cultural attractions charge no admission, and the number of free museums is staggering. The British Museum, National Gallery, Tate Modern, Natural History Museum, and Science Museum are a few from the top of the list (though there may be a fee for special exhibitions). You can dip in and out of these and then relax with the locals for free in Hyde Park, Regent's Park, or others.

Plan your airport transfer—it's not cheap. Tube, taxi, or the Heathrow or Gatwick Express are the most common ways to go, each with its pluses and minuses. Taking the Tube (London's underground subway system) is the cheapest way to reach most points in central London (£4.50 at this writing), but you'll have to lug your bags. Taxi trips from Heathrow can take more than an hour and cost £50-plus, depending upon traffic. From Gatwick (90 minutes), the taxi fare is at least £70 plus tip. Another option is the Heathrow Express train, which makes the trip to London Paddington in 15 minutes. Standard one-way tickets cost £16.50 (£32 round-trip). Gatwick has a similar train. But then you'll likely need a taxi to your city hotel.

Buy an Oyster card or Travelcard for the Underground and buses. To save money and get discounted fares, purchase an electronic Oyster card at a Tube station for £3, charge it with a cash value, and use it on the Tube or on buses around the city. You reload it with money as needed. Another option is a Travelcard, sold for a specific number of days (even one day) of travel and good for buses and for specific zones in the Tube system. Buses are a good way to see the town, particularly if you plan to hop on and off to cover many sights—but don't take a bus if you are in a hurry.

14

WORD OF MOUTH. "Having just got back from London, I'd recommend an Oyster travel card to anyone staying more than two days." —khunwilko

SCOTLAND

Take the ferry. Because Scotland has so many islands, ferry services are of paramount importance. Most ferries transport vehicles as well as foot passengers, although a few smaller ones are for passengers only. It's a good idea to make a reservation ahead of time, although reservations are not absolutely necessary. These are working ferries, not tourist boats. The main operator is Caledonian MacBrayne, known as CalMac. It sells an Island Rover runabout ticket, ideal for touring holidays in the islands, as well as an island-hopping scheme called Island Hopscotch. Fares range from £4 for a short trip to almost £50 for a longer trip with several legs.

Research bringing your own golf clubs. Call the golf course and your airline for details. Airlines may not necessarily treat golf clubs as typical luggage, and you may have to pay an extra fee or follow packing instructions in order to bring them over on your flight. When you book your tee time, which you should do in advance (many places let you book online), check about clubs. Except at the most basic courses, equipment is generally available for rent.

Beware the biting midge. Pack some insect repellent to deter this tiny biting fly if you're traveling in the Highlands and islands in summer; the Highland midge is a force to be reckoned with. You might want to set out on a hike after a windy spell, when the creatures have been temporarily beaten back. Antihistamine cream is helpful in reducing swelling of bites you do get.

GREECE

Be smart about choosing a ferry to the Greek Islands. Take into account the number of stops and the arrival time: Sometimes a ferry that leaves an hour later gets you there faster! Catamarans and hydrofoils are pricier, and you need to reserve in advance in summer, but they cut travel time in half. Remember that if the sea is choppy sailings are often canceled. The main ferry line is Hellenic Seaways; the main booking engine is *www.greekferries.com.*

Expect variable place-name transliterations. Examples: Agios or Ayios, Georgios or Yiorgos. Also, the English version may differ from the local Greek version: Corfu is known as Kerkyra; island capitals are often just called Chora (town); and Athens's boulevard Vasilissis Sofias (Queen Sofia) was renamed Eleftheriou Venizelou, but you'll likely get blank stares if you call it that.

Be careful with your gestures. The Greek "no"—a tipping back of the head, sometimes with the eyes closed and eyebrows raised—looks like our "yes." And Greeks often wave good-bye with the palm facing them, which looks like "come here" to English speakers, while our palm-outward wave may be interpreted as "come here" by them.

Check your expectations. Lodging is less expensive in Greece than in most EU countries, but, except in Athens, quality is often lower, too. Of particular note: In most low-end hotels (and restaurants, shops, and other public places) the plumbing is delicate enough to require that toilet paper be trashed rather than flushed.

Tip like a pro in Greece. For tipping in Greek restaurants, a 13% service charge is figured by law into the price of a meal. However, it is customary to leave an additional 8%-10% tip if the service was satisfactory. During the Christmas and Greek Easter holiday periods, restaurants will tack on an obligatory 18% holiday bonus to your bill for the waiters.

HOLLAND

Book well in advance. Accommodation in the incredibly popular Randstad region (the provinces of North and South Holland, and Utrecht) is at a premium.

Go to museums early. You don't want to have come all this way to see a Vermeer or Van Gogh and not be able to get close enough because of all the tourists and schoolchildren.

Avoid Amsterdam's Red Light District at night. The streets are jammed with noisy groups of young men who don't pose a serious criminal threat but who can behave obnoxiously (hence the outdoor lavatories and signs forbidding urination in the nearby canal).

Know what to expect at a coffee shop. Coffee shops might sell coffee and snacks, but the licensed ones also sell marijuana, hash, and drug paraphernalia, which can be used on the spot.

Don't worry about speaking Dutch. Most Dutch in major cities are bilingual in Dutch and English—if not a third or fourth language.

Know your station. Be sure of the exact name of the train station from which your train will depart, and the one at which you wish to get off. In some Dutch cities (including Amsterdam, Rotterdam, The Hague, and Delft) there are two or more stations, although one is the principle station.

Try local Dutch brews. The Dutch are especially fond of their pils, a light golden lager usually served with a large head. Locals claim that it tastes better if sipped through the foam, so asking for a top-up may offend. There are stronger beers, usually referred to as bokbier—typically seasonal, they're made with warming spices in the winter. In summer *witte bier* (white beer) is a refreshing drink, a zesty brew served cool with a twist of lemon. There's almost nothing better than a beer and sandwich taken at a canal-side café.

Go out for Indonesian rijstafel. This multi-ingredient dish with rice, vegetables or meat, and sweet and spicy condiments is a tasty legacy of Dutch colonialism.

Rent a bike. It's a magnificent way to see the city—the locals will agree. Never leave your bike unlocked, however: There is a rapid turnover of stolen bikes no matter what quality or condition. Use a D-lock, which can't be cut with the average thief's tools, and lock your bike's frame to something that can't be shifted, like a railing.

14

Know when to tip. Tipping 15% to 20% of the cost of a meal is not common practice in the Netherlands or in Belgium. Instead, it is customary to round off the total to a convenient figure to reward good service. If paying with a credit card, pay the exact amount of the bill with your card, and leave a few euros in cash on the table for the waiting staff.

IRELAND

Take public transit. Ireland's public transportation system was once one of Europe's worst, but the past decade has seen sizable improvements made in the national network of buses and trains. You can figure out most of the details from ⊕*www.busireann.ie* (buses) and ⊕*www.irishrail.ie* (trains). The Northern Ireland transport system is a lot better, at ⊕*www.translink.co.uk*.

Know that not all pubs are created equal. To distinguish the real gold from the sparkling pyrite, look for a qualified bar staff (a uniform of white shirt and black trousers is often a good sign you won't be waited on by a grubby student), at least one man over sixty drinking at the bar (he should know the good bars by now, right?), no TV, and no recorded music (a pub is a place to talk).

Get the full low-down on all of Ireland's festivals. Check out the Bord Fáilte Web site and its full calendar of events, provided on a month-by-month basis at www.discoverireland.ie.

Pack a bilingual map if you're heading to the Gaeltacht. English is now outlawed in road signs in these Gaelic-speaking communities, found along the western seaboard, on some islands, and in pockets in West Cork and County Waterford. So be sure to use a map with place names in both English and Irish (you can't rely on official Ordnance Survey maps, which now only print Irish place names in these areas).

Learn the ground rules for a traditional music session. Don't talk during the solo, and don't stare at the singer; most people look at the floor. Buy the musicians a drink if it's a small session, and if at all possible, have a party piece to contribute yourself—if you can't sing or play, recite a poem or tell a joke. It's the gesture that counts.

Don't be fooled by distance markers. Road signs in rural Ireland sometimes give distances in miles and sometimes in kilometers—even along the same route. And it's not always clear from the signs which measurement is being used.

Feel the pulse of the nation. Check out any of the RTÉ Radio 1's morning programs with well-known jocks like Pat Kenny and Joe Duffy. Allowing the nation to give full vent to their spleens across the airwaves, these radio shows have now become Ireland's modern confessional.

During the holidays in Ireland, tip your bartender in beer. You don't tip in Irish pubs, but for waiter service in a bar, a hotel lounge, or a Dublin lounge bar, leave about 1 euro for a tip. Around Christmas time, however, you can tip your bartender in a pub by telling them to "have one yourself," which translates as tipping them the price of a pint.

14

ITALY

Order multiple courses. A full meal in Italy has traditionally consisted of five courses, and every menu you encounter will be organized along a five-course plan. The crucial rule of restaurant dining is that you should order at least two courses. It's a common mistake for tourists to order only a second course, thinking they're getting a "main course" complete with side dishes. What they wind up with is one lonely piece of meat.

Don't plan to visit Italy in August. In much of the country the heat can be stifling, and many Italians are themselves on vacation, making major cities feel like ghost towns.

Keep your lodging expectations realistic. Hotels in Italy are usually well maintained, but in some respects they won't match what you find at comparably priced U.S. lodgings. Rooms are usually smaller, particularly in cities; if you're truly cramped, ask for another room, but don't expect things to be spacious. A "double bed" is commonly two singles pushed together. And in the bathroom, tubs are not a given—request one if it's essential. In budget places, showers sometimes use a drain in the middle of the bathroom floor. And washcloths are a rarity.

Pack binoculars for sightseeing. They will help you get a good look at wondrous painted ceilings and domes.

Have coins handy. You'll need them for the *luce* (light) machines that illuminate the works of art in churches.

Consider renting a car outside of cities. Having a car in Italian cities is almost always a liability, but outside the cities it's often crucial. An effective strategy is to start and end your Italian itinerary in major cities, car-free, and to pick up wheels for countryside touring in between.

If you drive in Italy, do so extra defensively. When you hit the road, don't be surprised to encounter other cars engaging in tailgating and high-risk passing. Your best response is to take the same safety-first approach you use at home. On the upside, Italy's roads are well maintained. Wearing a seat belt and having your lights on at all times are required by law.

Don't forget to tip. In monasteries and other sights where admission is free, a contribution (€0.50–€1) is expected. In restaurants a service charge of 10% to 15% may appear on your check. If service is not included, leave a tip of up to 10%. Always leave your tip in cash, even if there's a line item on your credit-card slip for a tip (otherwise the server will never see it). Italians rarely tip taxi drivers, but a euro or two is appreciated. Tip guides about €1.50 per person for a half-day group tour.

NAPLES

Beware of Naples's un-air-conditioned cabs. In the hot summer, hopping into a cab outside Naples's Stazione Centrale rail station can lead to a total meltdown, thanks to the city's constant traffic jams and global-warming temperatures. Solution? Head for the city's trams, trains, and buses, all of which—miracle of miracles—are nicely air-conditioned.

Forget the bus and take the ferry. If heading to Capri or the Amalfi Coast from Naples, remember that a vast network of boats and ferries leaves from Naples's Molo Beverello. Metro del Mare is just one of the companies that can whisk you to Positano or Amalfi in air-conditioned splendor, leaving the area's slower Circumvesuviana trains and SITA buses in the dust.

Avoid Naples in summer. Horror stories of torrid days and humongous crowds have driven more and more people to vacation here during the traditional "shoulder" times of May–June and September–October. The downside is that the region is now packed to the gills with travelers during those months— plan accordingly, or consider coming here in the winter, when crowds are gone and the weather is still delightful.

ROME

Save money with a Roma Pass. Since there is a lot of ground to cover in Rome, it's wise to plan your sightseeing schedule with possible savings in mind, and purchasing the Roma Pass (www.romapass.it) allows you to do just that. The three-day pass costs €23, and is good for unlimited use of buses, trams, and the metro. It includes admission to two of more than 40 participating museums or archaeological sites, and can help you jump to the head of the long line waiting to get into the Colosseum.

Ask for the bill in restaurants. In Rome the bill will not be brought until you ask for it. Unless otherwise written on the menu, service is included. However, it's customary to leave an additional 5%–10% tip for the waiter, depending on the quality of service.

Always check times locally for museum hours. They vary and may change with the seasons. Sightseeing in churches during religious rites is usually discouraged.

14

Mind the dress codes. They're especially strict for visits to the Basilica di San Pietro and the Musei Vaticani: Shorts, tank tops, and halter tops are taboo. Shoulders must be covered. Women should carry a scarf or shawl to cover bare arms if the custodians insist. Those who do not comply with the dress code are refused admittance.

Keep an eye out for purse snatchers. Different from pickpockets, they often work in teams on a single motor scooter or motorcycle: One drives and the other grabs.

VENICE AND THE VENETO
Do a gondola ride right. An enchanting diversion rather than a practical way to get around, *un giro in gondola* is a round-trip ride. Some consider these trips tourist traps; others wouldn't miss them. To make the most of it, request to go through more remote side canals, where you'll get an intimate glimpse of the city that can't be seen any other way.

Be ready to navigate via landmarks. Finding your way around Venice is complicated; a good map is essential, but for locals street names beyond the main thoroughfares are insignificant, so much so that many Venetians don't even know the name of the street they live on. Don't be put off if you are greeted with a shrug and an embarrassed smile if you ask a Venetian for directions to an address. Find out first which landmark your destination is near; you should have little trouble in getting directions to that point. Once there, you should be able to find your precise destination by searching out the house number.

PORTUGAL

Drive defensively. Portuguese drivers are notoriously rash, and the nation has one of Europe's highest traffic-fatality rates. Adding to the stress is the fact that many drivers don't have insurance.

Plan to shop. This is a country with a wealth of crafts—from superbly woven baskets to beautifully embroidered linens, to irresistible porcelain and pottery (you might want to pack your own bubble wrap and tape to get the latter home safely). Items made of cork, leather, and wood should make your list; so should port and other local wines. The fashion-design scene is thriving here as well: Top names include Ana Salazar, Fàtima Lopes, Maria Gambina, Manuel Alves, and Josè Manuel Gonçalves.

Try to catch a fado show. Fado means "fate," and, like the blues, fado songs are full of fatalism. The image of a black-shawled fadista, head thrown back, eyes closed with emotion, voice rising and falling with soulful song, is quint-essentially Portuguese. Many casas de fado are also restaurants; some offer a mix of fado and folk-dancing shows.

Tip in Portugal. Service is included in café, restaurant, and hotel bills, but waiters and other service people are poorly paid, and you can be sure your contribution will be appreciated. Never feel obligated to leave a tip. An acceptable tip is 5%–10% of the total bill, and if you have a sandwich or *petiscos* (appetizers) at a bar, leave less, just enough to round out the bill to the nearest €0.50. Cocktail waiters get €0.30–€0.50 a drink, depending on the bar. Taxi drivers get about 10% of the meter. Hotel porters should receive €1 a bag; a doorman who calls you a taxi, €0.50. Tip €1 for room service and €1–€2 per night for maid service. Tip a concierge for any additional help he or she gives you. Tip tour guides €2–€5, depending on how knowledgeable they are and on the length of the tour.

RUSSIA

MOSCOW AND ST. PETERSBURG

Avoid being robbed or mugged. Don't travel alone at night in unfamiliar areas, and stay reasonably sober. Don't attempt to spice up your experience by drinking with people you don't know well. Keep an expensive phone or camera out of sight as much as possible. Avoid very crowded metro cars, where pickpockets may operate, and don't linger outside train stations at night. Don't hang your bag on the back of your chair in cafés—keep it in sight.

Buy quality Russian vodka. There are hundreds of brands of vodka in Russia. Some are rough and best left alone; two of the best are Flagman and Russky Standart. Alcohol counterfeiting, which can lead to alcohol poisoning, is a problem, so try to purchase vodka from a reputable-looking store or, if buying from a kiosk, check to see that the seal has not been broken.

Drink vodka like a Russian. Vodka is drunk everywhere socially with the intention of producing a state of conviviality referred to as *dusha-dushe* (soul-to-soul). When a Russian taps his throat, be prepared to join in for a round. The "vodka procedure" is as follows: Prepare a forkful of food (pickles, herring, boiled potatoes) or chunk of bread, inhale and exhale quickly, then breathe in and tip the vodka down your throat all at once (no sipping here), breathe out and eat.

14

Tip waiters in Russia. Tipping is increasingly the norm in modern-day Russia. Add an extra 10%, or 15% to a restaurant bill for exceptional service. If you are paying by credit card, leave the tip in cash—the waiter is less likely to see it if you add it to the credit-card charge.

Mind your feet. Shoes are particularly important in Russia and must be kept clean, even when the weather conditions make this difficult. In some museums, galleries, and palaces, such as the Tretyakov Gallery, you may be asked to put on plastic booties similar to the kind surgeons wear over your shoes before entering the gallery. When entering a Russian home, always remove your shoes at the entryway.

Master the migration card and other official documents. Make sure you're given a migration card on the plane (cabin crew can be unreliable, and passport control doesn't stock them) and fill it out before getting to passport control, where they'll stamp it. Keep it with you until you leave the country. When you check in at a hotel, you'll be given a registration card with an official stamp, and you should carry that and your passport and a copy of your visa with you at all times in case you are stopped by the police—or an imposter looking to collect "fines" if you're not carrying these somewhat legally required items (the law's hazy on the subject; err on the side of safety).

Go with taxi companies, and ride solo. Get your hotel to recommend a taxi company and use it instead of gypsy cabs. If this is impossible, avoid taxis that already have occupants, and never allow your driver to stop to take an extra passenger after you have gotten in.

Drink only boiled or bottled water in St. Petersburg. The water supply in St. Petersburg is thought to contain an intestinal parasite called Giardia lamblia, which causes diarrhea, stomach cramps, and nausea. The gestation period is two to three weeks, so symptoms usually arise after you return home. Imported bottled water is widely available.

WORD OF MOUTH. "Prepare [your] kids so they won't have that culture shock that comes from not being able to read the [Cyrillic] alphabet [in Moscow]. It's only a couple dozen characters, and when you can decipher them, you can tell what a lot of words mean. Take them into the subway—outside of rush hour so you don't lose them—they will never forget the endlessly long and deep escalators for example. The ride down to the platform takes longer than the train ride.very cool!" —DalaiLlama

---

SCANDINAVIA

Look for discounts. Scandinavia is expensive; even if you don't consider yourself a budget traveler, investigate ways to save money. Check into fly–drive packages, air passes (which often must be purchased before leaving home), rail passes (which sometimes get you hotel and other discounts), and urban-transit passes. Research free days–nights at museums. Have lunch at high-end restaurants, rather than the more expensive dinner, and skip the wine; alcoholic beverages are heavily taxed and pricey. Make efforts to get V.A.T. refunds on purchases. If time and energy are limited, work with a brick-and-mortar travel agent who specializes in Scandinavia. He or she might have special deals and insider info on saving money all around.

Venture north of the Arctic Circle. Between early June and mid-July the sun doesn't set here—a phenomenon known as the midnight sun. Some of the prettiest places to take in this phenomenon are Boø, Narvik, and Nordkapp in Norway; or while skiing the King's Trail in northern Sweden. Equally moving (though in a less gleeful way) is the reverse experience at the height of winter, when the Arctic goes completely dark for a few months.

Drink aquavit. Aquavit, or akvavit, is a Scandanavian liquor of about 40% alcohol by volume. Its name comes from *aqua vitae* (Latin for "water of life"). Like other Scandinavian liquors, it's distilled from potatoes or grains and flavored with herbs like caraway seeds, cumin, dill, fennel, or coriander. It's an acquired taste; drink it as a shot—or as the Danes say, "snaps"—with meals, especially the appetizer. To really fit in, chase it with beer.

DENMARK

Talk to a Dane. The best way to discover Denmark is to strike up a conversation with an affable, hospitable Dane. It will most likely be *hyggelig*—a term that defies definition but comes close to meaning charming and pleasant. A summertime beach picnic can be as hyggelig as tea on a cold winter's night; the only requirement is the company of a Dane.

Explore outside of Copenhagen, especially if you're a Shakespeare buff. The surrounding countryside in the rest of Zealand is not to be missed. Less than an hour from the city, fields and half-timber cottages checker the land, and in the north you'll find Hamlet's Kronborg Castle crowning Helsingør. You'll find beaches, too—some chic, some deserted—all powdered with fine white sand.

Tip judiciously in Denmark. It has long been held that the egalitarian Danes don't expect to be tipped. That said, most people do tip, and those who receive tips appreciate them. Service is included in hotel bills. Many restaurants have started adding a gratuity to bills; always check to see whether it's been included. If not, leave a token tip. The same holds true for taxis—if a trip costs DKr 58, most people will give the driver DKr 60. If the driver is extremely friendly or helpful, tip more at your own discretion. Hotel porters expect about DKr 5 per bag.

FINLAND

Time your visit well. Starting in June, Helsinki, the Lakelands, and the southwestern coast come out of hibernation for long, bright days. A particular treat in the Lakelands is the Savonlinna Opera Festival, held in late July or August. But note that many restaurants close in July—especially in Helsinki. Northern Finland's tourism peaks in winter, and with good reason. In addition to snow sports galore, you can also take in Lapland, storied home of Santa Claus, during the Christmas season.

Rack up those passport stamps. A side trip from Helsinki to St. Petersburg, Russia, is made easier thanks to the Allegro train. It travels at roughly 140 mi an hour and makes the journey in 3½ hours. (Fingers crossed that it takes the same or less time to get that Russian visa.) In addition, Tallinn, Estonia, is only a two-hour ferry ride south of Helsinki.

Skip the tip in Finland—for the most part. Tipping isn't the norm, but is becoming more prevalent; use your discretion about tipping for a job well done. Service charges are generally included in hotel and restaurant bills, so employees don't generally expect tips. It's customary, though not required, to round up taxi fares to the nearest euro. Give one euro to train or hotel porters. Coat-check fees are usually posted.

NORWAY

Don't keep your cab waiting. If you called for one, an additional fee can be charged to your fare. Taxis are radio dispatched from a central office, and can take up to a half hour to get to you at peak times. A better bet might be to head to a taxi stand; in Oslo's city center these include stands at Stortinget in Karl Johans Gate, at Stortorget by the cathedral, at Youngstorget, and at Central Station.

Know how to tip like a Norwegian. Service is generally included in the bill in restaurants; leave up to an additional 10% if the service was exemplary. At a bar, round the tab up to the nearest 5 kroner or 10 kroner per drink.

Go hiking. We can't recommend this activity too highly— just be sure to pack a sturdy pair of hiking shoes. Hiking's the national pastime, and you'll never be too far from a well-marked mountain trail here. One of the best places for beginners is the gently sloping terrain of the Hardangervidda plateau.

Try the breakfast cheeses. Norway's famous brown goat cheese, *Geitost* (a sweet, caramel-flavor whey cheese made from goat and cow's milk), and *Norvegia* (a Norwegian Gouda-like cheese) are on virtually every table. They are eaten in thin slices, cut with a cheese plane or slicer—a Norwegian invention—on buttered wheat or rye bread.

Eat *middag* (dinner) early. Dinner is the only hot meal of the day and is early—from 1 to 4 in the country, 3 to 7 in the city—so many cafeterias serving home-style food close by 6 or 7. However, in Oslo it's possible to get dinner as late as midnight, especially in summer. Most restaurants in Oslo stop serving dinner around 10.

SWEDEN

Tip appropriately. Service is included in the bill in restaurants; only tip in very fancy restaurants, and then only an additional 5% to 10%. For drinks, round up to the nearest 5 krona or 10 krona. Taxi fares should be rounded up as well, though giving as much as 15 krona to 20 krona above the fare is very much appreciated.

Do as the Swedes do and indulge your wanderlust. The constitution upholds the right to roam; feel free to explore any beach, field, forest, lake, or river that strikes your fancy.

Always carry your bathing suit. Water is plentiful and irresistibly clean; be ready to take a dip at a moment's notice.

14

Take in the Jokkmokk market in February. Held on the first Thursday and continuing through Saturday, it features traditional Sámi (Lapp) artifacts and plenty of reindeer.

SPAIN

Don't tip more than 10% of the bill. Leave less if you eat tapas or sandwiches at a bar—just enough to round out the bill. Restaurant checks almost always include a service charge, which is not the same as a voluntary tip.

Specify whether you want an automatic rental car. Virtually all cars in Spain have a manual transmission—if you don't want a stick shift, reserve weeks in advance and specify automatic transmission. Call to reconfirm your automatic car before you leave for Spain.

Don't assume that holidays last just a day. If a public holiday falls on a Tuesday or Thursday, many businesses also close on the adjacent Monday or Friday. If a major holiday falls on a Sunday, businesses close on Monday.

Make parador reservations well in advance. Paradors, especially the Parador de Granada overlooking the Alhambra, are extremely popular with foreigners and Spaniards alike.

Don't flaunt your flesh in public (away from the beach, that is). Many women in Andalusia go topless on beaches, but even if you have a modest swimsuit, you will need to wear a cover-up when eating in nearby establishments. When visiting churches, don't wear shorts or anything risqué.

Don't expect kids' menus, or high chairs. In Spain children eat whatever their parents do, so it's perfectly acceptable to ask for an extra plate and share your food. Exceptions to this rule are the kid-friendly resorts along the Costa del Sol.

SWITZERLAND

Take it easy up high. Limit strenuous excursions on the first day at extra-high-altitude resorts, those at 5,248 feet and above. Adults with heart problems may want to avoid all excursions above 6,500 feet.

Pack smart. Even in July and August the evening air grows chilly in the mountains, so bring a warm sweater. And bring along a hat or sunscreen, as the atmosphere is thinner at high altitudes. Glaciers can be blinding in the sun, so be sure to bring sunglasses, which should have side shields especially for high-altitude hiking or skiing. Good walking shoes or hiking boots are a must, whether you're tackling medieval cobblestones or mountain trails.

Plan ahead for getting around with kids. All children under the age of 12 who are less than 150 cm (59 inches) tall must be fastened in an infant car seat, child seat, or booster seat while riding in a motor vehicle. There are no exemptions to this rule for taxis, and finding a taxi willing to provide the seats is nearly impossible. If you are traveling with children and renting a car, be sure to ask the rental-car company for the appropriate seats in advance, or plan on taking trains and buses instead.

When driving, remember the *vignette*. To use the semi-expressways and expressways, you must display a sticker, or *vignette,* on the top-center or lower corner of the windshield. You can buy one at the border or in post offices, gas stations, and garages. A vignette costs 40 SF or €27. Driving without a vignette puts you at risk of a 100 SF fine. Cars rented within Switzerland already have these stickers; if you rent a car elsewhere in Europe, ask whether the rental company will provide the vignette for you.

Know that it is polite to tip. Despite menus marked *service compris,* the Swiss *do* tip at restaurants, but it's not done as a percentage. Instead, they give quantities anywhere from the change from the nearest franc to 10 SF or more for a world-class meal that has been exquisitely served. If, in a café, the waitress settles the bill at the table, fishing the change from her leather purse, give her the change on the spot—or calculate the total, including tip, and tell her the full sum before she counts it onto the tabletop. If you're paying for a meal with a credit card, try to tip with cash. Bartenders are also tipped along these lines. Tipping porters and doormen is easier: 2 SF per bag is adequate in good hotels, 1 SF per trip in humbler lodgings. A fixed rate of 5 SF per bag applies to porter fees at the Geneva and Zürich airports. Tip taxi drivers the change or an extra couple of francs, depending on the length of the drive and whether they've helped with your bags.

TURKEY

Take the bus, not the train. Buses are much faster than most trains in Turkey, and provide inexpensive service almost around the clock between all cities and towns; they're fairly comfortable and often air-conditioned. Express buses between major cities are significantly faster and more comfortable than local buses. There are also more and more inter-city air flights available, which can save even more time.

14

Avoid driving in Istanbul and other major cities. Urban streets and highways are frequently jammed with vehicles operated by high-speed lunatics and drivers who constantly honk their horns. You should also avoid driving on highways after dusk, because drivers often drive without their lights on, and vehicles are known to stop in the roadway in complete darkness. In the countryside, watch out for drivers passing on a curve or at the top of a hill, and beware of carts—very difficult to see at night—and motorcycles weaving in and out of traffic while carrying entire families.

Know that Turks set great store in politeness. No one will expect you to have mastered the intricacies of polite speech in Turkish, but learn a few words—please (*lütfen* or lewt-fen) and thank you (*teşekkür ederim* or tay-shake-kur eh-day-reem) are useful—and you will be rewarded.

Be respectful when visiting mosques. For women, bare arms and legs are not acceptable inside a mosque, and men should avoid wearing shorts, too. Before entering a mosque, shoes must be removed. There is usually an attendant, and shoes are generally safe. You're best off avoiding mosques at midday on Friday, when attendances are higher and it's the equivalent of Sunday morning for Christians, or Saturday morning for Jews.

WORD OF MOUTH. "Istanbul . . . beautiful city, lots to see, great mixture of modern and old world, wonderful history and sights, great food, among the nicest people of all of my travels." —risab

Steel yourself for cigarette smoke. Although much of North America and Western Europe is going smoke-free, Turks still enjoy their chain smoking: Pack a clothes freshener like Febreze to get rid of the smell of Turkish cigarettes. And while you're at it, take some kind of hand sanitizer or moist wipes for on-the-go freshening up.

Know what to expect in the bathroom. Standards of restroom cleanliness tend to be lower in Turkey than most people are used to in North America, so be prepared. In public facilities and generally all but the fanciest restaurants, Turkish-style squatters are the norm, and toilet paper is often not provided. Sometimes it's possible to purchase some from the custodian, but you're well advised to carry a supply of your own.

Be ready to get lost in Istanbul. Even with a good map in hand, it's easy to lose your way along Istanbul's twisty streets. Don't hesitate to ask for help navigating; people are almost always happy to help.

WORD OF MOUTH. **"In the more touristed places in Turkey, all the guides had flashlights they were using to show their groups the frescoes, so we were glad we'd thought to take them." —julies**

Order by the plate. *Mezes* (small plates) are an integral part of the Turkish dining experience. Share a few as appetizers, or order a bunch and have a feast. There'll probably be more permutations of eggplant preparation than your imagination can conceive of.

Speak up if you want a double bed. Most accommodations tend to push two singles together, which some people find frustrating. That said, know that a double might not be available.

Tip like a local in Turkey. In restaurants, a 10%–15% charge is added to the bill in all but inexpensive fast-food spots, but since it doesn't necessarily find its way to your waiter, leave an additional 10% to 15%. Taxi drivers in Turkey are becoming used to foreigners giving them something; round off the fare to the nearest 50 kuruş. Dolmus drivers do not get tipped. At Turkish baths, staff members who attend to you expect to share a tip of 30%–35% of the bill: don't worry about missing them—they'll be lined up expectantly on your departure. Tour guides often expect a tip, usually YTL 5 to YTL 7 per day if you were happy with the guide.

MEXICO

Keep your Mexican tourist card. If you're arriving by plane from the United States or Canada, you'll get this on the way in. Ask for it if you don't; you'll need to present it when you leave the country, and not having it causes big headaches. They're also available through travel agents and Mexican consulates, and at the border if you're entering by land.

Use common safety sense everywhere in Mexico. Exercise particular caution in border towns like Tijuana and in Mexico City. Don't advertise that you're a tourist, and don't wear any valuables, including watches. Wear a money belt, put valuables in hotel safes, and carry your own baggage whenever possible, unless in a luxury hotel. Keep your passport in the hotel's safe. Take only registered hotel taxis or have a hotel concierge call for one—do not hail taxis on the street under any circumstances. Use ATMs during the day and in big, enclosed commercial areas. Avoid the glass-enclosed street variety of banks, where you may be more vulnerable to thieves who force you to withdraw money for them; abduction is also possible.

Don't pack valuables in checked luggage on flights to Mexico. There's a good chance you might not find them there when you get to baggage claim. Rarely, travelers are even ordered to check the larger of their carry-ons at the gate and not given time to transfer valuable items—which then go missing. Be sure your expensive things are in your smallest carry-on.

Know Mexican driving rules. Given the high levels of highway fatalities in Mexico, you're better off not driving. If you do opt to drive, know that you must carry Mexican auto insurance, which you can purchase near border crossings on either the U.S. or Mexican side. If you enter Mexico with a car, you must leave with it. Look into the other strict rules regarding bringing any car into the country.

Bring proper identification for children traveling to Mexico. All children must have proof of citizenship (a birth certificate) for travel to Mexico. All children up to age 18 traveling with a single parent must also have a notarized letter from the other parent stating that the child has his or her permission to leave their home country. If the other parent is deceased or the child has only one legal parent, a notarized statement saying so must be obtained as proof.

14

Watch what you eat in Mexico. Stay away from ice, uncooked food, and unpasteurized milk and milk products, and drink only bottled water or water that has been boiled for at least 10 minutes, even when you're brushing your teeth.

Buy Mexican silver like a pro. Real silver is weightier and is marked ".925" (indicating a silver content of at least 92.5%) for sterling and ".950" (at least 95% silver content) for finer pieces. When size permits, the manufacturer's name and the word "Mexico" should also appear.

Be Talavera savvy. These blue-on-white ceramics are named for the Spanish town where they originated; authentic Mexican Talavera is produced in Puebla and parts of Tlaxcala and Guanajuato. Look on the back or bottom of the piece for the factory name and state of origin; manufacturers throughout Mexico produce Talavera-style pieces, which should sell for much less.

Note that tipping is important in Mexico. The minimum wage is just about $5 a day, and that's what most maids, bellhops, and others in the tourism industry earn—be as generous as you can. Bellmen in international chain hotels think in dollars and know that in the United States porters are tipped about $2 a bag; they tend to expect the equivalent. Elsewhere 10 pesos–20 pesos per bag suffices. And it is best to tip using local currency whenever possible, so that service personnel need not go to the bank to exchange dollars for pesos. Here are some guidelines: waiters 10%–15% of the bill; tour guides 10% of the total; chambermaids 10 pesos–20 pesos per day; bartenders 10 pesos–20 pesos per drink. There's no need to tip taxi drivers, particularly if you've negotiated a fare; you can, however, round up to the nearest whole number.

CANCÚN

Consider booking your hotel online. A growing number of Cancún hotels encourage you to make reservations online. Some allow you to book rooms right on their own Web sites, but even hotels without their own sites usually offer reservations via online booking agencies, such as *www.docancun.com*, *www.cancuntoday.net*, and *www.travelcenter.com*. Besides being convenient, booking online can often get you a 10%–20% discount on room rates.

Consider the weather. The rainy season starts in mid-September and lasts until mid-November—which means you can expect afternoon downpours that can last anywhere from 30 minutes to two hours. Hurricane season occurs during these months (and even from June to November); notable past storms have included Hurricane Wilma and Hurricane Dean.

Avoid tortoiseshell. Refrain from buying anything made from tortoiseshell. The *carey*, or hawksbill turtles, from which most of it comes, are an endangered species, and it's illegal to bring tortoiseshell products into the United States and several other countries.

LOS CABOS

14

Mind those Los Cabos waves. Not all beaches are swimmable all the time (or ever). Flags on beaches alert you to the surf. Red flags warn of dangerous swimming conditions; yellow flags indicate that you should use caution; and green flags mark safe-swimming areas.

Stay safe at night, particularly in Cabo San Lucas. Never leave your belongings unattended—anywhere. Although resort areas are generally safe, do be cautious. There have been reports of people being victimized after imbibing drugged drinks in Cabo San Lucas nightclubs. Like momma always said: Don't drink alone or with strangers.

Plan to go whale-watching along the Baja Peninsula. Every December through March, gray whales swim 8,000 km (5,000 mi) south from Alaska's Bering Strait to the tip of the Baja Peninsula. Up to 6,000 whales swim past and stop close to the shore at several spots to give birth to their calves. Whale-watching boats—most of them *pangas* (small skiffs)—must get permission from the Mexican government to enter whale-watching areas.

WORD OF MOUTH. "[Los Cabos is] one of the best places in the world for marlin fishing (January is good for striped marlin). There's also several scenic challenging golf courses and a wild party scene downtown most nights. Rent a car and visit the smaller, quieter towns on either the Pacific side (Todos Santos) or Cortez side (Los Barilles, etc), or go snorkeling or whale watching or various other water activities." —Bill_H

PUERTO VALLARTA

For a walking vacation, stay in Old Vallarta or Marina Vallarta. This includes El Centro (with its hilly, cobblestone streets and excellent views) and the Romantic Zone south of the Cuale River (where you'll find more shops, restaurants, hill-free walking, and Los Muertos beach). Hotels here range from inexpensive to moderate. Marina Vallarta, too, is a place you can stay relatively car-free, though a bicycle is handy. Hotels here tend to be more luxury-oriented.

Get your ZZZs. Some accommodations in Riviera Nayarit and Jalisco are along the main highway and experience heavy traffic noise. And resort hotels often have lobby bars in the middle of an open-air atrium leading directly to rooms or rooftop discotheques, or outdoor theme nights with live music. When you book, request a room far from the noisiest part of the hotel.

Don't be time-share shark bait. If the time-share sales sharks smell interest, you'll be dead in the water. Salespeople are as unavoidable as death and taxes in PV. And almost as dreaded. Anyone calling you "amigo" as you walk down the street is probably selling. (Vallartenses are friendly, but they don't accost you in public.) Either walk away without a word or firmly say "No, thanks" as you continue walking. Ignore them when they yell after you.

Take the polite yet firm approach with beach vendors. If you don't feel like partaking of what the vendor's offering, don't feel pressured. Although it might feel rude, it's culturally permissible to smile and firmly say *"no, gracias"* only once with no further eye contact, or simply ignore itinerant vendors, especially if you're in the middle of a conversation. Being blatantly impolite, of course—that is, shouting at the vendor to take a hike—*is* rude, no matter where you're from.

SOUTH AMERICA

Prepare for health issues in South America. The Centers for Disease Control (⊕ *www.cdc.gov*) have country-specific information about health concerns and suggested or required inoculations, prophylactic medications, etc. Visit your doctor to be sure you're up to date on tetanus and any other shots. (Children should have current inoculations against measles, mumps, rubella, and polio.) Inquire about a hepatitis A inoculation, which can prevent common intestinal infections (though avoiding ice, uncooked food, fruits with peels, and tap water that hasn't been boiled for at least 10–20 minutes can go far toward preventing digestive distress, too). For tropical regions, get yellow fever shots and look into malaria medications.

Mind the altitude. Due to the high altitude in parts of Bolivia, Peru, Colombia, and Argentina, you may suffer from *soroche*, or altitude sickness. Symptoms include dizziness, fatigue, and shortness of breath. When you visit areas over 10,000 feet above sea level, take it easy at first. Avoid alcohol and caffeine, drink lots of bottled water and juice to stay hydrated, and rest for at least half a day. Symptoms usually disappear by the second day. If they don't, consult a doctor, especially if you have a history of high blood pressure. To fight soroche, locals swear by *mate de coca*, a tea made from the leaves of the coca plant.

Be wise about drinking water. In most countries it's best to drink only bottled water or water that has been boiled for at least 10 minutes, even when brushing your teeth. Order drinks without ice. Note that water doesn't boil sufficiently at high altitudes to kill bacteria, so in countries like Bolivia and Peru you'll have to use purification tablets.

Know when to drive—and when not to. In many cities streets are traffic-clogged, steep, or confusing. In the countryside many roads are unpaved or poorly maintained, and subject to floods in rainy seasons. And just about everywhere drivers are reckless. That said, there are some places where it truly makes sense to drive: say the Lakes District of Argentina, where roads are both decent and scenic.

ARGENTINA

Travel by bus at least once. Since the train system in Argentina went private and was drastically reduced in the late 1990s, tourists and locals alike tend to choose buses as their conveyance of choice within the country. Different companies cover different regions, and almost all feature toilets, videos, air-conditioning, cushy leg rests, and wide seats that recline to about a 145-degree angle—or flat if you choose first class. It's hugely cheaper than flying, and is a good way to get a feel for the country's vastness and take in some scenery you wouldn't see from the air.

Ladies, be ready for attention. Women can expect pointed looks, the occasional *piropo* (a flirtatious remark, usually alluding to some physical aspect), and some advances. These catcalls rarely escalate into actual physical harassment, so the best reaction is to do as local women do and ignore it. Reply only if you're really confident with Spanish swear words.

Know how to tip. *Propinas* (tips) are a question of rewarding good service rather than an obligation. Restaurant bills—even those that have a *cubierto* (bread and service charge)—don't include gratuities; locals usually add 10%. Bellhops and maids expect tips only in the very expensive hotels, where a tip in dollars is appreciated. You can also give a small tip (10% or less) to tour guides. Taxi fares can just be rounded off.

Change your money in cities. You may not be able to change currency in rural areas at all, so don't leave cities without adequate amounts of pesos in small denominations.

BUENOS AIRES
Be smart when you visit the ATM. Always use ATMs within bank hours (weekdays 10–3), or at least in populated areas in daylight, as they're common target areas for thieves (especially in Microcentro and Tribunales). Hail taxis far from banks and ATMs; robbers have been known to pose as taxi drivers and search for visitors who have just drawn money. Looking alert and savvy is often enough to avoid this situation. In the event you are held up, comply quickly and quietly.

Take domestic flight schedules with a grain of salt. If you're planning on using Buenos Aires's domestic airport—Aeroparque—and the international one—Ezeiza—on the same day, give yourself at least five hours between arrival in one airport and departure in another. A free shuttle is offered between the two airports, but a taxi might be the better bet, especially if traffic is particularly congested—which it's sure to be if you're in a hurry.

Know how to take the *colectivo* (city bus). Consult a *Guia T*, found at most larger kiosks for about 3 pesos, to figure out which line you need and which street you should walk on to find a *parada*, or stop. When you see your bus coming, hail it like a cab, wait for it to come to a rolling halt (at best), and say *"ochenta, por favor"* to the driver before plunking your 80 centavos (change given, but only coins accepted) into the ticket machine. As you ride, pay attention to where you are, as stops aren't routinely announced.

Push a stop request button when you see your destination coming up. Retain your ticket, as police occasionally board to check and impose fines.

Don't drink to get smashed. Porteños do love a good drink, particularly the very Argentine Fernet and cola, but young and old alike tend to put more emphasis on their conversational prowess and ability to look spectacular when they go out. To fit in, and to be sure you'll have energy left at 5 AM when the party's still going, try not to overdo on the alcohol.

Order *medialunas* like a local. These croissantlike pastries are a café breakfast staple, and come in two types: *de grasa*, which tend to be a little drier and skinnier but have a very delicate, mellow taste, and *de manteca*, which are plump, moist, sweet, and, like all good things, come in threes.

14

BOLIVIA

Get vaccinations. Unless you are traveling in a risk area, you won't need your yellow fever vaccination, but you will need the certificate if you are traveling on to some of the other countries on the continent, including the international hub airport at São Paulo. Don't get one from the health centers in-country—they're not recognized internationally.

Follow food safety measures. Do not drink tap water, and order beverages without ice. Avoid eating food from street vendors. Words to remember: "Boil it, cook it, peel it, or forget it."

Avoid the rainy season. From November to March heavy downpours make many roads in the lowlands virtually impassable. In the highlands the season brings dark, cloudy skies but little rain. If you plan to travel by bus or car—though this isn't recommended—it's best to go between April and October.

Understand hotel pricing. Some hotels have two pricing systems—one for Bolivians and one for foreigners. Even if you fall into the latter category, you'll find nice accommodations for $35 or less, particularly away from the cities. Do not be afraid to ask to see the room in advance—it's common practice in Bolivia.

Go for local crafts. Crafts shops are usually grouped together—in La Paz most can be found on Calle Sagàrnaga. It's always worth looking for cooperatives outside the capital, however. These sell traditional textiles made in rural areas, especially in the provinces of Chuquisaca and Potosì. The shawls, hats, and skirts worn by highland women are sold in most of the local markets and in some stores in La Paz, but shopkeepers sometimes refuse to sell some types of traditional garments to foreigners. However, the felt bowler hats are for sale everywhere and make an interesting fashion statement back home.

Understand tipping policies. Bolivia is not a tipping culture, but expect to pay for small favors and "help" everywhere. In restaurants a tip of 5% to 10% is in order if you are happy with the service. Taxi drivers do not expect tips unless you hire them for the day, in which case 10% is appropriate. Airport porters expect (Bs)5 per baggage cart they handle. Shoeshine boys, who pop up out of the cracks in the pavement on every corner, will try to charge you 10 times the going rate of (Bs)1—their roguish smiles may persuade you to tip more. If someone offers to watch your car, best to accept or they will steal it instead—again, (Bs)1 is standard for this "service."

BRAZIL

Don't forget that you need a visa to visit Brazil. Visas are required for U.S., Canadian, and Australian citizens. Go to the Web site for the Brazilian embassy or consulate nearest you for the most up-to-date information. At this writing, the tourist visa fee is US$160. Additional fees may be levied if you apply by mail. Among other things, you'll need to provide your airline ticket or other proof-of-travel documentation. Obtaining a visa takes time, and you must have every bit of paperwork in order when you visit the consulate, so read instructions carefully. (For example, in the U.S. the fee can only be paid with a U.S. Postal Service money order.) The good news: The visa is valid for five years.

Be ever vigilant against petty crime. Although there has been a real effort to crack down on tourist-related crime, particularly in Rio, petty street thievery—pickpocketing, bag snatching, etc.—is still prevalent in urban areas, especially in places around tourist hotels, restaurants, and discos. By day the countryside is safe.

Get peak-season tickets and reservations early for Brazilian buses. Bus travel is very popular (and often luxurious) in Brazil. Reservations are a must when traveling to resort areas during high season—particularly on weekends—or during major holidays and school-break periods. Arrive at bus stations early, particularly for peak-season travel.

Mind your hand gestures. Throughout Brazil, use the thumbs-up gesture to indicate that something is OK. The gesture created by making a circle with your thumb and index finger and holding your other fingers up in the air has a very rude meaning.

Know that tipping is customary in Brazil. A 10% tip may or may not be added to your bill in sit-down restaurants; always check and act accordingly. The same is true in bars. Taxi drivers don't expect tips, but it's customary to round up the fare to the nearest whole number. Tip tour guides 10%. Tip hotel porters–doormen 1 or 2 reais upon arrival and departure; tip the same amount for each bag. Leave chambermaids 1 or 2 reais per day at the front desk upon departure. Have spare change available to tip parking, bathroom, and gas-station attendants. Wages are low here, so if service is good, be as generous as possible.

CHILE

Learn how to tip. In restaurants and for tour guides, a 10% tip is usual, unless service has been deficient. Taxi drivers don't expect to be tipped. Visitors need to be wary of parking attendants. During the day they should only charge what's on their portable meters when you collect the car but, at night, they will ask for money—usually 1,000 pesos—in advance. This is a racket, but for your car's safety it's better to comply.

Be greeting-savvy. Females will probably greet you with a kiss on one cheek, while males will go with a firm handshake.

Pack for all seasons. No matter what time of year you're traveling, you'll need clothing to suit a wide range of temperatures.

Arrive at bus stations extra early in peak seasons. Companies are notoriously difficult to reach by phone, so it's often better to stop by the terminal to check on prices and schedules.

COLOMBIA

Take a taxi whenever possible. As you tour cities here, don't be carefree about strolling around, even during the day, or about lingering in places at night. It's simply not safe to do so.

Take the bus out of Bogotá. The massive Terminal de Transportes, where long-distance buses arrive and depart, looks more like an airport than a bus station. It's where you'll find all major bus companies (and plenty of thieves, so watch your bags). Buses depart for other major cities about every hour. Buses are the most common means of transportation for Colombians, so they are often more comfortable than those in the United States.

Breakfast like a local. Bogotanos like to start the day off with *santafereño*, a steaming cup of chocolate accompanied by a slab of cheese—you melt the cheese in the chocolate.

Tip—unless it's already on your bill. In finer restaurants, tip 10% to 15% if the charge isn't included. At more informal restaurants, 1,000 pesos to 2,000 pesos is the norm. If you hire a taxi driver more than once, or hire a tour guide, do tip. One-off taxi rides don't need to involve a tip (though if you round up a bit the gesture will be appreciated).

ECUADOR

Take care in Quito. Take all the precautions you would traveling in a large city in a developing country and your visit here can be hassle-free. Security in the Old City has improved dramatically with a beefed-up police presence, but streets are dark at night and you should take a taxi after sundown. Nighttime muggings have occurred in the New City's La Mariscal district. Exercise caution and take taxis, even if going just a couple of blocks. A growing number of casual eateries offer wireless Internet service to their customers, but we caution against whipping out a laptop computer in such a public, high-trafficked space.

Know when mealtimes are. Many restaurants close for a break between 3 and 7, and on Sunday some remain shuttered or close early.

Going to the Galapagos? Make sure you have your TCT card. All visitors must carry a transit control card (*tarjeta de control de tránsito*) issued by the Instituto Nacional Galápagos (INGALA, *www.ingala.gov.ec*) to enter the islands.

Your tour operator should take care of this step for you if you go with an organized group, though ask, as not all do.

Know that tipping isn't a huge thing in Ecuador. In nicer restaurants, a 10% gratuity is added to the bill; add an extra dollar or two if service was truly exceptional. Fifty cents ber bag is typical for those who help you with your bags at hotels. In Quito, give taxi drivers at least a full $1 even if the meter reads less than that; otherwise, tipping is not customary (despite what the driver might try to tell you). Do tip tour guides.

PARAGUAY

Don't forget that you need a visa. U.S., Canadian, Australian, and New Zealand citizens need to obtain a visa before arrival. Your application must be accompanied by the following: your passport with at least six months' remaining validity; two passport-size photos; and two copies each of your bank statement, your return plane ticket or itinerary, and the visa form (downloadable in PDF format from embassy Web sites). Fees, payable in U.S. dollars only, are $45 for a single-entry visa and $65 for multiple entries.

Load up on lace. Few words in the language begin with the tilded ñ. A tablecloth or placemat fashioned in *ñandutí* fashion is sure to elicit admiration from the folks back home, as well as comment on its unusual name. Artisans craft the delicate spiderweb lacework out of silk or cotton to create Paraguay's signature souvenir.

Try cold maté. This stimulating, bitter, traditional tealike beverage is taken communally as a social activity, and although Paraguay's neighboring countries—Chile, Argentina, Uruguay—drink it with hot water from a thermos, Paraguayans make and drink it cold (and often prefer to call it *terere*). You might see some people drinking it without a *bombilla* (straw with a filter at the end), too; true terere partakers drink right from the side of the hollowed-out gourd, filtering the looseleaf tea with their teeth.

Tip 10% in all restaurants. Keep some coins handy for tipping porters or anyone else who helps you out with a service you would customarily tip for at home.

PATAGONIA

Eat like a local. Chilean Patagonia is no gourmet haven, but the aura of sophistication that lingers in Punta Arenas, the region's largest city, is reflected in the variety of restaurants you can find here. In Puerto Natales it's harder, but still possible, to find a good meal. King crab is always expensive; it's worth the splurge only if it's fresh, rather than frozen (the waiters will be honest with you if you ask). If you hop the border into Argentina, the dining options are cheaper and often tastier. You'll find the same fire-roasted *centolla* and *cordero* (in Argentina it's *cordero a la cruz* or *al asador*—slow-roasted on wooden spits over an open fire) but you'll also get a chance to try the famous Argentine *parrillas* (grilled-meat restaurants).

Iron out an itinerary. Working out a rewarding itinerary can be relatively easy. If you want to begin your trip in Chile, fly into Punta Arenas, the region's principal city. If you'd rather begin your Patagonian jaunt in Argentina, El Calafate and Ushuaia are the two most popular jumping-off points. From any of these locations, you can travel to most of the other destinations by bus or car (or take the ferry from Punta Arenas to Tierra del Fuego). A few remote spots, such as Isla Magdalena or Puerto Williams, can be reached only by boat or airplane.

Raise a glass at world's end. In Chile's Puerto Williams, the southernmost permanent settlement in the world, a small Swiss freighter permanently moored at the dock and listing slightly to port is home to the rustic Club de Yates Micalvi. Sailors stop here for good company, strong spirits, and hearty food as they travel between the Atlantic and Pacific around Cape Horn. Stop by and mingle with whoever is there at the time. You might meet Aussies, Brits, Finns, Russians, Swedes, or even the occasional American.

Watch for those penguins. In late September about 2,000 Magellanic penguin couples begin to arrive at Pingüinera de Seno Otway, a desolate and windswept land off the Otway Sound, about 40 mi northwest of Puerto Arenas. They mate and lay their eggs in early October, and brood their eggs in November. The penguins depart from the sound in late March.

Get wise about the weather. Late November to early March—summer in the southern hemisphere—is high season in Patagonia. Demand for accommodations is highest in January and February, so reservations are vital. Summer weather is pleasantly cool. Bring an extra layer or two, even when the sun is shining. Windbreakers are essential. On or near Antarctic waters, stiff breezes can be biting. In spring (September to November) and fall (March to May) the weather is usually delightfully mild, but can also be downright cold. The region goes into virtual hibernation in the winter months of June, July, and August.

WORD OF MOUTH. **"We drove to Puerto Pyramides where w spent 2 hours on our whale-watching trip. It was wonderful. We had many mother whales with their calves come right up to the boat." —crzn 1**

14

PERU

Get vaccinated. No vaccinations are required to enter Peru, although yellow fever vaccinations are recommended if you're visiting the jungle areas in the east. It's a good idea to have up-to-date boosters for tetanus, diphtheria, and measles. A hepatitis A inoculation can prevent one of the most common intestinal infections. Those who might be around animals should consider a rabies vaccine. As rabies is a concern, most hospitals have anti-rabies injections. Children traveling to Peru should have their vaccinations for childhood diseases up-to-date.

Be smart about food safety. The major health risk in Peru is traveler's diarrhea, caused by viruses, bacteria, or parasites in contaminated food or water. So watch what you eat. If you eat something from a street vendor, make sure it's cooked in front of you. Avoid uncooked food, food that has been sitting around at room temperature, and unpasteurized milk and milk products. Drink only bottled water or water that has been boiled for 10–20 minutes, even when brushing your teeth. Order drinks *sin hielo,* or without ice. Note that water boils at a lower temperature at high altitudes, and may not be hot enough to kill the bacteria, so consider using purification tablets. Local brands include Micropur.

Watch out for altitude sickness. Known locally as *soroche,* altitude sickness affects the majority of visitors to Cusco, Puno, and other high-altitude cities. Headache, dizziness, nausea, and shortness of breath are common. When you visit areas over 10,000 feet above sea level, take it easy for the first few days. Avoiding alcohol will keep you from getting even more dehydrated. To fight soroche, Peruvians swear by *mate de coca,* a tea made from the leaves of the coca plant. Soroche is also a problem in the Andes. Spend a few nights at lower elevations before you head higher. If you must fly directly to higher altitudes, plan on doing next to nothing for the first day or two. Drinking plenty of water or coca tea or taking frequent naps may also help. If symptoms persist, return to lower elevations. If you have high blood pressure or a history of heart trouble, check with your doctor before traveling to high elevations.

Take precautions in the jungle. Mosquitoes are a problem in tropical areas, especially at dusk. Take along plenty of repellent containing DEET. You may not get through airport screening with an aerosol can, so take a spritz bottle or cream. Local brands of repellent are readily available in pharmacies. If you plan to spend time in the jungle, be sure to wear clothing that covers your arms and legs, sleep under a mosquito net, and spray bug repellent in living and sleeping areas. You should also ask your doctor about antimalarial medications. Do so early, as some vaccinations must be started weeks before heading into a malaria zone.

Plan to eat a big lunch. Most Peruvians think of lunch as the main meal of the day, and many restaurants open only at midday. Served between 1 and 3, lunch was once followed by a siesta, though the custom has largely died out. Dinner can be anything from a light snack to another full meal. Peruvians tend to dine late, between 7 and 11.

Understand the bus system. Second-class buses (*servicio normal*) tend to be overcrowded and uncomfortable, whereas the more expensive first-class service (*primera clase*) is more comfortable and much more likely to arrive on schedule.

Check out your hotel room. It's always good to take a look at your room before accepting it; especially if you're staying in a budget hotel. If it isn't what you expected, there might be several other rooms from which to choose. Expense is no guarantee of charm or cleanliness, and accommodations can vary dramatically within a single hotel. Many older hotels in some of the small towns in Peru have rooms with charming balconies or spacious terraces; ask whether there's a room *con balcoì* or *con terraza* when checking in.

Drink like a local. Peru's national drink is the pisco sour, made with a pale grape brandy—close to 100 proof—derived from grapes grown in vineyards around Ica, south of Lima. Added to the brandy are lemon juice, sugar, bitters, and egg white. It is a refreshing drink and one that nearly every bar in Peru claims to make best.

Plan to travel by boat in the Amazon. Passenger boats are the most important means of transportation in the jungle. If you visit a jungle lodge, your hosts will pick you up in an outboard-powered boat—some have thatched roofs. Larger boats make 4- to 10-day cruises on the Amazon from Iquitos. You can also make arrangements for an excursion with a native guide in a wooden dugout called a *pecka-pecka*. However, do get a reference from a reliable source in whatever river town you happen to be in.

Tip in Peru. A 10% tip suffices in most restaurants unless the service is exceptional. Porters in hotels and airports expect S/2–S/3 per bag. There's no need to tip taxi drivers, although many people round up the fare. At bars, tip about 50 céntimos for a beer, more for a mixed drink. Bathroom attendants get 20 céntimos; gas-station attendants get 50 céntimos for extra services such as adding air to your tires. Tour guides and tour bus drivers should get S/5–S/10 each per day.

14

WORD OF MOUTH. "On the topic of things to take to Peru, be sure to bring chapstick or similar for your lips. It's incredibly dry and dusty. I also wish I had brought something for my eyes. I wear contacts and was constantly getting dust in them." —yestravel

URUGUAY

See a criolla. Also known as *jineteadas,* these Uruguayan-style rodeos are held in every corner of the country, but the most spectacular one takes place in Montevideo's El Prado district every Easter. Gauchos (cowboys) from all over Uruguay come to display their riding skills.

Bask in colonial splendor. You wouldn't expect to find much ancient in this modern, progressive country, but the once-walled 1680 Portuguese settlement of Colonia del Sacramento makes up for it. Flowers spill over balconies, balladeers serenade their sweethearts, and lanterns illuminate the streets in one of the continent's best-preserved colonial cities. Be sure to wear shoes with decent soles to wander the cobbled streets of the older parts of town with ease; also watch for the occasional small sinkhole if you venture down to the grass by the water.

Keep praise of Argentine soccer teams to yourself. The *fútbol* pride is just as fierce here as it is across the Paraná Delta. Trust us.

Know taht tips are appreciated in Uruguay. In restaurants a flat 10% of the bill is adequate. Tour guides should also get 10% of the total. A 20-peso tip is fine for parking valets, hotel porters (per bag), and chambermaids (per night). Tipping cabbies is optional.

VENEZUELA

Come for the Caribbean. St. Bart's has nothing on Margarita, the continent's one true Caribbean island. Venezuelans call their favorite vacation destination *La Perla del Caribe* (the Pearl of the Caribbean), and the island, with its white-sand beaches, smart hotels, yummy restaurants, and historic sites, really does live up to the hype.

Be careful when in Caracas. The city well deserves its reputation as a dangerous place. The main tourist areas are generally safe during the day, but always be on your guard. Even residents do not go out alone in most neighborhoods after dark, when muggings and other violent crimes are shockingly frequent. Taxis are the safest means of transportation after dark.

Tip only if service is exemplary. Your restaurant bill will have the service charge built in, but do tip up to an extra 10% if your server or the food (or both) were above and beyond expectations.

SOUTH PACIFIC

AUSTRALIA

Be prepared to tip for some services. Australians don't tip nearly as much as North Americans. Waitstaff are the exception: Hotels and restaurants don't usually add service charges, so a 10%–15% tip for good service is normal. Room service and housemaids are only tipped for special services. Taxi drivers don't expect a tip, but leaving small change will get you a smile. Guides, tour-bus drivers, and chauffeurs don't expect tips either, though they're grateful if someone in the group takes up a collection for them. No tipping is necessary—indeed, it would cause confusion—in hair salons or for theater ushers.

Know how to read a menu. In Australia entrée means appetizer, and main courses are American main courses.

Get sporty. Catch a local sports event. Cricket in summer (October–March) or Australian rules football (think rugby meets soccer) in late autumn and winter are a blast. If you've never gone diving, there's no better place to try it than the Great Barrier Reef.

Look right before stepping into the street. Driving is on the left, and stepping off a curb can be dangerous if your instincts have you looking left.

Know the rules of the road. Pick up a copy of the Highway Code from the local automobile association for any state or territory in which you plan to drive. If you drive through the Outback, carry plenty of water and always tell someone your itinerary and schedule.

14

Make rail reservations well in advance. This is especially necessary during peak tourist seasons, roughly from November through February. Advance-purchase train fares, which afford a 10%–40% discount between some major cities, are best bought before departure for Australia, as they tend to be booked up far in advance. Contact your travel agent or the appropriate Rail Australia office.

WORD OF MOUTH. "I haven't been to the Grampians yet, but I can definitely recommend the Blue Mountains! You can easily spend 6 days in this area. do the Grand Canyon walk and visit Jenolan Caves. The easiest way is to rent a car, since public transport can be a bit of a hassle out there." —TravelSarah

FIJI

Present an offering to the village leader. If you visit any villages, carry with you a *sevusevu,* (offering) of *yaqona* (kava root) for the head of the village. He'll pound it into a powder, mix it with water to create a traditional (and mildly intoxicating) beverage, and serve you a small bowlful. Clap your hands once, accept the bowl, drink it in a gulp, then clap your hands three times and say, "*Muca!*" to express gratitude and satisfaction. You might think this is a situation you'll never find yourself in, but many hiking or rafting tours cross onto village-owned land, and tour operators must receive the chief's OK to do this. Thus, the yaqona ceremony may well be part of many a trip.

Mind the head. When venturing into the smaller villages, wearing hats and/or touching someone on the head is considered very disrespectful, so opt for sunscreen and a pair of shades, and keep your hands to yourself. In the larger towns hats are more acceptable, but still try to avoid the passerby's pate.

Dress modestly away from your resort. It's simple really, just toss a T-shirt over your swimsuit, or buy a *sulu*, like a pareu, to wrap around yourself. Men, take note, you can wear them, too!

WORD OF MOUTH. "On a recent trip [to Fiji], I rented a car and drove from the Coral Coast up to Ba. I went with friends to visit a traditional village and school and stayed overnight. Next day, back via Suva, stopping here and there. I thoroughly enjoyed it. Viti Levu's small, easy to drive around and has a very interesting history. Plus sparkling clear waters and climate perfect for year-round swimming/snorkeling/diving." —Bokhara2

Speak to the hotel manager before tipping. Often, directly handing money to an employee can cause confusion and embarassment, and there may be a more discreet way of rewarding the employee for his or her good service.

Tip in restaurants. About 10% is fine, even if the service was exceptional.

NEW ZEALAND

Mind the strong sun. Cover up with a long-sleeve shirt, a hat, and long pants or a beach wrap, because the primary health hazard here is sunburn or sunstroke. Likewise, avoid dehydration. The wisest approach when dressing is to wear layered outfits. Frequently, particularly at the change of seasons, weather can turn suddenly.

Don't plan to tour Auckland on foot. It isn't the easiest place to figure out. It was built out, rather than up, and the sprawl makes the greater city close to impossible to explore on foot. What might look like short walking distances on maps can turn out to be far longer.

Remember this simple axiom: Drive left, look right. That means keep to the left lane, and when turning right or left from a stop sign, the closest lane of traffic will be coming from the right, so look in that direction first. By the same token, pedestrians should look right before crossing the street. So repeat this several times: Drive left, look right.

Overestimate drive times. Due to the less than flat terrain, many New Zealand roads are "wonky," or crooked. So when mapping out your itinerary, don't plan on averaging 100 kph (62 mph) very often.

Know what's meant by "Kiwi." The word "kiwi" refers to either people (New Zealanders) or to the protected kiwi bird, but not the kiwifruit.

Navigate sheep talk smoothly. You might lose smarty points if you ask dumb sheep questions. "When do you cut their fur?" or "When do their tails fall off?" will elicit laughter: sheep have wool, not fur or hair, and their tails are cut off. You will also be considered quite tedious if you tell "sheep jokes." There isn't one that they haven't heard already.

Keep an ear out for Kiwis' eloquent use of understatement. This facet of Kiwi speech is both blessing and curse. Everything sounds relaxed and easygoing, but if you're trying to judge something like distance or difficulty you may run into trouble. For instance, no matter how far away something is, people often say it's "just down the road" or "just over the hill." Ask specific questions to avoid a misunderstanding.

Be considerate of Māori traditions. For instance, *marae*, the area in front of a meetinghouse, should not be entered unless you are invited, or unless it's in use as a cultural center. Also, it's best not to use *hongi* (touching foreheads and noses in greeting) unless someone initiates it.

Know that prostitution is legal in New Zealand. These are not establishments with blinking neon BROTHEL signs in the window; so be aware if you're seeking a massage that some parlors might not offer exactly what you had in mind. And Candy's on Shotover Street ain't sellin' jellybeans.

Beware of New Zealand's one health hazard. Although the country's alpine lakes might look like backdrops for mineral-water ads, some in South Island harbor a tiny organism that can cause "duck itch," a temporary but intense skin irritation.

Tip appropriately. Tipping is not as widely practiced in New Zealand as in the United States or Europe, but in city restaurants and hotels it's appreciated if you acknowledge good service with a 10% tip. Taxi drivers will appreciate rounding up the fare to the nearest $5 amount, but don't feel you have to do this. Porters will be happy with a $1 or $2 coin. Most other people, like bartenders, theater attendants, gas-station attendants, or barbers, will probably wonder what you are doing if you try to give them a tip.

TAHITI

Learn a little Tahitian. Although French and English are widely spoken, the Tahitian language, or reo Tahiti, has been experiencing a resurgence as islanders become increasingly interested in honoring their roots. "Hello" is *ia orana;* "good-bye" is *nana;* and "thank you" is *mauru'uru.*

Bring home a black pearl. But first stop by the Musée de la Perle Robert Wan to learn about the pearls and the man who jumpstarted the industry in the '60s. The museum will also give you some tips on how to ensure that you're picking out an authentic black pearl. For one, look at the pearl's depth of color; though black (or a shade of gray), it should show a certain iridescence.

Afford an overwater bungalow (OVB). You've surely seen pictures of Tahiti's signature auberge, perched on stilts out over the cerulean waters, but did you know that they can easily go for a grand a night? If you're willing to bypass sleeping on Bora Bora, you can find OVBs on Raiatea or Moorea for around 50% (or more!) cheaper.

Know that the French Polynesian islands are a casual destination. Comfortable, loose-fitting clothes, sundresses, and bright colors fit in everywhere. Bring what you'll need to stay covered from the intense tropical sun (brimmed hats, sunscreen, sarongs, and loose, long-sleeved shirts are essential), as well as what you'll need to play in the ocean (sturdy reef shoes, a few swimsuits, etc.). Mosquito repellent, a raincoat, and a first-aid kit are essential.

WORD OF MOUTH. "March is the low season [in French Polynesia and] many of the resorts offer special rates that include a free night and often a buffet breakfast. . . . As far as the weather is concerned it is towards the end of the hot humid season and its a bit more rainy." —uschi

Know that tipping is not expected in Tahiti. However, if the service is extraordinary, tipping as a compliment is always appreciated.

Contacts and Resources

Air Travel
Booking
Bus and Train Travel
Car Travel
Cruise Travel
Family Travel
Health and Fitness
Money Matters
Packing
Passports and Visas
Pet Travel
Research and Planning
Safety and Security
Technology
Visitor Information

www.fodors.com/forums

▌ AIR TRAVEL

Airplane Seats Seat Guru (⊕ www.seatguru.com).

Airport, Airline, and Flight Info Airline Quality (⊕ www.airlinequality.com). **Alternate Airports** (⊕ alternateairports.com). **Bureau of Transportation Statistics** (⊕ www.bts.gov/ntda/oai). **Do Hop** (⊕ www.dohop.com). **Flight Stats** (⊕ www.flightstats.com). **Official Airline Guides** (⊕ www.oag.com). **OrbitzTLC Traveler Update** (⊕ updates.orbitz.com). **National Air Traffic Controllers Association** (⊕ www.avoiddelays.com). **Sidestep.com** (⊕ www.sidestep.com/airportguides). **World Airport Codes** (⊕ www.world-airport-codes.com).

Airport Parking Airport Parking Reservations (⊕ www.airportparkingreservations.com). **Avistar/FastTrack Parking** (⊕ www.avistarparking.com). **ParkSleepFly.com** (⊕ www.parksleepfly.com).

Blogs and Community Sites Flightmemory (⊕ www.flightmemory.com). **Flightstory** (⊕ www.flightstory.net). **Flyer Talk** (⊕ www.flyertalk.com). **Frequent-Flier** (⊕ www.frequentflier.com). **Johnny Jet** (⊕ www.johnnyjet.com).

Booking ⇨ Flights under Booking, below.

Consumer Information Air Transport Association (⊕ www.airlines.org). **Air Travelers Association** (⊕ www.airtravelersassociation.com/). **Department of Transportation Aviation Consumer Protection and Enforcement** (⊕ airconsumer.ost.dot.gov). **Fed-eral Aviation Administration** (☎ 866/835–5322 Consumer Hotline, 866/289–9673 Transportation Security Hotline ⊕ www.faa.gov). **Unclaimed Baggage Center** (⊕ www.unclaimedbaggage.com).

Frequent-Flier Information Frequent Flier (⊕ www.frequentflier.com). **Points** (⊕ www.points.com). **Web Flyer** (⊕ www.webflyer.com).

Safety and Security AirSafe.com (⊕ www.airsafe.com). **Aviation Safety Network** (⊕ aviation-safety.net). **Clear Card** (⊕ www.clearme.com). **National Transportation Safety Board** (⊕ www.ntsb.gov). **Transportation Security Administration** (⊕ www.tsa.gov). **Trusted Traveler Programs** (⊕ www.cbp.gov/xp/cgov/travel).

▌ BOOKING

Aggregators Kayak (⊕ www.kayak.com). **Mobissimo** (⊕ www.mobissimo.com). **Quixo** (⊕ www.quixo.com). **Sidestep** (⊕ www.sidestep.com). **Travelgrove** (⊕ www.travelgrove.com).

Auction Site Information Bidding ForTravel (⊕ www.biddingfortravel.yuku.com).

Auction Sites LuxuryLink.com (⊕ www.luxurylink.com). **Priceline** (⊕ www.priceline.com). **Skyauction.com** (⊕ www.skyauction.com).

Booking Engines/Online Travel Agents Expedia (⊕ www.expedia.com). **Orbitz** (⊕ www.orbitz.com). **Travelocity** (⊕ www.travelocity.com).

Discounter Hotwire (⊕ www.hotwire.com).

Show and Event Tickets Opera Base (⊕ www.operabase.com). **Theater Development Fund** (⊕ www.tdf.org). **Ticketmaster** (⊕ www.ticketmaster.com). **Viator** (⊕ www.viator.com)

FLIGHTS

Airline Links Airlines of the Web (⊕ www.flyaow.com).

Fare Comparisons FareCompare (⊕ www.farecompare.com). **Smarter-Travel** (⊕ www.smartertravel.com). **TravelZoo** (⊕ www.travelzoo.com).

Multidestination Trips AirTreks (⊕ www.AirTreks.com). **Flylc** (⊕ www.Flylc.com). **Montrose Travel** (⊕ www.MontroseTravel.com). **Vayama** (⊕ www.Vayama.com).

ACCOMMODATIONS

Association American Hotel & Lodging Association (⊕ www.ahla.com).

Home Exchanges Digsville (⊕ www.digsville.com). **Exchange Homes** (⊕ www.exchangehomes.com). **Home Exchange** (⊕ www.homeexchange.com). **Home Link International** (⊕ www.homelink.org). **Intervac** (⊕ www.intervac-homeexchange.org). **Seniors Home Exchange** (⊕ www.seniorshomeexchange.com).

Hostels Hostelling International (⊕ www.hihostels.com).

Hotel Room Wholesalers Hotel Club (⊕ www.hotelclub.com).

Hotels.com (⊕ www.hotels.com).

House and Villa Rental At Home Abroad (⊕ www.athomeabroadinc.com). **Forgetaway** (⊕ www.forgetaway.com). **Home Abroad** (⊕ www.homeabroad.com). **Homeaway** (⊕ www.homeaway.com). **Mountain Lodges** (⊕ www.mountain-lodges.com). **Slow Travel** (⊕ www.slowtrav.com). **Vacation Home Rentals** (⊕ www.vacationhomerentals.com). **Villa Europe** (⊕ www.villaeurope.com). **Villas International** (⊕ www.villasintl.com).

RENTAL CARS

European Wholesalers Auto Europe (⊕ www.autoeurope.com). **Europe by Car** (⊕ www.europebycarblog.com). **Kemwel** (⊕ www.kemwel.com).

U.S. Rental Agencies Alamo (⊕ www.alamo.com). **Avis** (⊕ www.avis.com). **Budget** (⊕ www.budget.com). **Hertz** (⊕ www.hertz.com). **National Car Rental** (⊕ www.nationalcar.com).

▌ BUS AND TRAIN TRAVEL

BUS TRAVEL

Aggregator Go To Bus (⊕ www.gotobus.com).

"Chinatown Express" Companies Chinatown Bus (⊕ www.chinatown-bus.org).

North American Bus Companies BoltBus (⊕ www.boltbus.com). **Greyhound Bus** (⊕ www.greyhound.com). **MegaBus** (⊕ us.megabus.com). **NeOn** (⊕ www.neonbus.com). **Peter Pan Bus Lines** (⊕ www.peterpanbus.com). **Trailways** (⊕ www.trailways.com).

TRAIN TRAVEL

European Rail Pass Eurail Pass (⊕ www.eurail.com).

North American Rail Companies Amtrak (⊕ www.amtrak.com). **VIA Rail Canada** (⊕ www.viarail.ca).

Tourist and Scenic Railways Aggregator **U.S. Train Web** (⊕ www.trainweb.com).

▌ CAR TRAVEL

Audio Books **Audible** (⊕ www.audible.com). **Audio Bookstore** (⊕ www.theaudiobookstore.com). **Barnes and Noble** (⊕ www.barnesand noble.ebooks). **Cracker Barrel** (☎ 800/333–9566 ⊕ www.crackerbarrel.com). **iTunes** (⊕ www.itunes.com). **Simply Audiobooks** (⊕ www.simplyaudiobooks.com).

Automobile Associations **American Automobile Association** (AAA ⊕ www.aaa.com). **British Automobile Association** (AA ⊕ www.theaa.com). **Canadian Automobile Association** (AA ⊕ www.caa.ca).

Booking ⇨ Rental Cars under Booking, above.

Coupons for Unreserved-Only Hotel Rooms **Room Saver** (⊕ www.roomsaver.com).

Gas Prices **AAA Fuel Cost Calculator** (⊕ www.fuelcostcalculator.com). **Gas Buddy** (⊕ www.gasbuddy.com). **Gas Price Watch** (⊕ www.gaspricewatch.com).**United States Environmental Agency's Fuel Economy Web Site** (⊕ www.fueleconomy.gov).

GPS **Garmin** (⊕ www.garmin.com). **Magellan GPS** (⊕ www.magellangps.com). **TomTom** (⊕ www.tomtom.com).

International Driving **Association for Safe International Road Travel** (⊕ www.asirt.com).

Rest Areas **Road Notes** (⊕ www.roadnotes.com).

Restaurants **BooRah** (⊕ www.boorah.com). **Fodor's** (⊕ www.fodors.com). **MenuPages** (⊕ www.menupages.com). **Road Food** (⊕ www.roadfood.com). **Yelp** (⊕ www.yelp.com).

RVING

General Information **Good Sam Club** (⊕ www.goodsamclub.com). **Go Rving, Inc.** (⊕ gorving.com).

Rentals **Cruise America** (⊕ www.cruiseamerica.com). **El Monte** (⊕ www.elmonterv.com). **Idea Merge** (⊕ www.ideamerge.org). **Recreation Vehicle Rental Association** (⊕ www.rvra.org).

RVing in France **French Passion** (⊕ www.frenchpassion.com).

▌ CRUISE TRAVEL

GENERAL RESOURCES

Association **Cruise Lines International Association** (⊕ www.cruising.org).

Publications and Web Sites **Avid Cruiser** (⊕ www.avidcruiser.com). **Cruise Critic** (⊕ www.cruisecritic.com). **Cruise Diva** (⊕ www.cruisediva.com). **Fodors.com** (⊕ www.fodors.com/cruise). **Porthole Cruise Magazine** (⊕ www.porthole.com).

SPECIALTY CRUISES

Cruise Wedding Service Provider **The Wedding Experience** (⊕ www.theweddingexperience.com).

Group Cruises **Countryside Travel** (⊕ www.countryside-travel.com). **CruisePlanning.net** (⊕ www.cruiseplanning.net). **Skyscraper Tours Cruises** (⊕ www.skyscrapertours.com). **Whet Travel Inc.** (⊕ www.whettravel.com).

Nudist Cruises Bare Necessities Tour & Travel (⊕ www.bare-necessities.com).

Resources for Gays and Lesbians Atlantis Events (⊕ www.atlantisevents.com). **Olivia Cruises & Resorts** (⊕ www.olivia.com). **R Family Vacations** (⊕ www.rfamilyvacations.com). **RSVP Vacations** (⊕ www.rsvp.net).

Resources for Passengers with Disabilities Advanced Aeromedical (☎ 800/346–3556 or 757/481–1590 ⊕ www.aeromedic.com). **Care Vacations/Cruise Ship Assist** (⊕ www.cruiseshipassist.com). **Scoot Around** (⊕ www.scootaround.com). **The Seeing Eye, Inc.** (☎ 973/539–4425 ⊕ www.seeingeye.org). **U.S. Department of State, Bureau of Consular Affairs** (☎ 888/407–4747 ⊕ travel.state.gov/index.html).

Solo Cruising Cruise Mates (⊕ www.cruisemates.com/articles/single/). **SinglesCruise.com** (⊕ www.singlescruise.com). **Singles Cruise Resource** (⊕ www.solocruiseresource.com).

▌ FAMILY TRAVEL

Babies Babies Travel Lite (⊕ babiestravellite.com). **BabyAnt** (⊕ Babyant.com).

Changing Tables Changing Table Locator (⊕ www.changingtablelocator.com).

Entertainment Boardgames (⊕ boardgames.com). **Mom's Minivan** ⊕ momsminivan.com).

Family Reunions Reunions Magazine(⊕ reunionsmag.com).

Flying FlyingWithKids.com (⊕ www.flyingwithkids.com).

General Info and Community Sites DisneyFamily.com (⊕ www.family.go.com). **Family Travel Forum** (⊕ www.familytravelforum.com).

Safety American Academy of Pediatrics (⊕ www.aap.org). **National Highway Traffic Safety Administration** (⊕ www.nhtsa.dot.gov).

TRAVEL AGENCIES

Adventure Travel Adventures by Disney (⊕ adventuresbydisney.com). **Backroads** (⊕ www.backroads.com). **CoveredWagonVacations** (⊕ wagonswestwyo.com). **Dude Ranchers Association** (⊕ duderanch.org). **Kids Go Too** (⊕ www.kidsgotootravel.com). **ThomsonFamilyAdventure** (⊕ www.familyadventures.com).

Families General The Family Traveler (⊕ thefamilytraveler.com). **Personal Touch Travel** (⊕ www.personaltouchtravel.net). **Rascals in Paradise** (⊕ www.rascalsinparadise.com).

Grandparent/Grandchild Travel Grand Travel (☎ 800/247–7651 ⊕ www.grandtrvl.com).

▌ HEALTH AND FITNESS

Active Travel Great Outdoors Recreation Pages (⊕ www.gorp.com). **Travel Hub** (⊕ www.travelhub.com). **Voyage Trek Travel** (⊕ www.voyagetrek.com).

Diet and Exercise American Council on Exercise (⊕ www.acefitness.org). **Food Allergy & Anaphylaxis Network** (⊕ www.foodallergy.org). **United States Department of Agriculture** (⊕ www.usda.gov). **VegDining.com** (⊕ www.vegdining.com). **Weight Watchers** (⊕ www.weightwatchers.com).

Fitness Gear Jfit (⊕ *www.jfit.com*). **Lifeline USA** (⊕ *www.lifelineusa. com*). **Power Systems** (⊕ *www. power-systems.com*).

General Information American Academy of Dermatologists (⊕ *www.aad.org*). **Centers for Disease Control** (CDC ⊕ *www. cdc.gov/travel*). **Deep-vein thrombosis (DVT)** (⊕ *www.dvt. net*). **MaxLifestyle.net** (⊕ *www. maxlifestyle.net*). **World Health Organization** (WHO ⊕ *www.who.int*).

Health Clubs, Gyms, and Pools Airport Gyms (⊕ *www.airportgyms. com*). **Athletic-Minded Traveler** (⊕ *www.athleticmindedtraveler.com*). **Healthclubs.com** (⊕ *www.health-clubs.com*). **Run the Planet** (⊕ *www. runtheplanet.com*). **Swimmers Guide** (⊕ *www.swimmersguide.com*). **Yoga Finder** (⊕ *www.yogafinder.com*).

Insurance Access America (⊕ *www.accessamerica.com*). **CSA Travel Protection** (⊕ *www. csatravelprotection.com*). **Expedia Package Protection Plan** (⊕ *www. expedia.com*). **HTH Worldwide** (⊕ *www.hthworldwide.com*). **International Medical Group** (⊕ *www. imglobal.com*). **Travel Guard** (⊕ *www.travelguard.com*). **Wallach & Company** (⊕ *www.wallach.com*).

Insurance Comparison Info InsureMyTrip.com (⊕ *www. insuremytrip.com*). **QuoteWright. com** (⊕ *www.quotewright.com*). **Squaremouth** (⊕ *www.squaremouth. com*). **Total Travel Insurance.com** (⊕ *www.totaltravelinsurance.com*).

Medical-Assistance Companies Air Med (⊕ *www.airmed. com*). **International SOS** (⊕ *www.* *internationalsos.com*). **MedJet Assist** (⊕ *www.medjetassist.com*).

Spas International Spa Association (⊕ *www.ispaexperience.com*). **Spa Finder** (⊕ *www.spafinder.com*).

Travel Medicine International Association of Travel Medicine (⊕ *www.istm.org*).

❚ MONEY MATTERS

Budgeting Tools AAA Fuel Cost Calculator (⊕ *www. fuelcostcalculator.com*). **U.S. State Department** (⊕ *aoprals.state.gov/*).

Currency Exchange International Currency Express (⊕ *www. foreignmoney.com*).

Currency-Exchange Rates Google (⊕ *www.google.com*). **Oanda** (⊕ *www.oanda.com*). **XE** (⊕ *www.xe.com*).

Tipping The Original Tipping Page (⊕ *www.tipping.org*).

PRICE COMPARISONS

Airfare Airfare Watch Dog (⊕ *www. airfarewatchdog.com*). **Fare Compare** (⊕ *www.farecompare.com*). **Which Budget** (⊕ *www.whichbudget. com*). **Yapta** (⊕ *www.yapta.com*).

General Travel Kayak (⊕ *www. kayak.com*). **Mobissimo** (⊕ *www. mobissimo.com*). **Quixo** (⊕ *www. quixo.com*). **Sidestep** (⊕ *www. sidestep.com*). **Travelgrove** (⊕ *www.travelgrove.com*).

❚ PACKING

Bags and Accessories The Container Store (⊕ *www.containerstore. com*). **Flight101** (⊕ *www.flight101. com*). **Hartmann** (⊕ *www.hartmann.*

com). **L.L. Bean** (⊕ *www.llbean. com*). **Luggage.com** (⊕ *www. luggage.com*). **Magellan's** (⊕ *www. magellans.com*). **Miminus** (⊕ *www. minimus.biz*). **Pro Travel Gear** (⊕ *www.protravelgear.com*). **Solu- tions** (⊕ *www.solutions.com*). **Trav- elsmith** (⊕ *www.travelsmith.com*).

Clothing Chicos (⊕ *www.chicos. com*). **Coldwater Creek** (⊕ *www. coldwatercreek.com*). **J. Jill** (⊕ *www. jjill.com*). **Orvis** (⊕ *www.orvis.com*). **Spiegel** (⊕ *www.spiegel.com*). **Til- ley Endurables** (⊕ *www.tilley.com*). **Travelsmith** (⊕ *www.travelsmith. com*).

Luggage Shipping Services Luggage Concierge (⊕ *www. luggageconcierge.com*). **Lug- gage Free** (⊕ *www.luggagefree. com*). **Sports Express** (⊕ *www. sportsexpress.com*). **Virtual Bellhop** (⊕ *www.virtualbellhop.com*).

Outdoor and Adventure Gear Campor(⊕ *www.campmor.com*). **Eastern Mountain Sports** (⊕ *www. ems.com*). **Land's End** (⊕ *www. landsend.com*). **L.L. Bean** (⊕ *www. llbean.com*). **Patagonia** (⊕ *www. patagonia.com*). **REI** (⊕ *www.rei.com*).

▮ PASSPORTS AND VISAS

Applications and Information U.S. State Department (☏ *877/ 487-2778 for an appointment at a passport office* ⊕ *travel.state.gov/ passport*).

Passport and Visa Expeditors A. Briggs (⊕ *www.abriggs.com*). **National Association of Passport & Visa Services** (⊕ *www.napvs. org*). **Passport Express** (⊕ *www. passportexpress.com*).

Passport Copies for Safekeep- ing Passport Support (⊕ *www. passportsupport.com*).

Passport Photos Online Photos (⊕ *epassportphotos.com*).

▮ PET TRAVEL

Air Safety Reports Thirdamend- ment.com (⊕ *www.thirdamendment. com/animals.html*). **U.S. Department of Transportation** (⊕ *airconsumer. ost.dot.gov/reports/index.htm*).

Air Travel Pet Policies Air Trans- port Association (⊕ *www.airlines. org/PassengersCargo*).

Air Travel with Pets Pet Airways (⊕ *www.petairways.com*). **PetFlight** (⊕ *www.petflight.com*).

Boarding Recommendations Pet Care Services Association (⊕ *www.petcareservices.org*).

Community Association of Pet Dog Trainers' Annual Conference (⊕ *www.apdt.com/conferen.htm*).

Cruising with Pets QM2 (⊕ *www. cunard.com/QM2*).

General Information DogFriendly. com (⊕ *dogfriendly.com*). **Doggone Good!** (⊕ *www.doggonegood.com*). **Go 2 Pets** (⊕ *www.go2pets.com*). **Humane Society of the United States** (⊕ *www.humanesociety. org*). **Petfriendlytravel.com** (⊕ *petfriendlytravel.com*). **Petsonthego.com** (⊕ *www. petsonthego.com*). **Tripswithpets. com** (⊕ *www.tripswithpets.com*).

Hotels with Pets Dog Friendly (⊕ *www.dogfriendly.com*). **Official Pet Hotels** (⊕ *www.officialpethotels.*

com). **Pets Welcome** (⊕ www. petswelcome.com).

Pet Sitting The National Association of Professional Pet Sitters (NAPPS) (⊕ www.petsitters.org).

Resorts for You and Your Pet **Camp Gone to the Dogs** (☎ 888/364–3293 ⊕ www. campgonetothedogs.com).

HEALTH AND WELL-BEING
24-Hour Pet Loss Assistance and Prevention **Help 4 Pets** (☎ 800/435–7473 ⊕ www.help4pets. com). **National Dog Registry** (⊕ www.nationaldogregistry.com).

Vet Referrals **American Animal Hospital Association (AAHA)** (⊕ www.healthypet.com). **American Veterinary Medical Association** (⊕ www.avma.org).

RULES AND REGULATIONS
International **EU Quarantine Rules** (⊕ www.ec.europa.eu/comm/ food/animal/index_en.htm). **Animal and Plant Health Inspection Service (APHIS)** (⊕ www.aphis.usda. gov/animal_welfare/pet_travel/ pet_travel.shtml).

United States **Hawaii Department of Agriculture** (⊕ www.hawaii. gov/hdoa/ai/aqs). **UK Pet Travel Scheme (PETS)** (⊕ www.defra.gov. uk). **U.S. Customs** (⊕ www.cbp.gov). **U.S. Department of Agriculture** (⊕ www.usda.gov).

▮ RESEARCH AND PLANNING

Beaches **Blue Flag Programme** (⊕ www.blueflag.org).

Events **City Search** (⊕ www. citysearch.com).

General Info **Central Intelligence Agency** (CIA ⊕ www.cia.gov). **World-Newspapers.com.** (⊕ www. world-newspapers.com).

Public Transportation **Hop Stop** (⊕ www.hopstop.com).

Restaurants **Chow Hound** (⊕ www. chowhound.com). **DinnerBroker** (⊕ www.dinnerbroker.com). **Fodor's** (⊕ www.fodors.com). **Open Table** (⊕ www.opentable.com). **Road Food** (⊕ www.roadfood.com).

Restrooms **Bathroom Diaries** (⊕ www.bathroomdiaries.com).

Theme Parks **Theme Park Insider** (⊕ www.themeparkinsider.com).

Tour Operators **National Tour Association** (⊕ www.ntaonline.org). **United States Tour Operators Association** (⊕ www.ustoa.org).

Travel Agents **American Society of Travel Agents** (ASTA ⊕ www.asta. org ⊕ www.travelsense.org).

Travel Blogs and Forums **Fodor's** (⊕ www.fodors.com). **Gusto** (⊕ www. gusto.com). **IgoUGo** (⊕ www.igougo. com). **RealTravel** (⊕ www.realtravel. com). **ravBuddy** (⊕ www.travebuddy. com). **TravelChums** (⊕ www. travelchums.com). **The Travel Insider** (⊕ www.thetravelinsider. info). **Smarter Traveler** (⊕ www. smartertravel.com). **VirtualTourist** (⊕ www.virtualtourist.com).

Weather **Weather Channel** (⊕ www.weather.com). **World Meteorological Organization** (WMO ⊕ severe.worldweather.wmo.int/). **World Weather Information Service** (⊕ worldweather.wmo.int).

SAFETY AND SECURITY

Advisories and Alerts Australian Department of Foreign Affairs & Trade (⊕ www.smartraveller. gov.au). **ComeBackAlive** (⊕ www. comebackalive.com). **Foreign Affairs and International Trade Canada** (⊕ www.voyage.gc.ca). **U.K. Foreign & Commonwealth Office** (⊕ www.fco.gov.uk). **U.S. Embassies** (⊕ usembassy.state.gov). **U.S. State Department** (⊕ travel.state.gov).

Airports Transportation Safety Administration (⊕ www.tsa.gov).

Emergencies State Department's emergency assistance numbers (☎ 888/407–4747 or 202/647–5225).

State Department's Travel Registry State Department (⊕ travelregistration.state.gov/ibrs).

TECHNOLOGY

AV Equipment Rental InMotion (⊕ www.inmotionpictures.com).

Cell-Phone Plans and Rentals All Cell Rentals (⊕ www. allcellrentals.com). **Cellular Abroad** (⊕ www.cellularabroad.com). **International Cellular** (⊕ www. internationalcellular.com). **My Japan Phone** (⊕ www.myjapanphone.com). **Travel Cell** (⊕ www.travelcell.com).

General Info Steve Kropla's Help for World Travelers (⊕ www.kropla. com).

SIM cards Brightroam (⊕ www. brightroam.com). **Rebel Fone** (⊕ www.rebelfone.com). **WORLDSIM** (⊕ www.worldsim.com).

Wi-Fi Hotspots iWire (⊕ www. jiwire.com). **Wi-Fi Free Spot** (⊕ www.wififreespot.com). **Wi-Fi Hot Spot List** (⊕ www.wifihotspotlist. com).

VISITOR INFORMATION

AFRICA AND THE MIDDLE EAST
Egypt Egyptian Tourist Authority (⊕ www.egypt.travel).

Israel Israel Ministry of Tourism (⊕ www.goisrael.com).

Kenya Kenya Tourist Board (⊕ www.magicalkenya.com).

Morocco Moroccan National Tourist Office (⊕ www.visitmorocco.com).

South Africa South Africa Tourism (⊕ www.southafrica.net).

Tanzania Tanzania Tourist Board (⊕ www.tanzaniatouristboard.com).

ASIA
Bali Bali Tourism Board (⊕ www. balitourismboard.org).

Cambodia Tourism of Cambodia (⊕ www.tourismcambodia.com).

China National Tourist Office (⊕ www.cnto.org). **Hong Kong Tourism Board** (⊕ www.discover-hongkong.com). **eBeijing** (⊕ www. ebeijing.gov.cn). **Shanghai Municipal Tourism Administrative Commission** (⊕ www.meet-in-shanghai. net). **Tibet Tourism Bureau, Shanghai** (⊕ www.tibet-tour.com).

India Ministry of Tourism (⊕ www. incredibleindia.org).

Japan Japan National Tourist Organization (⊕ www.japantrav-elinfo.jp).

Laos Laos Tourism Administration (⊕ www.tourismlaos.org).

Nepal **Nepal Tourism Board** (⊕ *www.welcomenepal.com*).

Singapore **Singapore Tourism Board** (⊕ *www.yoursingapore.com*).

Thailand **Tourism Authority of Thailand** (⊕ *www.tourismthailand. org*).

Tibet **Tibet Tourism Bureau, Shanghai** (⊕ *www.tibet-tour.com*).

Vietnam **Vietnam National Administration of Tourism** (⊕ *www. vietnamtourism.com*).

BERMUDA, BAHAMAS, AND THE CARIBBEAN
Bahamas **Bahamas Ministry of Tourism** (⊕ *www.bahamas.com*).

Bermuda **Bermuda Department of Tourism** (⊕ *www. bermudatourism.com*).

Caribbean Tourism Organization **Caribbean Tourism Development Company** (⊕ *www.caribbeantravel. com*).

CANADA
Canada General Info **Canadian Tourism Commission** (⊕ *www. canada.travel*).

Montreal and Québec **Québec City Tourism** (⊕ *www.quebecregion. com*). **Tourisme Montréal** (⊕ *www. tourisme-montreal.org*). **Tourisme Québec** (⊕ *www.bonjourquebec. com*).

Vancouver and Victoria **Tourism Vancouver** (⊕ *www. tourismvancouver.com*). **Tourism Victoria** (⊕ *www.tourismvictoria.com*).

CENTRAL AMERICA
Belize **Belize Tourism Board** (⊕ *www.travelbelize.org*).

Costa Rica **Costa Rica Tourism Board** (⊕ *www.visitcostarica.com*).

El Salvador **Ministry of Tourism** (⊕ *www.elsalvador.travel/ingles*).

Guatemala **Guatemalan Tourism Comission** (⊕ *www.visitguatemala. com*).

Honduras **Honduras Institute of Tourism** (⊕ *www.letsgohonduras. com*).

Nicaragua **Nicaraguan Institute of Tourism** (⊕ *www.visitnicaragua. com*).

Panama **Panama Institute of Tourism** (⊕ *www.visitpanama.com*).

EUROPE
Austria **Austria Tourist Office** (⊕ *www.austria.info*). **Vienna Tourist Office** (⊕ *www.wien.info/*).

Belgium **Belgian Tourist Office** (⊕ *www.visitbelgium.com*).

Croatia **Croatian National Tourist Board** (⊕ *croatia.hr*).

Denmark **Danish Tourist Board** (⊕ *www.visitdenmark.com*).

Europe General and by Destination **Europe Tourist Office** (⊕ *www.europe.or*).

Finland **Finnish Tourist Board** ⊕ *www.visitfinland.com*).

France **French Government Tourist Office** (⊕ *us.franceguide.com*). **Paris Convention and Visitors Bureau** (⊕ *en.parisinfo.com*). **Provence Alpes Tourism International** (⊕ *www.provenceguide.co.uk*).

Germany **Berlin Tourism** (⊕ *www. berlin-tourist-information.de*).

Germany Tourist Board (⊕ *www. germany-tourism.de*).

Great Britain British Tourist Authority (⊕ *www.visitbritain.com*). **London Tourist Board** (⊕ *www. visitlondon.com*). **Scottish Tourist Board** (⊕ *www.visitscotland.com*). **Welsh Tourist Board** (⊕ *www.visitswales.com*).

Greece Greek National Tourism Organization (⊕ *www.visitgreece.gr*).

Holland Netherlands Board of Tourism and Conventions (⊕ *www. holland.com*).

Hungary Budapest Tourism Office (⊕ *www.budapestinfo.hu/en*). **Hungarian National Tourist Office** (⊕ *www.gotohungary.com*).

Iceland Icelandic Tourist Board (⊕ *www.icelandtouristboard.com*).

Ireland Fáilte Ireland (⊕ *www. discoverireland.ie*).

Italy Italian Government Tourist Board (⊕ *www.italiantourism.com*). **Naples Tourist Board** (⊕ *www. inaples.it*). **Rome Tourist Board** (⊕ *en.turismoroma.it/*). **Venice Tourist Office** (⊕ *www.turismovenezia.it*).

Moscow and St. Petersburg Russia National Tourist Office (⊕ *www.russia-travel.com*).

Norway Norwegian Tourist Board (⊕ *www.visitnorway.com*).

Poland Polish National Tourist Office (⊕ *www.poland.travel*).

Portugal Turismo de Portugal (⊕ *www.visitportugal.com*).

Scandinavia Scandinavian Tourist Boards of North America (⊕ *www. goscandinavia.com*).

Slovenia Slovenian Tourist Board (⊕ *www.slovenia.info*).

Spain Tourist Office of Spain (⊕ *www.spain.info*).

Sweden Swedish Tourist Board (⊕ *www.visitsweden.com*).

Switzerland Swiss National Tourist Office (⊕ *www.myswitzerland. com*).

Turkey Ministry of Tourism (⊕ *www.tourismturkey.org*).

MEXICO
General and by Destination Consejo de Promoción Turística de México (⊕ *www.visitmexico.com*).

SOUTH AMERICA
Argentina Secretariat of Tourism (⊕ *www.turismo.gov.ar/*). **Undersecretariat of Tourism, Buenos Aires** (⊕ *www.bue.gov.ar*).

Bolivia Embassy of Bolivia (⊕ *www.bolivia.usa.org*).

Brazil Brazil Tourism Office (⊕ *www.braziltourism.org*).

Chile Embassy of Chile (⊕ *www. chile-usa.org*).

Colombia Tourism Colombia (⊕ *www.turismocolombia.com*).

Paraguay Paraguay (⊕ *country. paraguay.com*).

Patagonia Embassy of Chile (⊕ *www.chile-usa.org*). **Secretariat of Tourism, Argentina** (⊕ *www. turismo.gov.ar*).

Peru Peru Export & Tourism Promotion Board (⊕ *www.peru.info*).

Uruguay Ministry of Tourism and Sport of Uruguay (⊕ *www.turismo. gub.uy/*).

Venezuela **Embassy of the Bolivarian Republic of Venezuela** (⊕ *venezuela-us.org/*).

SOUTH PACIFIC
Australia **Tourism Australia** (⊕ *www.australia.com*).

Fiji **Tourism Fiji** (⊕ *www.bulafiji. com*).

New Zealand **Tourism New Zealand** (⊕ *www.newzealand.com*).

Tahiti **Tahiti Turisme** (⊕ *www.tahiti-tourisme.com*).

UNITED STATES
General Info and by State **Offical Travel and Tourism Web Site of the United States** (⊕ *www. DiscoverAmerica.com*).

WORLDWIDE
Links to Tourist Boards Worldwide **Tourist Offices Worldwide Directory** (⊕ *www.towd.com*).

INDEX